THE BRANDON BURLSWORTH STORY

GREATER

THE INCREDIBLE BIOGRAPHY OF THE GREATEST WALK-ON IN THE HISTORY OF COLLEGE FOOTBALL

JEFF KINLEY

REVISED & UPDATED VERSION

"THROUGH THE EYES OF A CHAMPION"

First printing: August 2016

Greater Productions, LLC
509 W. Spring Street, Suite 310
Fayetteville, AR 72701

ISBN: 978-0-9978839-5-4

Cover design by Jonathan Holder
Cover photo of Chris Severio as Brandon Burlsworth by Art Machine
Back cover photo of Brandon Burlsworth by Marty Burlsworth
Both inside flap photos of Brandon by Wal Beazley

Printed in the United States of America

This book is lovingly dedicated

to my three sons,

Clayton, Stuart, and Davis.

Here is an example you can follow, boys:

"Do it the Burls way."

Acknowledgments

This book could not have been written apart from the contributions of dozens of people who provided unique perspectives on Brandon and the events surrounding his life. I am so grateful to the entire Burlsworth family, who opened their homes and hearts to me, allowing access to personal family memories and artifacts. No sacrifice I have made in writing this book remotely compares to what they have suffered. To Barbara, Marty, Grady, Vickie, and Jeannie, my deepest appreciation for your complete cooperation over these past several months. To Brandon's extended family, childhood and family friends, teachers, and citizens of Harrison, Arkansas; you were a huge source of important background information for me. You showed me why Brandon remains your "favorite son." Thanks to Tommy Tice, for giving me insight into Brandon's formative high school years and athletic career.

I would also like to thank Frank Broyles and Houston Nutt for opening every door for me in the University of Arkansas Athletic Department. The Razorback coaching staff and administrative personnel were enormously helpful to me in my research.

I am also thankful for my time spent in Indianapolis, which provided me with a perspective on Brandon's brief stint with the Colts. To Craig Kelley, Jim Mora, Bill Polian, and the entire Colts football club goes a special note of thanks.

Brandon's former teammates, coaches, and friends were especially helpful as they gave me a behind-the-scenes tour of life with Burls.

Thanks also goes to my "silent partners," who, without desire for recognition, gladly funded the research of this book. Guys, without you I could never have done it. To Rachelle Rexer, who graciously offered to type my final revisions of this manuscript as I stared at a rapidly approaching deadline — no doubt God sent you at just the right time. Very special thanks goes to my good friend and father-in-law, Charles Basham, who first encouraged me to write this book. To my precious wife, Beverly, and our three boys, thank you for not complaining as you gave up time with me over the past several months. Instead, you encouraged and believed in me, praying diligently for this project every step of the way.

Contents

Foreword 9
Preface 11
Introduction 15
1. Almost Home 17
2. Bobby Sox and Baby Boys 21
3. Six and "Superchurch" 27
4. Autograph 39
5. Best Friends 51
6. Kicked Around 57
7. Goblins 69
8. Walk-On 81
9. A New Football Player 97
10. Calling the Hogs 109
11. Going "Nutts" 127
12. All-American 155
13. Behind the Glasses 167
14. Upward Draft! 177
15. An Impressive Start 195
16. Quality Time 213
17. "It's Over" 229
18. A State of Shock 243
19. Where Are the Heroes? 257
20. "How Bad Do You Want It?" 271
Afterword 281

Foreword

I have had the privilege to be a part of the Razorback program for more than 44 years. In that time, I have worked with many outstanding administrators, coaches, student-athletes, and fans. Undoubtedly, one of the finest individuals that I have ever been associated with was Brandon Burlsworth.

Brandon was a great example of what every student-athlete should be. He was an outstanding competitor, a committed student, and a devoted son. His determination and commitment to be the best he could be on and off the field of play were evident to anyone that had the pleasure to know him.

His story continues to serve as an inspiration to many involved in collegiate athletics as well as those in other walks of life. Brandon was a special person, and he will always be a treasured member of the Razorback family.

J. Frank Broyles
Athletic Director
University of Arkansas

Preface

Making a movie about a person's life is an enormous responsibility – even more so if that individual is a beloved, genuine hero with an amazing personal story. Such was the situation in which I found myself when I was asked to co-write and direct *Greater,* the biopic about the life of Brandon Burlsworth. Brandon is not only the greatest walk-on in the history of college football, he's also a Hall of Famer in that cosmic game in which we've all taken the field as walk-ons … life. The fact that I reside in Brandon's home state of Arkansas made the duty all the more daunting. As I told Brian Riendl, the writer, producer and general driving force behind *Greater*, we simply could not allow ourselves to make a bad Brandon Burlsworth movie. We had to get things right.

Jeff Kinley's book, *Eyes of a Champion*, was a huge help to us in that regard. It was not our only source of information about Brandon — Brian had spent a few years interviewing just about everyone involved in Brandon's life, from players and coaches to media personalities and friends. We also had access to Marty, Barbara, Vickie, and the rest of the Burlsworth family, who were unfailingly gracious and tremendously helpful. But the focus of Mr. Kinley's book, I felt, provided something invaluable: an intimate look at the man underneath the helmet.

In *Eyes of a Champion,* one gets to know both Brandon Burlsworth, the underdog hero with the Herculean work ethic and remarkable character, whose poster any father would be glad to hang on his son's bedroom wall, and "Burls," the gentle, quirky young college student, pestered by the same day-to-day fears and insecurities common to us all. Though Mr. Kinley certainly illustrates the scope of Brandon's many achievements, his emphasis most often seems to be on showing us the everyday Brandon … the normal guy with whom one might hang out, argue with about the big game, or tussle with over that missing piece of cake in the refrigerator. I attended the University of Arkansas at the same time as Brandon, and though I did not have the honor of knowing him, we had several friends and acquaintances in common. I can attest that the picture *Eyes of a Champion* provides of Brandon Burlsworth comports very well with my impression. Complicated and flawed, "Burls" was, in many ways, not that much different than you and I … except for the ways in which he *was* different; and those are the ways which forge legends.

Communicating the essence of a consequential life in a two-hour movie is hard. Though narratives seem obvious once all the work has been done, things are very far from clear while they are being ironed out. One has to find the "best" direction out of a near-infinite number of possibilities. Determining what should be left in and what should be left out is a constant struggle. Emotional transactions which took months to unfold in real life need to be dramatized in one-minute scenes. Time must be compressed, real people combined into composite characters, and innumerable other choices made. Give a hundred different filmmakers the same life story to make into a movie and you will get a hundred very different pictures at the end of the day. Brian and I easily could have written entire movies about Brandon which concentrated solely on his relationships with Ed Robinson or Grant Williams, but unfortunately neither of these men, nor many others who had a big impact on Brandon's life, are featured in our narrative for *Greater.* We just didn't have the time to do it all.

Happily, the longer format of a book will allow you to get to know these men and many others who influenced Brandon. You will find details and clarifications about Brandon's life in this book that we couldn't include in *Greater.* This makes *Eyes of a Champion* a wonderful companion piece to our film.

Likewise, the copious research Brian did for *Greater* uncovered many events and facets of Brandon's life which do not appear in *Eyes of a Champion.* Some of the most cinematic lines in the movie, such as coach Ford's "Make it? I just hope he lives!" or coach Tice's "I'm sure that I'll get over his death but I'm not sure I'll ever get over his life," or Grant Garrett's "They'll let ANYBODY walk-on," may seem like screenwriterly invention, but they were actually said in real life. Brandon really did dive at the quarterback during a youth football game only to lay prone, ineffectually clutching his ankles, rather than taking him down. Brandon's walking through a construction site rather than altering his normal route to class, much to the glee of his cackling teammates, is also actual Burlsworth lore. We uncovered numerous great stories about Brandon and did our best to get as many as we could into the movie, though there were many we simply could not fit. In this way, *Greater* is also a nice supplement to *Eyes of a Champion*. Looking at both our film and Mr. Kinley's book should provide one with a complementary picture of Brandon Burlsworth and his life.

Greater is my second feature film. I pray God favors me with many more, but even if I were to make a hundred future pictures, I should not be likely to ever again encounter a subject as worthy as Brandon Burlsworth. Bringing his story to the screen has been, and will continue to be, one of the great honors of my life.

David Hunt
Director, Co-Writer and Editor of *Greater*
April, 2016

Introduction

Writing this book was not something I originally pursued. Rather, it pursued me. After it was initially suggested that I consider writing this story, I began casually investigating the facts concerning the life of Brandon Burlsworth. The more I uncovered, the more I was compelled to write. After I met with the Burlsworth family and after much prayer, it became clear to them that I was the right person to pen the book. By this time it had also become crystal clear to me that America had to hear this story. Opening my laptop, I began writing about a young man whom I had never met, but who would soon greatly impact my life. Five months later, and after thousands of miles of travel, I am even more convinced that his story is a must-read.

Brandon's life demonstrates there are still some great young people left in the world. He was a man's man, a hulk of a physical specimen. But housed within that massive frame was a gentle and tender heart. His humble demeanor stood in stark contrast to his passion and zeal on the gridiron. He could just as easily drive a defensive lineman into the turf as he could open the door for a lady or bend down to pick up a child. In some ways, the story of Brandon's life is an anchor of hope in a time when cynicism seems to rule the day. With all that is bad in the world, and in the midst of continual reports of corruption in both collegiate and professional athletics, Brandon's story is a breath of fresh Ozark Mountain air. I trust you will breathe deep as you read.

The purpose of this book is not to exalt Brandon Burlsworth. Nor is it to catapult him into some kind of sainthood. Brandon would never have wanted that — that just wasn't his way. But what this book attempts to do is honor the life and legacy of an extraordinary young man, and point others to the faith he so strongly embraced. I trust the pages that follow will clearly show you "Burls' worth," to coin a phrase. There is no debate that his is a memory that will perpetually live on in Arkansas Razorback history.

This book had to be written. It's a story worth telling because it's about an example worth following. So whether you're in an easy chair at home, a seat on an airplane, or a break table at work, sit back and enjoy. Don't be afraid to laugh, but also don't hesitate to shed a tear or two. Get ready for the challenge of seeing things a little differently from now on.

Prepare to see life through the eyes of a champion.

ONE

Almost Home

Tommy Tice is not a happy man. In fact, he's downright annoyed. Tapping nervously on his steering wheel, he glances at his watch — 4:45 p.m. *I'm gonna be late*, he thinks to himself. Tice knows this road, having driven it countless times before. But never has he seen it lined with so many cars, backed up to a crawl. Brake lights blink on and off as if the drivers are attempting to communicate by Morse code. Bumper to bumper, the seemingly endless line of vehicles slowly progresses onward, much to the disappointment of those on this wooded stretch of road. The frustration index is rising. You see, it's not normal to be caught in a traffic jam on this rural Arkansas highway. In fact, the congestion looks more like Saturday night vacation traffic in nearby boomtown Branson, Missouri.

Increasing Tice's irritation is the fact that he is so close to his home in Harrison — just a few miles away from his doorstep. He would love to be walking through his front door about now, smelling a hot supper. Instead, he's forced to smell the exhaust fumes of the car ahead of him. Impatient and unwillingly parked on rural Highway 412, he will have to settle for a cold supper by the time he makes the city limits.

Without much else to do in a situation like this but wait, Tice begins thinking about his upcoming schedule, part of which includes a big sports assembly the high school has planned for the end of the year. Being the athletic director and head football coach at Harrison High, Tice will naturally have a huge part in the assembly. But with plenty of time on his hands at the moment, he flashes forward to the gathering, wondering how he might involve his favorite former football player in the festivities. Brandon Burlsworth's name and face have been a staple in Arkansas sports headlines for the past year, having won national accolades and acclaim. His storybook rise from small town walk-on to All-American and recent selection in the NFL draft has made him a statewide hero. The former Harrison High Goblin star has gladly agreed to come back and help his old coach with the upcoming festivities. Now it is just a question of how.

Tommy can't help but smile as he thinks of Brandon, as the two have grown close over the years. Every coach looks for a shining example toward which he can point his players, inspiring them to greatness on and off the field. For Tice, that example is Brandon.

Inching his way toward Harrison and home, the coach reminds himself that patience is a virtue. After some time, the seemingly endless column of cars slowly makes its way around a curve in this asphalt artery which connects a scattered assortment of small mountain communities. Rounding that bend, Tice notices a roadside park on the right. Peering into the distance up ahead, he finally realizes what has caused the long delay… there has been a wreck. A very bad one.

By this time the wreckers have arrived at the scene, along with the Arkansas State Police who are directing traffic and trying to move along the line of cars, which crawl by at a snail's pace. Each vehicle's occupants attempt a peek at the reason they have been held up so long. It's human nature to look, and they feel a passing glance is due them considering the amount of time they have invested. As Tice creeps by, he sees a white car that has been totaled by the impact of the accident. Passing the crash, he is struck by the devastating scene. Though he, like most, has been exposed to footage of similar accidents on television, nothing on the tube could have prepared him for the shock of being so close to such a tragedy. The sight of that wreck is accompanied by an unanticipated feeling of mortality that sweeps over the high school football coach.

As if in a funeral-like procession, trucks and cars file past the crash site, some drivers gawking, some gazing, others just grateful it wasn't them. Sympathetically, Tommy shakes his head as traffic begins speeding up past the bottleneck. Tice wastes no time heading for his home in Harrison. Being only 30 minutes outside of town, it won't take him long to get there. Arriving home, Tice has hardly come through the door when the phone rings.

That rural traffic jam, he would soon realize, has just changed the rest of his life.

TWO

Bobby Sox and Baby Boys

In the late 1950s, life in a small Arkansas town like Harrison didn't offer much promise for a bright and attractive teenage girl like Barbara Long. Raised modestly in a typical middle-class home, her dad eked out a respectable living as a rural mail carrier. He was responsible for the postal route in Snowball, a tiny town not much bigger than what its name suggests. Folks knew Sumlar Long simply as "Slim." As you might guess, he didn't much care to be called by his given name, and since he could turn sideways and almost disappear, friends dubbed him "Slim." The nickname stuck. Barbara's mom, Audrey, worked hard doing what most moms did in those days — staying at home, taking care of the house and the family.

It was during her senior year in high school that Barbara landed a job working as a waitress at a local cafe after school and on Saturdays. One day a girlfriend and co-worker approached Barbara with a proposition. "I have someone I'd like you to meet," she said. She offered to set Barbara up on a blind date with a young man she knew named Leo Burlsworth, who lived in Ridgeway, just a stone's throw from Harrison.

Barbara agreed to that initial blind date, and enjoyed her time with Leo. One date led to another, and an initial friendship rapidly grew into a serious courtship. Just weeks before her high school graduation, the two became husband and wife.

Yet even with the blessings of their contemporaries, there were still no matrimonial guarantees in those days. (Come to think of it, there still aren't any.) Being so young didn't make married life any easier for Barbara and Leo. The test of getting to know your spouse when you barely know yourself is not an easy assignment for anyone, let alone a teenage girl. The Burlsworth newlyweds struggled as all couples do, regardless of age, personality, intelligence, or background. Marriage is quite possibly the biggest challenge most of us face in this short life.

A uniquely gifted musician, Leo could play most any instrument, but he focused on guitar. Having never received any formal music training, he possessed a natural ability to play by ear. Leo traveled with several different bands, and as a result, he and Barbara moved around quite a bit in the early months of their marriage. Ask any musician and he'll tell you life on the road is hardly a life at all. When your home is a bus and your dining room is the next cafe down the road, there isn't much room for stability. The Burlsworths soon grew tired of this lifestyle and eventually decided to return to Harrison and make a permanent home.

Not long afterward Leo received a call from a headliner act at the Ozark Opry, located at Lake of the Ozarks in central Missouri. Because of his instinctive talent, he was asked to direct the house band as well. The ongoing gig included appearing on live TV, which ultimately meant long hours of rehearsing and performing and more time away from home.

After a few years, the stress of having to perform to perfection in two live shows a day eventually caught up with Leo. There was a physical and emotional price to pay for all this work, and Leo was living on credit. Seeking some relief from the stress brought on by such a grueling work schedule, Leo began taking prescription drugs. Before long he also started drinking, then drinking heavily. This, as you would expect, brought additional frustration to his already-tense marriage to Barbara, who by this time was caring for two small children, Marty and Grady. The strain ultimately became too heavy for the couple to shoulder, and they divorced.

In spite of the divorce, Barbara was still optimistic that there might be some help for Leo and hope for reconciliation. *It is possible there could be healing in a broken relationship like ours*, she thought. She wondered if perhaps the painful memories of the past would fade away over time, just enough to give them incentive for a new start.

This proved to be the case, and in 1970 Leo and Barbara remarried. But though they made a courageous attempt to take a sad song and make it a better one, their situation did not much improve.

Complicating matters further, Barbara was surprised to discover she was expecting child number three. She remembers being more than a little concerned, being pregnant at 36, an age when most women have bid farewell to the childbearing years. She had lived nearly half her life already, and now she would have to start all over again with a new baby. In some ways she felt like the world was closing in on her.

Sensing the anxiety brought on by the impending birth of a third child, a friend and work associate approached Barbara one day with an unusual, if ultimately unserious, proposal. "Barbara, listen. You're 36 years old and considering all you've been through, the last thing you need right now is another child to feed and take care of. Let me take the baby for you and I will raise him as my own." Had her friend been serious with the offer, this could have been a good deal. Not having to take on the responsibility of another child and knowing he would be well-cared for was in some people's minds a good offer. But Barbara, though grateful to her friend for the "offer," never even entertained the thought.

"Absolutely not," she replied. "This is my child, and I'm going to raise him." And that was that.

Not for a moment did Barbara even consider giving up the baby. To her, it just wasn't an option. Having never run from responsibility in her life, she wasn't about to start now. Besides, she wanted this baby. She also believed there was a greater purpose in all that was happening. She was confident God had a special plan for this child. *Otherwise, why would He have allowed this to happen?* she reasoned.

The fall of 1976 came in Northwest Arkansas. In typical fashion, glowing red-colored leaves mixed with a purple-orange hue to create an almost fluorescent effect as the autumn sun burst through. In this season the Ozark foliage resembles a master artist's brush stroke on a canvas of gentle, rolling country hills — a picturesque portrait of Creation.

America was celebrating its bicentennial. There had been two hundred years of freedom since our nation's birth. A new sense of patriotism and rediscovered love for the red, white and blue swept across the land. But in the Burlsworth house there was an altogether different kind of celebration taking place.

On September 20 Barbara welcomed the arrival of yet another boy into the family. Brandon Vaughn Burlsworth was born at Boone County Hospital and was quite a hefty baby, weighing in at nine pounds, fourteen ounces. Years later, after achieving notoriety with the Razorbacks, a sort of urban legend was born, stating that because Brandon was a rather large infant, nurses had dubbed him the "football baby."

From the start, life would be somewhat different for this new baby boy. His big brothers, Grady and Marty, were 13 and 16 years old when he was born. And life would be different for Barbara as well. It had been over a decade since she had cared for a newborn baby. It's one thing to raise three children. It's another thing altogether to raise three boys. There is a certain unique dynamic (or dynamite!) that boys bring to a household.

The presence of even one girl in the home is at least some measure of comfort to a mom. There is always the hope that having one other female with which to identify might bring a calming influence to family life. But peace and quiet are usually the first of many casualties associated with an all-boy family. A mom must possess the patience of Job, the wisdom of Solomon, and the tenacity of General Patton if she is to survive the ordeal.

Barbara's days of cooking, washing, and cleaning for a husband and two on-the-go adolescent males would now also be filled with caring for an infant: changing diapers, washing bottles, bathing the baby. Her nights would now be interrupted with midnight feedings.

Things will be different from here on out, she told herself. And she was right.

But "different" didn't necessarily mean worse. Unexpected change can sometimes be a blessing in disguise. Though the packaging may not necessarily impress us, the best gifts in life often arrive in the most unexpected ways. "Little" Brandon proved to be both a blessing and a gift, which is what children are meant to be in the first place. They're treasures to be cherished, lives merely on loan to parents for a short while. Countless times over the course of his life, Barbara would remind her son, "Brandon, if I ever doubt that God is in control, all I have to do is look at you." From the day of his birth, there was a special bond between this mother and her new boy. It was a bond that, though tested at times, would grow stronger with each passing year.

For Marty and Grady, suffering at the hands of their kid brother was something the two teenagers would simply have to live with. More than once, while lying on their stomachs watching TV, a two-year-old toddler would come out of nowhere and without provocation launch a surprise attack. Resembling a kamikaze pilot, Brandon would charge up behind them and dive-bomb into their backs as if they were human beanbags. "While we screamed in surprised pain," Marty recalls, "Dad would just sit back and laugh. I guess Bran was a little spoiled in that way."

Before long, however, things went south again in the Burlsworth marriage, only this time it would be a permanent situation. Bad habits are hard to break, especially when they escalate into enslaving addictions. Leo had tried unsuccessfully to conquer his dependence on alcohol. Enduring for as long as she could for the boys' sake, Barbara felt a split was the only option left to her. There would be no more reconciliation this time. The couple divorced in 1979. Brandon was two.

In spite of his struggle with alcohol, Leo Burlsworth was basically a good and gentle man who loved his sons. He recognized the detrimental impact his addiction had on his ability to be a good father and role model. After his divorce from Barbara, Leo spent the next eight years keeping some distance from his youngest son. This was a self-imposed removal from Brandon's life, as he and Barbara remained friends. While some divorced couples entertain an ongoing hostility, Leo and Barbara's civility towards one another was a measure of consolation to the boys.

Consequently, with his father now gone and his brothers so much older than he, Brandon was raised for all intents and purposes as an only child. Starting over again in life with a new baby and without a husband was, of course, not the plan Barbara had envisioned. But as her nature dictated, she welcomed the challenge with all the tenacity and perseverance she had evidenced previous to this point in her life. She had not allowed the surprising setbacks of life to sidetrack her from her long-held faith in God. And if her relationship with Him had taught her anything, it had shown her that, through Christ, she could handle any challenge the new day might bring.

And make no mistake about it. This was a new day.

THREE

SIX AND "SUPERCHURCH"

"Brandon, wake up! Wake up!" Barbara shouted nervously. Her six-year-old son's body lay motionless on the ground. "Brandon, honey! Talk to me!" Her voice was louder this time, carrying a tone of panic. Wild thoughts race across a mother's mind when her child is unconscious. In those seconds that seem to linger forever, incoherent random images flash like lightning through the brain.

Is he alive? Is he going to live? What do I do? Oh God, please help!

Brandon had been riding his bike across the yard, and like a typical six-year-old male had not paid attention to where he was going. An electrical cord was strung across the backyard, connecting power to a freezer inside a rear building. Pedaling furiously across the lawn, Brandon never saw the cord or even knew it was there until it caught him under the chin, flipping him violently back onto the ground. The impact of his head hitting the hard surface immediately knocked him unconscious.

He was out cold.

Emerging out of that back building, all Barbara Burlsworth saw was her son's lifeless body lying on the grass. Racing across the yard as fast as her feet carry her, she began calling out his name. When her boy failed to respond, she quickly scooped up his limp frame and ran inside, where she threw water on his face. Suddenly, the young lad's eyes flew open. Dazed and disoriented, Brandon blinked, unsure of exactly where or who he was. One thing he had no doubt about however … he had a headache the size of Texas.

Soon after that bicycle accident, Brandon began complaining to his mother of a strange feeling in his head. "My head just feels funny, Mom," he would say. But then as quickly as the feeling came, it would pass, only to return unexpectedly at a later time. This caused growing concern for Barbara, as it would for any parent. *Falling backwards and being knocked unconscious like that may have damaged his brain in some way*, she thought. To be on the safe side, Barbara drove her son three hours south to Little Rock for an examination. Once there, doctors ordered a CAT scan, which can be a frightening experience for anyone, particularly for a first grader. But both Brandon and Barbara's fears were relieved as it was concluded that no brain damage was evident. His "funny feelings" were something his doctors predicted would eventually just go away. Even so, his physician felt it necessary to recommend medication to prevent the possibility of suffering a seizure in the near future.

Barbara was not fully convinced medication was necessary for her six-year-old since Brandon had not shown any evidence of experiencing seizures to that point. So for added peace of mind she obtained a second opinion from a doctor in Fayetteville. He confirmed the previous physician's recommendation concerning the prescription. That was good enough for Barbara, and Brandon never suffered a single seizure, taking the preventative medication until he was twelve.

The good news was that the bike accident apparently in no way affected Brandon's normal development and activity as a youngster. Like most preadolescent boys, Brandon had his share of runny noses, muddy shoes, dirty hands, torn jeans, and bedtime protests. Barbara was all too familiar with the reality that boys are very different from girls. Take sense of humor, for example … a group of boys can watch old "Three Stooges" episodes and howl with laughter while girls just shake their heads in confusion, wondering what's so funny. Boys' eating habits are also very different than girls'. It's not that one is right and the other wrong. It's just that a boy finds nothing strange about a ketchup-and-peanut butter sandwich, a cold piece of pizza for breakfast, or jamming French fries inside his hamburger. In a boy's room, it's not altogether unlikely to discover a petrified chicken bone or a year-old empty Coke can stuffed into the back of a sock drawer.

Brandon attended elementary school eight miles south of Harrison in Valley Springs, which at that time basically consisted of a convenience store and a post office. There, Brandon blended in with the other children, proving to be a typical primary school student. In those early years, he was not the near obsessive-compulsive "neatnik" he would later become. In fact, he was just the opposite. His teachers were not in the least amused at his lack of organization. When it came to homework, Brandon was a scatterbrain, papers were strewn everywhere and difficult to find, if one could find them at all. Sometimes his work was discovered in a pile at the back of the classroom. He would also forget to turn in required assignments.

As a child, Brandon was not immune from the other characteristic challenges of growing up. He was at times an overactive child who could be quite a handful to control. Raising him as a single mother, working multiple jobs to keep their heads above water, was not easy. *When this one gets to be a teenager, he's gonna kill me!* Barbara would jokingly think to herself between her many duties a mother and breadwinner.

Brandon's disorder in the classroom was not the only evidence that he needed a little more "managing." Cases in point were his episodes of boyhood bravado played out on the school bus. There was a certain boy who rode the same bus with Brandon, and for some unknown reason the two lads simply did not get along. In plain language, they fought a lot … about twice a week. From Brandon's perspective, this kid possessed the unique ability (it was actually more of a gift) to get under his skin. Most of us know someone like this. Through words, actions, and even facial expressions, they push all the right buttons necessary to get you upset, angry, or frustrated, needling you non-stop until they get the response they want. For reasons unknown, they somehow gain a sort of perverse pleasure out of making you upset.

Barbara never quite figured out who was the initial instigator of these bi-weekly bus brawls, though she had her suspicions. Parents instinctively want to believe their own children are innocent victims and the other kid is the real "bully in blue jeans," but whatever the case, Brandon and this boy proved to be thorns in each other's sides for the duration of their elementary bus career.

When Brandon was six years old, his brother Marty married Vickie Martin. As is often customary, family members are part of the wedding party, and Marty's wedding was no exception. The couple had dated for 18 months, and Bran was always somewhere close by, hanging around them. So, at age six, Brandon was asked to be in Marty and Vickie's wedding, and he would later be in brother Grady's as well. In fact, because he was considered such an adorable little boy, Brandon was asked to be in several weddings. It became a normal thing to him, and in his mind he actually expected to be in any ceremony involving a family member. On one occasion, when an extended family member was married and Brandon wasn't asked to be in the wedding party, he got offended and confused as to why he wasn't the ring bearer.

Like most children his age, Brandon believed the world revolved around him. As in every kid's world, Brandon's perspective was small and limited. The bedroom was his domain, the backyard his world and the neighborhood his solar system. Beyond that, as far as he was concerned, was the vastness of interstellar space. Brandon would soon understand he was not the center of his own universe, but merely a planet in Someone Else's solar system.

Naturally reclusive, Brandon spent more time by himself than he did hanging out with other kids. That meant more time in front of the television, which for Brandon meant more afternoon snacks. Junk food meant more pounds, and big brother Marty was not very sympathetic when it came to Brandon's weight. Having a different body structure and metabolism, Marty could eat all he wanted and hardly gain a pound. This was a sore spot for Brandon, who was forced to carefully watch what he ate. But the pounds piled on as he grew, which didn't make things any easier for Brandon socially.

It was at this time that Brandon got involved with a program called "Superchurch," an all-day Saturday activity for area kids sponsored by his church, First Assembly of God. The program's purpose was to reach out to as many kids in the community as possible, rounding them up on a bus and bringing them to church on Saturday for a day of fun. There they would get to play games, participate in competition, eat, and hear a story from the Bible.

Though still a kid himself, Brandon volunteered to not only participate but also be a program helper to the church's youth pastor, Rick Watts. He was accepted there, no matter where he came from or what the scale said each morning. He assisted with games and activities for children his own age, helping gather the others onto the bus, sitting with them, and making sure they felt welcome and accepted. Superchurch lasted a good part of the day as the kids weren't brought home until around 1:00 p.m. Afterward, Brandon and the other boys who had been helping out would hang around, playing football in the church yard with their youth pastor. Whenever adults praised Brandon for his servant spirit in helping the other kids in the program, he would typically respond, "It's no big deal." Even at this young age, Brandon felt uncomfortable having attention drawn to himself.

Much of Brandon's love for church and God came during those Saturdays. He learned how fun church can be and that it is supposed to be that way for a kid. Like most children early in life, Brandon drew his impressions and conclusions about God from experiences at church. While there, he found some of the answers to life's most important questions like:

Does God really exist?
If so, what is He like?
Can I know Him personally?
Does He really care about me?

Whether verbalized or not, these and other questions about God can buzz around in a youngster's mind like an annoying fly. It was important for Youth Pastor Rick Watts that his "Superchurch" kids have a good time, but beyond that, his goal was to create an environment that combined faith with fun. It was his desire to communicate that there was no contradiction between the two and they were mutually inclusive. He was aware that far too often there is a negative association about church in the minds of young people, and he was resolutely intent on changing that perception.

From his understanding of Scripture, he understood that God had become a man and revealed himself to mankind in a language we could understand. He didn't ask us to comprehend the incomprehensible, but instead spoke ordinary language to the common men, women, and children of His day. Jesus told stories, not about the esoteric mysteries of eternity, but rather about birds, flowers, farming, and family which communicated the reality of God and His ways. Along with healings and other miraculous deeds, Christ brought the truth to man without compromise. He entered our world so that we might eventually enter His. He did for us what we could never do for ourselves.

He brought us to God.

Rick figured that if this approach of being relevant to people's needs was good enough for Jesus, then it was good enough for him. He endeavored to reflect the reality of God to his youths, producing a positive image of the Almighty in their minds. Believing the 11th commandment was "Thou shalt not bore," Saturday "Superchurch" soon took on a life of its own, involving hundreds of area youngsters. Brandon Burlsworth was one of those kids. He was taught that serving others was more important than serving oneself. He began to enjoy serving in the background, unnoticed and unrecognized.

Another positive by-product of those Saturdays spent at church was that Brandon found a role model in Rick Watts. Though he rarely said much, young Brandon was always taking mental notes, soaking in everything Watts said. And he filled an internal notebook with the life lessons he learned watching Rick lead those kids. For a chubby little kid growing up without a father in the home, that was exactly what Brandon needed. Perhaps he also observed in Rick how a person could make an impact on other lives when they have a platform of influence. Rick moved on to another church when Brandon was 13, but he had an up-close influence on the boy during his formative years. That influence would not be lost with the passing of time, as Barbara later credited much of Brandon's early spiritual development to his time spent with Rick.

That exposure to a godly example and healthy early church experience imparted lessons that sank deep into Brandon's heart, taking root and helping to form his developing character. In later years he would often draw from those lessons as he himself became an example to others.

Though he was not a resident father, Leo Burlsworth was not completely nonexistent in Brandon's life. Brandon's dad did have gradually increasing contact with his son. Though up to this point he had played a minor role in Brandon's life, the truth is the elder Burlsworth cared very much for his son, so much so that in 1987 he was motivated to put his biggest problem in the past once and for all. He joined and committed himself to an alcohol recovery program. Like his son would later do with football, Leo demonstrated a fierce determination to the goal set before him. Once he set his mind on something, it was as good as done. Daily he began focusing his energy on recovery with dedication previously unseen in his life. He recognized that a person's daily actions, whether good or bad, become habits which grow into patterns of behavior. And it is those very patterns of behavior and lifestyle that determine who we are. Leo wanted to change what those patterns of behavior had done to him.

To his credit, and with God's help, he conquered this demon that had for so long held him in its powerful grip. It was a victory that brought not only a great sense of accomplishment to Leo, but also a huge relief to the family. For some, it was a long-awaited answer to prayers offered over the course of many years. But the good news was that the victory was not temporary, as Leo remained sober for the last ten years of his life. This was a key win at a time when it mattered, and at the only game where winning really counts.

After his recovery, Leo occasionally came by on Saturday and picked up Brandon for a sleepover at his house. The two headed back to his apartment where pizza was usually the cuisine of choice, followed by a movie or a game. Since neither of them was particularly known for his gift of gab there wasn't a whole lot of dialogue between them. Leo was a quiet man who preferred a few close friends and family rather than a crowd. In fact, just like Brandon, he felt rather uncomfortable in a large group setting. How ironic that his first chosen profession was playing guitar in a band before thousands of people each week, and his son's chosen profession was likewise a very public one as well.

But aside from their shared reserved personalities, another trait Brandon inherited from his dad was an attention to detail and love for routine. A person doesn't become an accomplished musician by watching other people play. He becomes successful by himself, playing and practicing … daily … every day … for hours on end. Calloused fingers and cramping hands are just some of the inherent costs of becoming a guitar player. He spends the majority of his time tucked away in a back room, mastering his craft. It can be a lonely lifestyle that to some degree seemed to fit a man like Leo. When he was learning a song or a particular lead part, Leo would often sit and play the same riff over and over for hours. If he made a mistake, he did it again. If he played it perfectly, he did it again. To those who knew him, Leo's constant practice and almost religious repetition appeared to border on the obsessive. And perhaps it was, for most great musicians are often born from a lifetime of daily, grueling practice. This type of dedication is characteristic of anyone who desires to be great at something, whether they be musicians … or athletes. But that was Leo. And that was precisely why he received offers to play with some of the top country performers and entertainers of his day, like Charlie Rich and Marty Robbins.

Shunning the public eye and opting for simplicity, Leo spent the last years of his life working mostly alone in a die casting factory. This very talented man, who at one time was asked to play with the industry's brightest stars, let his demons overcome his God-given professional potential. Though he conquered those demons later in life, one couldn't help but see the trajectory of Leo Burlsworth's life as a "what might have been" story. Brandon, who inherited his father's obsessive drive, would eventually resolve to keep constant vigil against the forces of decay which always lurk at the gate and which tore deep into his father's life. Brandon was gradually transformed by Leo's example, emulating the good and guarding himself from the bad. He would not repeat his father's mistakes.

Though Leo Burlsworth may not have been there for most of Brandon's youth, he never gave up on himself or his family, making sure he finished his race strong. In the end, Brandon would learn much from his loving, yet complicated, father.

Like his dad, Brandon had a great love for history. He loved to read and as a child had an insatiable hunger for knowledge, particularly history — the presidents and the great wars. Of particular interest to him were the Civil War and World War II. This attraction to history later came to the attention of brother Grady when Brandon was in high school. Brandon and his mom joined Grady, his wife Jeannie, and their son Jeff, on a summer vacation to Destin, Florida. The family and the future All-American piled into the car for a week-long stay at the beach. Along the way they took a slight detour, stopping in Vicksburg, Mississippi. There they planned on taking a quick tour of the Civil War museum and burial monuments before hitting the road again on the way to their Destin destination. But what was supposed to be a short rest from the road turned out to be a day-long adventure. Like a magnet to metal, Brandon was drawn to each exhibit where he curiously and carefully read the fine print on every monument. He became engulfed and engrossed in a world of his own, oblivious to others around him. Impatient and anxious to continue with their trip, Grady had to all but pry Brandon off the exhibits with a crowbar. It would come to no one's surprise that later, after entering the University of Arkansas, when he was asked on a questionnaire to list his favorite class, Brandon wrote "American History."

Growing up, Brandon's evenings were often spent reading books — non-fiction, history, the Bible, even encyclopedias. His ability to retain facts made him somewhat of a walking almanac – a human search engine of information. His thirst for knowledge was never satisfied, becoming something of a joke when anyone had difficulty finding the answer to a historical or biblical question. Inevitably, somebody would quip, "just ask Brandon." Often he spent so much time with his head buried in books that his mom used to worry about him keeping too much to himself. She was concerned he might not develop sufficient friendships with other kids.

When Brandon would spend the night with his dad, it would be on Saturday, which meant the following morning was Sunday. And Sunday meant church. Because of his earlier experience, Brandon had grown to love going to church. Though he wasn't legalistic about his attendance, Brandon had an unwavering commitment to not miss a Sunday service if at all possible. Church was a choice, not a chore, and for Brandon, it was a weekly routine that never became "routine." For his part, Leo faithfully woke up his son, got him dressed, and drove him to the church where he would meet up with his mom. Immediately upon entering the building however, Brandon rushed straight to the men's room, brushing his clothes in a frantic attempt to remove the smell of his dad's cigarettes. He was afraid of being embarrassed if someone smelled the smoke.

While at church, the youth ministry played a pivotal role in Brandon's life, and he was careful to take advantage of camps, trips, and retreats whenever they were offered. It was on one of those trips to a youth camp at age ten that a group of boys decided to play a practical joke on Brandon. Being a bit "different" from the other boys and trusting to a fault, it was the first of many such pranks young Brandon would endure. He had decided to go to bed around nine in order to get plenty of sleep before the following day's activities. The other three boys sharing his room came together and devised a trick to play on their target, putting their plan in motion around midnight.

"Brandon, get up. It's morning. Time to wake up," one of the boys called out, shaking the slumbering youth out of his sleep.

"Huh? What? What are you talking about," Brandon mumbled, squinting at the glaring lights in his eyes.

"You have to get up. We're running late and the meeting is about to start," replied the boy as his other two accomplices attempted to contain their snickering.

"Okay, I'm getting up," Brandon said as he stumbled toward the bathroom.

Brandon showered and got dressed, then gathered his Bible and notebook and started to head downstairs. Just as he reached for the doorknob the boys unveiled their deception to Brandon with knee-slapping delight. He looked at the clock, realizing it was just midnight. The joke was on him, and he was now wide-awake and fully dressed for the coming day. Such boyhood pranks are a part of any childhood, but given his shy and reserved nature, Brandon often became an easy target for bullies and practical jokers. He usually found consolation in his mother.

"Mom," he would say, "you love Marty and Grady more than me, don't you?"

Seizing the moment, Barbara would respond, "No, honey, I love you all the same," then quickly adding, "but you are my baby, and that makes you special."

A parent's words contain a power that can blast a child's fears and insecurities into oblivion. And sometimes that's just the kind of reassurance a little boy needs.

FOUR

AUTOGRAPH

Change was something for which Brandon never cared too much. As a matter of fact, change was downright irritating to him. A personality trait that would color most of his life, Brandon's preference for routine and regularity became a dominating factor in his decision-making. Giving him a sense of security, he comforted himself knowing that things would roughly be the same tomorrow as they were today. Some people tend to live each day wide open, playing it by ear. They feel confined and restricted by life when it is predictable. Instead, they prefer spontaneity, and an unplanned, spur-of-the-moment approach to living.

Not Brandon Burlsworth.

He liked things to stay pretty much the same. Same house. Same shoes. Same kinds of food. Same school. And if you were going to change something about his life, you had better have good reason for doing it. So when Barbara Burlsworth decided to transfer her son from the school at Valley Springs to Harrison Junior High for his ninth-grade year, she was met with some initial opposition. Though the move would mean it would be more convenient to get to and from school, that wasn't much comfort to Brandon. Transferring to another school posed a real threat to his world and his way of coping with it. A move meant making new friends, getting to know new teachers, and adjusting to new surroundings. For the overweight shy kid with few friends, not much money in his family and a mostly-absent father, this move to another school was like a defensive lineman charging into the backfield of his life, and Brandon felt as if he was about to be sacked. His instincts screamed, *Scramble and avoid the tackle!* And so, calling upon a maturing strong will, Brandon blocked his mom's protests with as much verbal resistance as he could muster.

In fairness, though, no child likes to have his life rearranged from one school year to the next. Change is difficult for anyone, but even more so for an insecure adolescent. Like an air traffic controller monitoring blips on a screen, a teenager is constantly tracking his small place in a big world, asking himself:

Am I accepted by my peers?
Do they like me?
Am I ugly?
How's my hair?
Will I be popular?

Adolescent insecurity can be a devastating plague for a youngster, especially ones whose bodies are growing faster than their emotional and social maturity. One misstep can spell disaster from which recovery is next to impossible. Drop your books in the hall once between classes. Trip going up the school steps. Let a facial blemish emerge on the wrong day. Your voice cracks in class while asking a question. Suffer through the accusation of liking someone of the opposite sex. And pray hard that you don't wear the wrong clothes to your first dance. All these near-fatal mishaps can mark you forever in your classmates' eyes, socially branding you with a label that sticks like super-glue throughout your grade-school career. Most adults can recall childhood classmates who failed to make the grade socially. Even today, though a former classmate may be a physician, she is still remembered for the time she cried and ran off stage during the school talent show. Or the successful businessman is forever known as the boy who wet his pants and had to go home early from school. We can still name the girl who always sat out recess games because she was athletically uncoordinated.

The awful reality of life is that kids can sometimes be ruthless toward one another. Kidding, teasing, taunting, and mocking with sadistic sarcasm, they have exterminated innumerable self-esteems. You're either too fat or too skinny. Too poor or too snobby. Too academic or too dumb. You can be ridiculed for being too religious or for appearing to have the "perfect" family. Or you are beaten down socially because you come from a single-parent home. In some circles, if you're not athletic or a part of the cheerleading squad, your reason for even being here is secretly questioned. But then for you there's always the school band … if you can stand the stigma. Whether vocal or unspoken, direct or passive, it's always destructive. Like an arrow, the rejection a young person feels plunges deep within, causing a wound that can take decades to heal.

For Brandon, his situation carried a bonus handicap, as he would now be the "new boy" in school. For a child in his situation, this can be quite a disadvantage as he starts the game with a negative score. You don't yet know the rules. You haven't had the chance to work off penance for previous social blunders. Instead of starting with a clean slate, you begin your new school career under a cloud of suspicion. As the new kid, you are entering the fight for acceptance and significance with one hand tied behind your back. You are on trial.

It's tough being a kid, and parents can be clueless to their child's feelings, especially when a change is imminent. That's because you're messing with their lives, and that produces a natural defense in their instinct to survive socially … not to mention some arguing, whining, and pouting along the way.

Brandon was no different in this respect. In his mind his mom was introducing an unwelcome variation to his routine that just didn't compute. However, his protests didn't last for long. Barbara knew her son well, and her knowledge of what was best for him was tempered with a sensitivity inherent in a loving mother's heart. She was well aware of the awkwardness a change like this would bring in Brandon's life, but she also understood the opportunities the new school would bring. Brandon was a big boy for his age. In fact, he had always been a little larger than his peers, a reality that had its advantages and disadvantages.

Brandon had played "T-ball" when he was six and seven years old. And though being bigger than the rest of the kids didn't mean he ran the bases with lightning speed, when he stepped up to the plate the opposing team's outfielders sprinted toward the fence in fear and anticipation. It didn't help them much though, for Brandon typically crushed the ball well over their heads. Though awkward in so many other areas, this is something he was good at. Experiencing success with his Babe Ruth impression gave young Brandon the confidence to begin searching for his place in the world. Sports just might be the answer… his "ticket to ride."

To look at him, you wouldn't think Brandon was much of a baseball player. But that's when having older brothers definitely has its advantages. Though they were separated by 16 years, Marty and Brandon shared similar traits. They both possessed very systematic and deliberate personalities. Early on, Brandon had shown an aggressive and competitive spirit, which was fueled in part by his older siblings. His strong will oftentimes produced a stubborn streak which proved to be a benefit on the playing field. And though he was never a problem child, his bulldogged determinism caused him to butt heads with his mom on many occasions.

Marty, still living in Harrison, was around to hang out with his kid brother. Initially, his involvement came in the form of unofficial baseball coach. Marty and Grady had grown up playing baseball and didn't want their baby brother to miss out on the experience. It was as natural as breathing for three boys from an all-American town to play the all-American game. But though Brandon had done well in T-ball, the chubby pre-adolescent experienced some difficulty consistently hitting a pitched ball. His awkwardness was growing into him rather than the other way around.

When Brandon was about ten years old, Marty coached a team in the local Babe Ruth League. Brandon tagged along, watching the big boys play and serving as the team's batboy. Sometimes he would even run with the team after practice. That, of course, was his first mistake.

Because Marty had acquired an eye for spotting potential in young athletes, he saw something in his brother that other people overlooked … a developing grit. The often-lazy kid who couldn't finish mowing the lawn was gradually giving way to a boy who wanted more. While coaching the team with one eye, he would keep the other focused on his not-so-little brother. He recognized the growing desire within Brandon to excel in athletics. Over a short period of time it became apparent that what Brandon lacked in natural ability, he was willing to compensate for through hard work and desire. That's when Marty's "in-house," informal coaching clinics began. You could call them coaching clinics, "athletic tutoring," whatever you like. But in reality, it wasn't much more than an older brother looking out for a younger one. Considering that Brandon was growing up during the most impressionable years of his life without a true father figure, Marty stepped in and filled the gap.

He began with the basics: conditioning, fielding, throwing, batting, hand-eye coordination. Brandon idolized St. Louis Cardinals shortstop Ozzie Smith, and had hung a huge poster of the superstar in his bedroom. But Brandon's build and lack of speed limited his acrobatic prowess on the dirt. His position of choice would land him instead on the pitching mound, and because he expressed the desire to pitch, Marty began working to develop his arm. To this point, ten-year-old Brandon had not yet earned the title "a coach's dream" he would later receive. He was still hard to coach and figured he knew much more about baseball than his big brother. Both Marty and Grady would take Brandon out in the front yard to work with him, helping him improve his game. Inevitably, they sought to critique, instruct, and advise their brother, which was not usually well-received. Angered by their constructive criticism, Brandon stormed back inside the house. Practice was officially over for the day, leaving the two older Burlsworth brothers staring at each other in frustration. Brandon wasn't the least bit grateful for his big brothers' insight into the game of baseball, particularly his game.

However, life has a way of doling out some poetic justice from time to time. Baseball season rolled around once again, and eager to play, Brandon could hardly wait to sign up for the local Babe Ruth League. Many of his friends and former teammates were a part of the league, and he was anxious to get on a team and start playing. Sign-up day came, and the teams were divided and assigned to coaches. Brandon's coach? You guessed it. Big brother Marty. But nepotism didn't rule in this kingdom, Brandon soon discovered, as there would be no favoritism from Big Bro. He would have to earn his right to play just like all the other boys. Brandon was taller than most of the kids on the team but heavier as well. Because Marty was committed to getting his team into shape for the season, he created incentives for them to earn playing time on the field—Brandon included. He challenged his kid brother to lose two pounds a week until he achieved a stabilized playing weight. The rule was "lose the weight or ride the bench." Extra weight on Brandon meant extra waiting on the bench. Losing the weight to play was just the leverage his coach needed to move Brandon from lethargy at home to leadership on the team. And it was a strategy that worked.

While traveling back from a trip to Blytheville, Marty decided to put his newly developed conditioning program to the test. Riding alone in the car together afforded the two brothers a chance to talk to one another. Because Brandon kept things to himself, even Barbara would often have to dig things out of him. But when he did open up, he was faithful to share exactly what he thought, even if it meant he offended in doing so. It was during some of those drives alone with Marty that Brandon would open up, allowing his brother to see what he was really thinking and feeling. Beyond the expected chitchat about sports, the two enjoyed real talk. They talked about life, faith and family; things that really mattered. The brothers valued those times for the bond it cemented between them.

And so, traveling back from Blytheville that day, Marty pitched an idea to his passenger. "Brandon," he said, pulling over and parking in front of a friend's house. "Why don't you just get out of the car and run home from here?" Brandon turned to his brother, raising his eyebrows as if to say, *Hmm, that's an idea.* "Sure. Okay," he said reluctantly.

Climbing out of the car, Brandon began trotting down the road toward home. Following closely behind him in the car, Marty looked like a Secret Service agent escort. But the gambit worked, and Brandon soon grew to understand both the value and benefits of a consistent conditioning program. Not long after this, he began running on his own without any prompting from his brother.

This running and dieting developed into a regimented routine. Between intermittent complaints that his decreased girth caused him to get pushed around in football, Brandon also saw some positive results in his performance, and that motivated him to keep up the good work. Through determined effort he had managed to salvage a permanent position on the team.

Now that his general conditioning was improving, it was time for Brandon to concentrate on the specifics of his game. Since his throwing mechanics weren't very good, work was needed if Brandon was to be a competitive pitcher. At 14 he had the ability to throw a baseball very hard, but struggled with his control. "Couldn't hit the backstop," Coach Tice remembers. That meant he would need practice, and lots of it. So Marty and Vickie filled a milk crate full of baseballs and headed out into the yard. At first, Brandon practiced throwing the ball into a chain link fence. This was to build up his arm strength. Then they pulled the car out of the garage, setting up a makeshift "batter's box" inside against the back wall. With a softer, little league baseball, Brandon would practice throwing into the square over and over, again and again. At night, they shined the car's headlights into the garage, giving him the light he needed to keep throwing. When it rained, he continued to throw using the garage as a makeshift indoor training facility. Vickie set up the video camera and they recorded Brandon's wind-up and delivery. Afterwards, they watched those films with religious repetition until both Marty and Brandon felt he had mastered the desired technique and accomplished his goal. The determination and drive that would one day become legendary was starting to take shape as he locked in on the goal of becoming an excellent pitcher and worked doggedly to achieve it.

Brandon's hard work began paying dividends at the end of the season as he was chosen to be a part of an area all-star team. The team traveled to Casper, Wyoming, where they competed in the NBC (National Baseball Congress) World Series. Harrison had periodically played host to the series, which brings teenage boys and their teams from all over the country together for a few days of highly competitive baseball. The team representing Harrison was coached by Jerry Maland. Maland was a former professional ballplayer with the Baltimore Orioles who loved the game and brought much-needed experience to the team. Together with Assistant Coach Mike McFarland, the group of 17 players chosen from city teams formed an all-league roster. These local standouts had, through their season's performance, earned themselves a spot on the squad.

Barbara Burlsworth was unable to make the trip that year, and since Marty and his family were vacationing in Baltimore at the time, Barbara asked Coach Maland to keep an eye on Brandon for her. Any time a parent sends her youngest child over a thousand miles away from home it's a comfort to know he is looked after by an adult. Jerry more than happily complied with her request, as he was fully aware that being responsible for Brandon would be an easy assignment. The once sloppy and rambunctious boy was becoming known as a conscientious, highly disciplined young man.

The 17-member team made the two-day trek in a caravan of cars. Brandon, Coach Maland, his son, Coach McFarland, and another player climbed into the coach's van and began the trip to faraway Casper. As far as Brandon knew, the town may as well have been what its name suggests — a ghost town. He hadn't spent too much time out of Arkansas, so any trip beyond its borders was a genuine adventure.

Nevertheless, in the 18 hours it took to get there, Brandon said just about as many words, keeping mostly to himself. Always speaking when spoken to, the reserve pitcher used his words as he did his pitches — endeavoring to make each one count.

But Jerry Maland wasn't the only former pro at the series that year. Invited to throw out the first pitch in the games was former Baltimore Orioles third baseman and Hall of Famer Brooks Robinson. Longtime faithful baseball fans remember Robinson for his trademark full-bodied dives down the third base line. He achieved legendary status partially due to winning Gold Gloves every year from 1960 to 1975, making more putouts, assists, and double plays than any third baseman in history. He also spent a record 23 years with one team, the Orioles. Sportswriter Gordon Beard said, "He never asked anyone to name a candy bar after him, but in Baltimore, people name their children after him." He played in four World Series and was named MVP in one of them, prompting the great Johnny

Bench to say, "I will become a left-handed hitter to keep the ball away from that guy." He was nicknamed "Hoover," after the vacuum cleaner, due to his ability to "suck up" every ball hit towards third base. Robinson set the standard as one of the game's premier infield superstars, defying any ball traveling on the ground or in the air to get past him. And he did all this in an era when players' salaries were modest compared to today's multi-million dollar contracts.

Besides throwing out the first pitch, the baseball great also spoke to all the players and coaches at the pre-series banquet held the night before opening ceremonies. Because Robinson was originally a Little Rock native and had the Oriole connection with Maland, he was invited to attend a special private meeting with the boys from Harrison. Happy to oblige, Brooks spent some quality time with the team, casually signing a few baseballs that would later find a permanent home on the tops of bedroom dressers all across a small town in the Ozarks. No fanfare here. Just a living legend taking a few moments to bring a little inspiration to a few boys. Robinson was attentive and extremely gracious with his time. Taking time to sign each ball, Robinson was unaware that at least one of those boys was watching with more than just eyes full of admiration. Standing silently in the crowd that night, one of the seventeen teenagers from Harrison jotted down a mental note. *Even though he's famous, we're still important to him.*

Moments like that impressed Brandon, teaching him valuable life lessons he would never forget. Years later, Brandon achieved celebrity status of his own as an Arkansas Razorback and All-American football player. As Brandon walked through his mom's front door carrying an armload of footballs, Barbara would ask, "Brandon, what in the world are you doing with all those?"

"The kids from church asked me if I would autograph them. I have to sign them all so I can bring them Sunday," he would explain.

During his career with the Hogs, Brandon came home occasionally to watch his old high school team play on Friday nights. Unfortunately, he never got to see much of the Goblin's games, as he spent most of his time on those nights signing autographs for little kids. Brandon was a bigger-than-life giant to those kids, a local legend who never said no to an autograph request. It was an example modeled for him years earlier on a hot summer night in Casper, Wyoming — one player, long past his prime and glory days showing the way for another who was yet to realize his own potential for greatness.

Yet, in spite of the inspiration of that evening, the baseball team from Harrison was easily defeated in the double-elimination tournament. Brandon, along with the other pitchers, saw limited playing time as they were shuffled in and out in an attempt to somehow reverse what proved to be an 0–2 showing at the series. It wasn't that the team was all that bad. They were just out-manned and out-played by better ball clubs that week. For Brandon, the ride home was as quiet as the trip up. Though he hated losing, he had pocketed two things worth keeping from the series — an autograph and an example. For a baseball fan and impressionable boy like Brandon, those two things were well worth the trip.

Perhaps his mind was already fast-forwarding to football. It was by this time August, and Tommy Tice's Goblins were scheduled to practice at 7:00 a.m. the following morning. The caravan from Wyoming wouldn't arrive back in Harrison until around 2:00 a.m., so Coach Tice graciously gave the baseball players a special exemption from the early-morning practice due to their long and exhausting ride home. Even so, most of the young athletes rose at five the next morning after only a couple hours' sleep, sluggishly making their way to the school's practice field. Not to be outdone, so did Brandon.

Though he would play baseball his sophomore year of high school, that trip to Casper proved to be among Brandon's last big baseball experiences. Being on the mound would soon take a back seat in his life. But Brandon still remained an avid baseball fan — watching games on television and talking about them with whomever would listen. He also retained an uncanny ability to recall facts regarding players and teams — win-loss records, batting averages, trades, positions, etc. It didn't matter. Brandon was a personal computer on legs with a seemingly limitless memory chip. Right up until he graduated from college, Brandon and Marty continued playing catch in the front yard, pitching to imaginary batters, dueling as if to outthrow the other. Barbara would come out onto the front porch to watch her boys. In her mind's eye, it was a flashback experience, almost like they were kids again.

Later, after being drafted into the NFL by the Indianapolis Colts, Brandon pitched an idea to Marty. "When I get to the NFL, and you come watch me play, we'll just bring our gloves along and play catch, just like we used to do."

Marty liked that idea.

FIVE

Best Friends

Though he had trouble with the game when he was younger, as Brandon grew it became evident that football would be the main sport at which he would excel. His rapid growth and ever-developing size and strength slowly guided him from the diamond to the gridiron. He enjoyed a short stint on the track and field squad, throwing both the discus and shot put, but Brandon's body was telling him in no uncertain terms he was destined to play football. That's where his future lay. Something deep inside him was stirring, like a black hole of desire, drawing him in. As in his other pursuits, Brandon subconsciously searched for a model and example to follow. Fortunately for Brandon, help was on the way.

Ed Robinson was also a homegrown product of Harrison, Arkansas. An Ozark country boy raised to answer "Yes ma'am" and "No sir," Ed carried himself with the same manner of rare but genuine humility that characterized Brandon. He wasn't the kind you'd see out partying with the local rabble-rousers on Friday night. Ed was a good boy with high moral standards, the kind of example every parent hopes their kid chooses as a friend. As a senior, Ed was a popular student and football star enjoying his last year in high school while Brandon was still enduring life as the new sophomore kid on the block. In the eyes of most seniors, sophomores are the bottom feeders in the Darwinian struggle that is the social food chain. Fortunately for Brandon, Ed didn't believe in evolution. To Brandon, Ed was his friend, the guy who had room in his world for an unimportant underclassman.

Ed was a member of First Assembly of God and a part of that Saturday "Superchurch" crew who stayed afterwards to play football with Youth Pastor Rick Watts. For Ed, Brandon, and the rest of the regular Saturday squad, football became more than just a way to pass the time on weekend. It grew to symbolize real friendship. Sports has a way of doing that, creating a bond that transcends social status or academic prowess. Guys have their own ways, methods, and mannerisms, which often make them alien to the fairer sex, and sometimes only men can really understand one another.

Guys generally bypass the emotional exchange they feel often characterizes relationships between girls. Guys don't usually hug. They "high-five." They don't tell their friends they love them. They say, "good game" or "good job" or "way to go." "How are you doing?" is replaced by "Wassup, man?" A boy demonstrates his affection for a buddy by blindsiding him on the football field, driving him three inches deep into the wet, Saturday-soaked backyard turf. Guys are more likely to exchange well-meaning insults than to exchange gifts, and in the rare event that a boy's mom buys a present for his friend's birthday, it had better be a sports-related offering or a macho action figure that shoots deadly laser beams – no sissy stuff allowed. Boys are rough with each other to the point of near-violence and can walk precariously close to the precipice of cruelty in their interactions. But they all know the unwritten rule — "no harm, no foul." Brandon and his buddies spoke this "guy dialect."

Just ask a boy who his best buddy is and he will likely reply that it's the guy who runs and sweats with him at recess or on the field. And though he doesn't possess the security and maturity to verbalize it yet, he loves his friend deeply. All political correctness aside, guys are different from girls. In their own twisted and insecure way, they still communicate. It's their way of expressing their God-implanted need for significance through the affirmation of others. This is part of what Brandon found in his friendship with Ed Robinson.

Having Ed as a buddy was a major coup for Brandon. It was like having friends in high places. In the world of a sophomore, having a senior friend is the equivalent of knowing someone in the Oval Office. It means you have an automatic "in," an advantage of sorts, a heads-up on the rest of the rabble that pave the road upon which upperclassmen tread. It's almost like skipping a grade in the cutthroat sub-culture of teenage society. And when you're shy and still a few pounds overweight, having this friend means you just won the social lottery.

Brandon may not have been consciously thinking all this, but he sure felt it inside. He did know that Ed was someone to look up to. Brandon admired Ed's athletic ability as well as his Christian character. He couldn't have cared less about social standing or popularity. He wasn't interested in achieving recognition for being a "big man on campus." He was just happy to have a friend, an ally, and most of all, a role model. But though he valued the friendship, the shy sophomore rarely called Ed on the phone. Ed made up for it, though, by calling Brandon, regularly coming by to pick him up in his truck. The two would go get pizza, pass the football around, or just go to Ed's and hang out where they would play pool, catch a game on TV, or rent a movie. For a kid who had trouble making friends, Brandon may as well have stumbled on buried treasure hidden in the Ozarks, so important to him was his friendship with Ed.

They nicknamed each other "Big." "Hey, Big." "What's up, Big?" It seemed a simple way to identify a guy who was your best friend, and it fit because they were both "big boys."

But more than that, they each played a big part in one another's life. It was an appropriate alias for two Arkansas country boys.

Ed Robinson had gained quite a reputation as a player on the Harrison High football team. Coach Tice and his Golden Goblins were fast becoming a force to be reckoned with in the competitive Class AAA division of Arkansas football. Tice had come to Harrison High in 1982 as head coach and athletic director. Since that time he had steadily built an athletic program that rivaled any in the state. During his tenure the school had not seen a single losing season. Ed was an outstanding lineman and one of the star players on the team.

At the close of his senior year, Ed was selected to play in the Arkansas high school all-star game, traditionally held at War Memorial Stadium in Little Rock. High school athletes compete all season for the chance to be selected from among their peers as the state's finest football players. A special kind of pride swelled within the 18-year-old Robinson, knowing the state's coaches believed him to be the best at his position and one of the best in the state. It was the pinnacle of Ed's football career to date, and a good showing in this game would increase his chances of being recruited by a major college. But the day before the all-star game all that changed in an instant. Ed seriously injured his knee during practice, tearing his anterior cruciate ligament. A season-ending injury for any player, it meant Ed would certainly miss the all-star game. But beyond that it cast a serious cloud over his hopes of being recruited by a Division I school. Disappointed and disheartened, Ed was forced to watch the game from the bench, sporting an uncomfortable pair of crutches. He had so hoped to star in the game, but real life had other plans. Ed's role and career on the football field would prove to be effectively over. But his greatest role was the one he was playing in Brandon's life.

Brandon and his mom came down to watch the game and to lend moral support to Ed. While there, Brandon was inspired beyond watching two high-school teams battle it out at War Memorial Stadium. Though the athletes were playing on artificial turf, there was nothing artificial about what Brandon saw in his mind. What he saw was as real as the players themselves. Even as a young teenager, Brandon was envisioning long-term goals. Objectives. Aspirations. Mentally, he projected himself down onto that field. His point of focus moved beyond making the varsity squad back up in Harrison. It even went beyond becoming a high school all-star. Though it was hardly full that chilly autumn day, Brandon imagined the 53,727 stadium seats packed to overflowing with cheering Arkansas Razorback fans. For a brief moment, he was captivated by a vision that took control of him. Filled with this inspiration, and amid the roar of the crowd, Brandon calmly yet confidently turned to his mom declaring, "I'll be here one day, Mom."

Unprepared for such a statement, as anyone would be, Barbara paused for a second, then with a maternal smile lovingly affirmed her son. So real was this image in Brandon's mind, it may as well have been announced over the public address system or flashed in lights on the scoreboard. Barbara turned again and looked at her son. Though he was now topping the six-foot mark, to her Brandon was still her baby boy. And she had no reason not to believe in him. His birth had been an unexpected but blessed one. God's plan had been evident from the beginning of his life. And who was she to doubt that plan would include something great for him? With the fresh oracle of his unexpected "pigskin prophecy," Brandon had decided his destiny then and there in that stadium. His mind was now made up. His course was set. For Brandon, there would be no second-guessing, doubt or reservations. And though the road ahead would be fraught with obstacles and involve a long, uphill climb, for Brandon, there would be no turning back.

SIX

KICKED AROUND

Had you been the proverbial fly on the wall the first time 15-year-old Brandon walked into the weight room at Harrison High School, you might not have recognized the former chubby kid from Cherry Street. Like most boys his age, Brandon was experiencing a growth spurt. A transformation was taking place, morphing his former frame into a 6-foot, 160-pound figure. While part of his new look was attributable to the typical pubescent surge in height, another contributing factor was Brandon's own conditioning program. Following brother Marty's initial push to begin running, Brandon had begun taking ownership of the discipline and shedding pounds in the process. However, losing weight also had its disadvantages, with Brandon complaining to his big brother, "I'm getting kicked around out there on the field, Marty. Now that I've lost that weight, the other guys are bigger than me."

This was a first for Brandon, who had grown quite accustomed to dominating teammates with his weight advantage. In his mind, his physical presence and performance was now failing to intimidate or impress anyone. But unknown to him, he was catching the attention of the ones who really mattered. The Harrison junior high team had already begun their practice season when Athletic Director Tommy Tice decided to visit the field and give the team a look. After all, it would be this same group of athletes that would become his future varsity squad. Spotting a lanky kid from across the field, Tice strolled up to Junior High Coach Inky Williams.

"Inky," Tice said with a hometown chuckle in his voice, "who is that kid over there?" pointing to Brandon.

"Coach," Williams immediately replied, "that kid right there is going to be a great football player one day."

A great football player? thought Tice. *How in the world could he make a statement like that?*

By all accounts, Brandon wasn't exactly tearing up the opposition at this point. In fact, just the opposite was taking place. It was a simple matter of math, actually. When an object weighing 160 pounds comes into contact with another weighing 210 pounds, the laws of physics dictate that the heavier object has the right of way. Translated, this means the bigger players were using Brandon to sod the practice field.

To make matters worse, his deficiency in size was equally matched by a lack of coordination. In Tice's words, "Brandon couldn't walk and chew gum at the same time." But though he was not naturally gifted, Brandon had already got it in his stubborn mind he was going to be a starter for the Goblins. He had developed a certain intensity, an ability to latch onto a goal like a snapping turtle onto a stick, not letting go … even during thunder. Derailing him from a decided objective required a blowtorch, sledgehammer and the "Jaws of Life." Nothing would deter him now. He wanted to play.

Of course, that didn't mean it would be easy for him. Few things worth having in life come easy. But goal-oriented individuals know that if it's worth having then it's worth the work and sacrifice it takes to get it. For Brandon, it would be a simple-yet grueling equation of labor and pain plus time. It would mean, as Tice told him, he had to be the first on site and the last to leave. While some athletes cruise on natural God-given ability, other less-talented individuals are forced to work twice as hard and long. Like a public speaker that spends little time in preparation or a gifted student who never studies, the "natural athlete" may need minimal practice time to maintain a level of play that outshines his opponents and teammates. But the rest, who don't possess that inborn quality, are forced to become overcomers, even overachievers. It's that or they are sentenced to ride the bench.

But what Brandon lacked in natural ability he made up for in an almost Marquis de Sade-like approach to discipline. Becoming a starter on the team was now his goal, an all-or-nothing proposition. He knew he was capable of more as a player, that there was potential bottled up inside him screaming to get out. That positive attitude had been drilled into him by his family and modeled for him by friends like Ed Robinson. As a result, a maturing determination was now present within him, a steadfastness of spirit, a fierce sense of focus. Like a locomotive charging down the tracks, this desire caused Brandon to surge full-speed ahead toward his vision with reckless abandon. And heaven have mercy on anyone who got in his way.

At the outset of his sophomore year, Brandon and his fellow third-stringers on the football team were used as a practice squad for the starting offensive line. These upperclassmen starters were bigger, stronger, more experienced, and smarter on the football field than were Brandon and his fellow greenhorns. And it's not easy being green. The end result was that the older guys would pound their younger teammates with such a beating that Brandon left most practices with tears in his eyes. But he always came back the next day. And the next.

When an athlete does that, he earns the attention and respect of his coaches. Brandon knew he had to "do his time" on the JV and practice squads if he was to gain enough merit to start for the Golden Goblins one day. But he reasoned it was worth it. *Set a goal before you and let it motivate you*, he thought. Having seen the district trophies prominently displayed in the entrance hall of Harrison High, Brandon was reminded every morning of the winning tradition the Goblins had established over the years. And he was also well aware of the reputation of a coach like Tommy Tice.

There are advantages to being the only "anything" in a small town. The only bank. The only grocery. The only orthodontist. The only church. When there is just one of your kind, you get all the business — and all the attention. But if you're the only high school football coach in town, it's a good news/bad news scenario that can be a blessing or a curse, depending on the direction of the wind on a particular day. You can be a local hero, basking in the light of your own glory. You can stroll down Main Street, greeting and waving at adoring townsfolk and fans. On the other hand, you can become fodder for editorial satire and the target of brutal insults. In the latter case, it becomes the better part of wisdom to avoid those streets, especially when they're laying fresh tar.

That's where Tommy Tice lived. In the community of Harrison High School athletics, he was the law, and everybody knew it. Those who knew him saw Tice grow older as the Harrison athletic program got better. His once dark hair had turned gray, and although he was outwardly masked by the wrinkles in his face, inside lived a youthful spirit that still energized this country boy.

Through his longevity and (more importantly) his winning tradition, Tice had become the "sheriff of football" in town — When he spoke his words were taken seriously by the local media, by students, athletes, parents, fellow high school coaches, and by recruiting scouts from major colleges. But Tice's credibility wasn't handed to him on a silver clipboard. He earned it the old-fashioned way — hard work plus time. There are no shortcuts to respect. That is one medal only awarded after a community has watched several years of game films. No flash-in-the-pan, overnight sensation here. Tice had a statewide reputation for bringing out the very best in his players, and the reflecting gold shine on his championship trophies were proof of it.

But the high school coach had learned there was far more to coaching than just X's and O's. He also had a personal touch that made all the difference in the lives of his players. Coach Tice was not so naïve to think every athlete on his team came from a healthy and affirming home life. Along with a coach's cap and clipboard had come the intangible expectation of being a role model and sometimes surrogate father to certain teenage boys. Even for the ones whose emotional tanks are regularly filled by plenty of love and attention at home, coaches still have the opportunity to reinforce a young man's self-worth and value.

So in an effort to be a positive influence on his players, Coach Tice had inaugurated a little custom he occasionally employed with his players. As they arrived for practice each day, Tice made an effort to be the first person his players saw. He would smile and tell each boy he was glad they were there. Then before they left for the day he made sure they saw that same smile again, recognizing the time in between he probably wouldn't be smiling too much at them! On the contrary, he would be riding them like crazy, whipping them into shape. It's hard to smile while simultaneously criticizing and critiquing. For some of his players, Coach figured, it just might be the only time during the day they got a smile from anybody. But in addition to his friendly greeting and in a further effort to bond with his team, Tice also had another custom of sorts, occasionally commenting to a player, "Hey, have I told you I loved you lately?" And when the athlete responded "No Coach, you haven't," Tice would smile and say, "I'll get back to you on that." It was a "macho-lite" method of communicating a love he had for each one of his boys. And over the years it had helped build a unifying bridge between the coach and his athletes.

For Brandon, Tice was just what he needed to help him take his game to the next level. To hear the coach talk, Brandon hardly needed anyone's help, so strong was the teenager's will to win. But that was Tice's humility showing itself. At this stage in his development, Brandon desperately needed the direction of a veteran instructor who knew how to uncover hidden talent. He needed someone who was an "old hand" at molding playground wannabes into gifted young athletes. Tommy Tice was the man. He still is.

Of course it helps a coach to have some raw materials with which to work. Between Brandon's sophomore and junior year in high school, he went through yet another physical change. Though he continued to steadily grow in height, he began "beefing up" over the summer as well. Tice saw Marty Burlsworth the following fall and quizzed him regarding Brandon.

"Marty, what in the world have you been feeding that boy?"

Confused, Marty replied, "Coach, what are you talking about?'

"I'm talking about Brandon. Just look at him. He's grown taller and gotten twice as big," Tice responded.

"Hmm. Well I haven't really noticed. You know I see him every day, and I guess it happened gradually," Marty said with a smile.

Marty proceeded to go straight home and confront his baby brother. "Hey Bran. How did you get bigger than me all of a sudden?"

Without missing a beat, Brandon replied matter-of-factly, "Eatin' and lifting weights."

That fall the *Harrison Daily Times* had written a feature article of a preseason football forecast. In the article, the writer had made mention of Brandon's increased growth and size. He had been hitting the weights and it was starting to show. His time spent pumping iron and his dedication to conditioning had guaranteed at least one thing for sure: Brandon wasn't going to be kicked around any longer.

But that wasn't the only way he had shown improvement. He had begun hitting the books as much as he was hitting the weight room and his academics were steadily improving as well. Again it was a case of part Brandon, part mentor. This time it was a teacher named Grant Williams. Williams had been teaching business law for over 20 years at the high school, just the kind of thing you'd expect in towns like Harrison. When he wasn't teaching, Grant worked at home on his cattle farm.

Williams is an amiable man, easy to get to know. He ran his classes effectively but informally and students were drawn to his personable nature. By his own admission, Williams had always tried to communicate the message that every person in his class is important, that every student has value and potential. One student who got the message was Brandon.

Having been a high school quarterback in his day, Williams had at one time been an excellent athlete. Fortunately for him, working the cattle farm had kept him from going the way of most men in their late thirties. Williams had kept in relatively good shape, and he proved it by periodically challenging some of his students to arm wrestling matches after class. One particular day saw big Brandon step up to the table to show up the teacher in front of his fellow students (and football players).

If I can't beat this little ole teacher, Brandon must have inwardly grinned, *I'll never be able to show my face around here again. No sweat, though. This will be a cakewalk.*

The two squared off, sitting in facing desks. The teacher and his student clasped right hands tightly together as a small gallery of onlookers encircled the desks. They secured their elbows on the desktops while positioning their arms at a 90-degree angle. They stared intently into each other's eyes, waiting for someone to give them the go-ahead. Finally, after a tense moment, someone yelled "Go!" and the match began. The two hands pressed together. Squeezing each other with much greater force than either of them had anticipated, Brandon's brow immediately became furrowed and a glimmer of surprise momentarily flashed over his face. *Man! He's not supposed to be this strong.*

Brandon had not anticipated the soft-spoken, smaller-bodied business teacher to possess such upper body strength. He had much less body mass than Brandon, and besides, the football player was the one who had been working out with weights, not the teacher. The contest went on, progressing rapidly into the "red-faced, vein-protruding" stage. Brandon decided it was time to end this thing, so he turned it up a notch, flexing his developing bicep. But when he did, Williams did the same. He was matching Brandon pound for pound, muscle for muscle. That's when most contestants lift out of their chair a little in an attempt to gain the advantage through leverage. But Brandon would stick to the unofficial rules of classroom arm-wrestling, keeping his rear end firmly planted in his seat. Their forearms began shaking as they exerted even more force.

By this time, the small crowd had grown and was becoming vocal, with students cheering for their favorite.

"C'mon, Mr. Williams. You can do it! Stick it to him!" yelled one student.

"Brandon, what are you doing, man? You're not gonna let this old man beat you, are ya?!" shouted another.

The noise level continued to rise as the match lingered on. What Brandon at first thought would be a test of initial quickness and strength had turned into an enduring battle of bulging biceps. For a while, it looked as though the match might end in a deadlock, then as if drawing from an unseen reservoir of power, Grant Williams clenched his jaw and body-slammed Brandon's wrist onto the hardwood desk.

That action sent cheers from the crowd reverberating down the emptying hallway outside the room. Williams raised his fist in triumph while an exhausted and heavy-breathing Brandon hung his head, shaking it in disbelief. And as the blood slowly began returning to their extremities, the two shook hands, smiling at one another. An inaudible exchange took place, the look in their eyes speaking for their mouths.

"You didn't think I could do it, did you?" asked Williams.

No sir, Mr. Williams. But I'm gonna get you next time. You just wait.

Brandon remembered his thought about not being able to show his face anymore if he lost. So he decided to show his face somewhere else for a while, particularly in the weight room. *Maybe one extra set of curls today*, he would think, recalling his humiliating loss to the man old enough to be his father. He would challenge Mr. Williams many more times over the course of the year. Understandably, these were usually private, after-school matches scheduled when the other students had left for the day. And Williams kept beating him again and again.

Months passed and Brandon's investments in the weight room steadily began paying dividends. By the end of the school year Brandon was able to consistently conquer his older arm-wrestling nemesis. But apart from their heated contests, Grant Williams became Brandon's favorite teacher. Having taken two classes under Williams, Brandon did something that, as far as Williams can recollect, only a handful of students have done during his 23-year teaching career.

"Mr. Williams, can I ask you a favor?" Brandon asked as graduation day drew near.

"Sure, Brandon," Williams replied. "Anything. What can I do for you?"

"Well, sir. I was wondering if I might have the textbook we used this year," he said.

Williams was caught off guard, but managed to hide his surprise. "Of course, Brandon. Here, you can take it with you."

"Thanks, Mr. Williams. I really appreciate it," Brandon responded.

Most students at this point in the year are scheming ways to make up assignments or trying to work for extra credit to raise their grade. Some are thinking up ways to skip the last few classes. Burlsworth asked for the textbook. For a "by-the-book" guy like Brandon this was no big deal, really. But given the fact that most teenagers wouldn't request to take a textbook home unless it was for kindling to start a fire, Williams was pleasantly surprised at Brandon's request. The business law teacher was also honored that he had somehow helped create an interest in Brandon for business. It felt good as a teacher to know that what he had taught actually made a difference in a student's life. Williams' personal attention to Brandon had built a bridge to him, and no matter what he carted across that bridge, whether it was academics, athletics, or arm-wrestling, this particular teenager was going to listen.

Brandon got that textbook and a whole lot more.

Fortunately for Brandon, Williams was another link in a chain of character-builders who was passing through his life. This is not unique to Brandon Burlsworth's experience. Many, if not most young people encounter such potential mentors as they mature. What made Brandon different was that he didn't waste these opportunities as they arose. While other kids were blowing off advice from their elders, Brandon had the foresight to take notes and put what he learned into action, seizing on every chance he had to learn from the role models he encountered. Teenagers famously think they know everything. Brandon Burlsworth had the humility to know he had much to learn and the innate respect and wisdom to be diligent in listening to those who had traveled life's road ahead of him.

In the case of Williams, he had the ability to see through a different set of lenses when it came to Brandon. He knew and appreciated the teenager for who he was, shy or not. He didn't challenge him to become someone else, but rather endeavored to help him become who he was meant to be. Brandon always addressed him as "Mr. Williams" or "Sir." That was the respectful thing to do. Because of this respect, Brandon believed almost everything told to him by Williams and other adults he admired. That prompted his coaches and teachers to be careful what they said to him. Tommy Tice would later tell the Razorback coaching staff, "You had better watch out what you tell Brandon to do, 'cause he'll do it. If you tell him he needs to gain about 60 pounds before next season, be sure it's 60 and not really just 20, 'cause he'll gain 60!"

Obey your elders. Believe the best in people. That is what Brandon was taught to do at home. That was the right way to live.

That was Burls' way.

SEVEN

Goblins!

There is a distinctive dynamic about high school football in this country that isn't recreated or duplicated at any other age or in any other sport. It's a fall ritual, as real as religion in some parts, and sometimes just as serious. In small towns all across America, this autumn drama is played out from tiny two-bleacher arenas in rural South Carolina to college-sized high school stadiums in metropolitan Texas. Parents, students, and hometown fans shell out a few dollars to come and root for their favorite team. It's a place to see friends, a grand social event in a small community. It's a chance to cheer on your old alma mater and reminisce back to when you sat in the stands with a Friday night date. It's a time to wrap up in a wool blanket to fend off a bitter October chill. Kids disinterested in the action on the field run under the bleachers playing tag or throw miniature footballs just outside the end zones. Cheerleaders brave the cold in pleated skirts, performing their well-rehearsed routines on the running track, which encloses the field. Parents of players wear booster club buttons depicting their sons' numbers. Team mascots provide amusing pre-game entertainment. Girlfriends watch as uniformed boyfriends give it their best effort, hoping for that one spectacular play that will impress their love interest. And in the event he should get hurt, she'll assume her rightful place as head nail-biter, anxiously awaiting the moment he is lifted back to his feet and helped off the field amid polite applause from both grandstands.

But the game itself is only part of the evening's excitement. The building anticipation leading up to the kickoff also plays a key role in the drama. Players hang up their jeans and letter jackets for a few hours on Friday night and outfit themselves in pants, pads, and helmets. The pre-game meal is finished. The locker room pep talk is over. The team prayer is done and the group huddles together one last time before taking the field. Assembling in the end zone, you could launch the space shuttle with the energy running through those young men. Then, like a galloping herd of wild mustangs, the team bursts through the paper banner held by the school's cheerleaders. Usually there is a victory slogan painted on that banner, something that motivates a stadium full of fans.

Beat Central!

Slay the Dragons!

Tame the Tigers!

Pound the Patriots!

As the home team charges through the banner, the hometown crowd erupts like a smoldering volcano, sending an avalanche of applause. It's fall and it's Friday night, and that means high school football. Is there anything more American than that?

In Harrison, Arkansas, you'll find only one place to play high school football … Goblin Stadium.

Known both regionally and statewide, the home turf of the Harrison High football team may as well be a landmark on the National Historical Register, so treasured is the edifice to local residents. The stadium is located next to Crooked Creek, which winds its way northward through the city. People say there is something special about those waters. No, not healing power to "cure what ails you," but something entirely different. That water has "winning power." It's the "Magic of

Crooked Creek," as Coach Tice calls it. And Harrison High football teams have been winning on it for years.

Ironically, the high school itself is several miles away on a new campus. The old school, now the junior high, is located on the property adjacent to the stadium. When the new high school was constructed in the mid-eighties, the decision was made to keep the home stadium at the former site because of the rich tradition established there. As a result, high school teams all over Arkansas now know about "the stadium beside the creek," having experienced repeated drownings in its nearby waters.

Brandon had begun his junior year alternating at positions with a senior, and did that for half a season. This was fine with him, given the fact he had spent the previous year wearing out the grass on the sidelines. Not yet a shadow of what he would later become physically, Brandon's skinny legs didn't quite seem to fit the rest of his developing frame. He looked like a pear on a couple of toothpicks. Barbara was plenty ready for her son to move from the sidelines to more time on the playing field. "Brandon, honey, I don't like to go to all these games and watch the back of your head the whole time," she would say.

Brandon began raising the bar on his personal goals and performance. He had started a new weight room regimen that was contributing to his improved play on the field. Not content to merely work out with the rest of the team, Brandon decided he would get up early in the morning, beginning his day while most of his friends were still "sawing logs" back home in bed. He asked Coach Tice if he could get into the weight room before school to work out, a request the coach was more than willing to grant. A typical morning went something like this: Tice would arrive at the school, driving around to the weight room back entrance. It was 6:15 and dark many of those mornings. Shutting off his headlights, Tice would see a lone figure silently sitting by the door in the pre-dawn darkness. Brandon's standard greeting never changed. "Coach, you sleep in again this morning? I've been here for 15 minutes waiting on you."

Without fail, he was the first to arrive and the last to leave the weight room, which had become a second home of sorts to Brandon. From the coach's vantage point, Tice observed Brandon's gradual but decisive development through his plate glass office window which overlooked the weight room. He knew he was seeing Inky Williams' prediction of Brandon becoming a great player come true before his own eyes. That pseudo-prophecy's partial fulfillment was taking place right there on the weight bench as Brandon grinded it out alone every morning at 6:15 a.m.

Brandon finally earned himself a spot in the Goblins' starting lineup. The offensive line position seemed to fit him best, and he quickly grew to love his role, soon becoming a typical lineman. The front line of the Goblins adopted the traditional short sleeve jersey, which made them look a little tougher than the opposing players, particularly in cold weather when many players dressed for warmth.

The Harrison Goblins had posted an impressive 11-2 record Brandon's sophomore year, winning the 3-A district title, thanks in part to players like Ed Robinson. The following year saw the team go 9-3. That was Brandon's junior year, and he progressed enough to make the all-district team. Up to this time he had played only one side of the line (offense). But during his senior year Coach Tice decided to give the rapidly developing athlete multiple jobs on the team. And so Brandon made the adjustment to play both defense and offense, with a spot on the kickoff team to boot.

It became almost a pre-game ritual for Tice to walk up to #54 and say, "Well, Brandon. I guess I'll see you when the game is over." Brandon would be on the field for the majority of the game serving in his three assignments, and he loved it. He also loved it when, during the week prior to a game, the media would tout the greatness of the opposing team's running back or defensive tackle. That only served as fuel to his fire, motivating him to make sure they didn't shine during the contest against the Goblins. His ever-increasing size and strength caused him to dominate his opponents, particularly while he was on offense.

During his sophomore and junior years, when a player would be down on the field hurt, Barbara Burlsworth would anxiously ask, "Is that Brandon down there? Is he hurt?" But throughout his senior year, when a player lay hurt on the field she would say, "Did Brandon do that?" She feared his growing strength and passion for the game was a little too much at times, and she didn't like that. She voiced her concern to Marty. "He's hurting those kids," she would typically say.

But the other players weren't the only ones he hurt. During one practice, Coach Tice decided to teach his defensive linemen the proper method of rushing on a certain play. Rather than draw on a clipboard, he strapped on a helmet and proceeded to give them a live example. Lining up against Brandon, who was playing on the offensive line, Tice called for the play to be run. Burlsworth came charging off the line like a bull out of the chute, smashing Tice across his facemask and sending the coach crashing to the ground where he hit his head, hard.

Stunned and dazed, Tice staggered back to his feet, and with his head still spinning said, "Now, Burlsworth. Don't ever make me show you how to do that again." That incident put Tice's playing career into permanent retirement, and he hasn't put on a helmet since.

Though he made significant contributions as a defensive tackle, Brandon lacked the necessary speed and quickness to effectively and consistently penetrate the backfield in time. Still, he knew that if he could get to the quarterback just after he released the ball, he could pop him hard, "ringing his bell." For a defensive lineman, there is no greater thrill than to sack the quarterback, knocking him into another time zone. A really good hit would cause the quarterback to wonder what day of the week it was. Unfortunately for Brandon, those sacks were few and far between, as he recorded a lot of "almost" sacks. It's still true that "almost" only counts in horseshoes and hand grenades.

In Brandon's last year to play for the Goblins, the team from Harrison managed a better-than-respectable 8-3 record. One moment during that year stuck out in Brandon's mind above all others. Harrison High was playing a big game against rival Alma, another small town some two hours southwest of Harrison. It was a home game but also a crucial one that season. Late in the contest, the score was 7-0 in favor of Harrison, with Alma threatening to score. Brandon was playing defensive strong side tackle that game, and he and the Goblin defense had stood strong, preventing Alma from making a first down. Now it was fourth down, and for the Alma Airedales, there was no debate as to what they should do. They were going for it. This would be a make or break play. If you know anything about football, you are well aware coaches don't normally go for it on fourth down unless it's absolutely necessary or the game is on the line. And that's exactly the predicament in which Alma found itself. With a loss looming, they would have to do something big to turn the tide. The next snap would pretty much decide the outcome of the game.

The Airedale offense broke from their huddle with a united handclap and trotted to the line of scrimmage. In a fourth down scenario the offense typically tries to draw the defensive line offsides, throw a Hail Mary pass, or confuse with a misdirection play. But since Alma needed more yards than an offside penalty would provide, that left the offense choosing one of the latter options.

The two teams met face to face on the line as the quarterback took his position behind the center. "Down!" shouted the team leader, scanning the defense as he barked out his signals. “Set!” he continued, trying to lift his voice above the enthusiastic roar of the hometown fans, who had by this time risen to their feet. Throughout the stadium fans and players alike anxiously awaited the play’s outcome. Brandon tensed impatiently, poised in his defensive stance, anxious to make something happen. Clenching his mouthgaurd tighter, he gave the opposing lineman an intense stare. Then, in rapid succession, the quarterback blasted out his cadence, “HUT! HUT!” The Alma team leader dropped back, and it looked for a split second as though they had called a pass play. Harrison’s defensive secondary, terrified of getting beat on a game-winning play, took the bait and sprinted downfield in anticipation of the final throw. But just as quickly as he had dropped back, the quarterback threw a quick inside pitch to the tailback, who had remained in the backfield as a blocking decoy. With the majority of the defense having bit on the pass play, they were caught with their momentum headed in the wrong direction. The d-linemen were caught off guard as well, cleats digging into the turf, engaged in hand-to-hand combat with the offensive line. Nobody saw the pitch, or if they did they were already too committed to change course and do anything about it. This was going to be a big play and a first down for sure, perhaps even a game-tying touchdown run.

Fortunately for the Goblins, there was one defensive lineman who had not been duped by the misdirection. Number 54 had kept a laser-beam lock on the quarterback, simultaneously engaging the offensive lineman while also watching the quarterback’s eyes from the snap to the feigned pass. By the time the tailback touched the leather, Brandon had already Fed-Exed himself into the backfield, nailing the ball carrier for a huge loss and giving Harrison possession. Prior to the play, brother Marty had been nervously roaming the sidelines, looking more like one of the coaching staff than a spectator. Upon seeing the result of the play, as the ball was blown dead, Harrison fans exploded into a standing ovation.

On the sidelines, Marty ran through a horde of high fives, slapping every hand he could find. It was the play of the game and eventually made the difference for Harrison as they went on to kick a field goal, sealing the victory.

Final score: Goblins 10, Alma 0.

It was during that same game when an Alma defensive lineman came off the field and returned to the sidelines, where he threw his helmet to the ground with such force he sent his chinstrap flying. The Alma coach reprimanded the player, who immediately responded, "I'm just mad 'cause we're losing, Coach." Shaking his head, the coach responded, "No. You're mad because Burlsworth has been whipping your tail all night!" The truth hurts. Like watching a recurring game film, that fourth-down play screened in the theater of Brandon's mind many times in the years to come, ultimately becoming his favorite high school football memory. But to keep from becoming too proud, Brandon reminded himself of the same advice he gave his Goblin teammates: "Be humble or stumble."

But it wasn't all guts and glory… one memory he tried hard to forget was the Goblins final home game loss to Malvern. The Malvern High School Leopards possessed an established running game, and were padding their reputation by running all over Harrison this particular night. That Friday saw rain, and lots of it, but for reasons unknown, the waters of Crooked Creek were running low for the Golden Goblins. The premier running back for the Leopards was somewhat of a showman, and the field was his stage that evening. Play after play, he managed to avoid tackles and scramble out of the backfield, virtually untouched by the defense, stepping around them like stationary cones in a practice drill. It proved embarrassing as time after time he rambled and juked his way downfield for another gain.

On one particular play, the Malvern star tailback broke free for a long run, and to add insult to injury, glanced back, giving the Harrison defense a mocking smile. Left in his wake, all the Goblins could do was watch through the pouring rain as the lone figure sprinted effortlessly toward a rain-soaked end zone.

The Harrison defensive line had struggled that year, and by Coach Tice's own admission, "weren't all that good." Even so, it still frustrated them to get beat so badly by this cocky running back. But nobody was more frustrated than Brandon. He hated to get beat by a guy like that. Worse, he hated to lose. He absolutely despised it. Defeat always produced a hollow feeling in the pit of his stomach, leaving him and often those in his presence feeling kind of sick. Though not a sore loser, Brandon was still not very good company when he lost. Most champions aren't. Winning represents many things to athletes like that. Winning is a focal point. A destination. A driving motivation. For some, it's more than an objective. It's an obsession. For Brandon, a loss meant a goal was not achieved, and to a goal-oriented young man like him, that was a frustrating experience. Because of the physical and emotional intensity exhibited by these championship-caliber athletes, they sometimes need time to process a loss, let their emotions settle, and put the defeat into the big picture of the season and life.

Brandon was no different. And even though he lived just blocks from the stadium, it was a very long ride home that night. Ironically, Brandon was unaware at the time that he would see this running back again after graduation from high school. In fact, he would see him almost every day for the next five years. Only this time, he wouldn't be trying to tackle him. Instead, this star tailback would be lining up behind Brandon, not against him. Soon he would help running back Madre Hill score touchdowns for the Arkansas Razorbacks, clearing a path for him as he rambled downfield. This time Madre would be looking back at Division I defenders with that mocking glare, as eventually he became an outstanding tailback for the Hogs. A nice enough guy in real life, Hill effortlessly dodged defenders on the field, causing some of them to look like they belonged back on the high school squad. And Brandon would be cheering his teammate on as he ran, pumping his fist in the air in triumph instead of helplessly watching him set land speed records.

Once again, all Brandon's hard work paid off as #54 won numerous accolades his senior year. He was voted the Outstanding Football Player in his hometown and had already been a two-time all-conference choice in addition to making all-state. But then came the High School All-Star Game. Coach Tommy Tice had been a fixture in the Arkansas High School Coaches' Association, so much so that he almost went to work for them at one point. But his blood still ran Goblin blue, so he decided to continue coaching at Harrison. Had Brandon needed some lobbying to gain a spot on the all-star team, Tice would have been a worthy and influential advocate. But Burlsworth's performance his senior year was convincing enough for the high school coaches who selected the team roster.

In the fall of '93, War Memorial Stadium was undergoing a field upgrade, replacing the well-worn artificial turf for real grass. Most Division I schools were returning to the more traditional playing field, and since the Hogs played several of their games down in Little Rock the decision was made to make the change. Unfortunately for that year's high school all-stars, it meant the game would have to be moved to another location. Since it was also centrally located, the field at the University of Central Arkansas in Conway was chosen. The field was a logical choice, as it was familiar to the coaches, having been used as the practice facility for the all-star game each year. Mildly disappointed, in the end it didn't matter all that much to Brandon, just as long as he was allowed to strap on a helmet and play offensive line. And play he did, his most satisfying block of the game coming on a quarterback roll-out. Brandon's responsibility was to pull and lead the way for the quarterback. But as he began clearing a path, a defensive end came charging hard, intending to swat Brandon out of his way like a fly in order to get the quarterback. Burlsworth, who seemed to be aware of what was going on around him at all times, saw the end coming and prepared himself for a head-on collision. When the two met, Brandon never even slowed as he plowed right through the defender, busting him up into the air and knocking him back on the turf where he landed on his rear. That powerful display of strength sent a domino effect of elbowing and laughing between Tice and his coaching buddies.

Though Brandon loved to win, he lived for something even greater. What motivated him was more than just walking away without a defeat. From as early as he could understand the concept, he was taught to work hard, be the best he could be, and do it all for God's glory. This is not to say Brandon didn't balk at working hard at times, especially during those early conditionings with brother Marty. But eventually the teenager took personal ownership of his work ethic and approach to life. As a result, he became a quarterback's best friend, doing more than just blocking for him. Brandon developed an "extra mile" attitude on every play, not stopping until he heard the referee's whistle blow.

But though he had a superb showing at that all-star game, the award for outstanding lineman was given to someone else. Prior to the game, Brandon made the comment that it always seemed that the award was given to an incoming scholarshipped football player at the University of Arkansas. Winning that award would take him one step closer to his goal of becoming a Razorback. But things didn't quite turn out the way Brandon had planned; though he was right about the scholarship, as the award was given that year to Grant Garrett. Once again, irony prevailed as Brandon and Grant went on to become teammates and very good friends, playing side-by-side on the Hogs' offensive line. However, Brandon remained unconvinced Garrett was the better player that day in Conway, often jokingly quipping to his buddy, "You got my award."

Brandon had played his last high school football game. He would never again wear a Harrison High School football uniform, never again hear a pre-game talk from Coach Tice. He was closing a chapter in his life. He knew there were no guarantees concerning his future in sports, not even one. He had seen his best friend Ed Robinson's career effectively end in a single play. But this was no time to dwell on the past, for Brandon had to begin setting his sights on getting a scholarship of his own if he were to play college football, and as it currently stood, he had very little in the way of offers, and nothing at all for Division I, as he was considered too small to play at that level. But he also was fully convinced that with Christ in his life all things were possible.

Hanging up his Goblin jersey for the last time, Brandon wondered what his Heavenly Father had in store for his future, what His divine plan included for him, and specifically, just how much football would play a part in it.

EIGHT

Walk-On

Like many would-be football players growing up in the Natural State, Brandon had an obsession with making it big with the University of Arkansas football team. To be sure, there are smaller colleges and universities that inspire allegiance in their own fan base, but none comes close to equaling the enormous support enjoyed by the U of A. Travel anywhere in Arkansas and you'll likely find a faded Hog bumper sticker on the back of a pickup truck or a youngster wearing a Razorback T-shirt. Scattered everywhere from Fordyce to Fort Smith and from Texarkana to Toad Suck are restaurants, souvenir shops, carwashes, and convenience stores all proudly displaying the Razorback name or logo. Hogmania is omnipresent in Arkansas, and having grown up just a stone's throw on the map from Fayetteville, Brandon was conscious from an early age of the imposing shadow cast by the university's athletic program.

Arkansas' football tradition dates back as far as 1894 and has a proud history, producing 47 All-Americans, 41 bowl appearances, 6 members of the College Football Hall of Fame, 2 members of the Pro Football Hall of Fame and one national championship. Oddly enough, however, they weren't always known as the Razorbacks.

Until 1909, the team's mascot was the Cardinal. Following a winning streak in 1909, then coach Hugo Bezdek gave a speech to the student body, referring to his team as a "wild band of razorback hogs." The moniker stuck and soon afterward the student body voted to officially change the mascot, marking 1910 as the first official season for a Razorback team. There's another tradition which states that during the Civil War, confederate soldiers from Arkansas were also known as "razorbacks." It wasn't until the 1920s that local farmers celebrating a Razorback win gave a hog call, eventually becoming what we now recognize as "Woo, Pig! Sooie!" If you're not a Razorback fan or from the state of Arkansas, calling the Hogs is something you may likely never understand. In fact, it may confuse or even frighten you. It's the school's war cry, a battle charge used to motivate as well as celebrate. It is as much a part of the school's athletic tradition as the Razorback hog itself.

In the 1960s an actual live Razorback mascot was introduced. The current live mascot is named Tusk IV, a Russian boar who most closely resembles a true razorback. He is housed in the Little Rock Zoo some three hours southeast of the campus in Fayetteville. His predecessors included such hogs as Tusk 1, II and III, and Big Red III, who unfortunately escaped from an animal exhibit near Eureka Springs in the summer of 1977. He was subsequently shot and killed by an irate farmer as the wild boar broke into one of his animal pens. Following the pig's untimely passing, a wild hog captured in south Arkansas was dubbed Ragnar and became the official mascot. Over the course of the next year, Ragnar reportedly killed a coyote, a 450-pound domestic pig and seven rattlesnakes. He died in 1978 of unknown causes — probably indigestion!

As a supplement to the real thing, Arkansas also has uniformed mascots who serve to heighten and help sustain an already fever pitch present at all Razorback football games. Over the years, some of the men who have helped create that football fervor bear recognizable names to Hog fans. Names such as Glen Rose, Jack Robbins, Jim Benton, Coach John Barnhill, Olympic medalist Clyde Scott, Pat Sumerall, Lance Alworth, Chuck Dicus, Bill Montgomery, Joe Ferguson, Bobby Burnett, Bill Cunningham, Steve Little, Ken Hatfield, Dan Hampton, Billy Ray Smith, Gary Anderson, Steve Atwater, and Wayne Martin. All of these evoke grand memories of past glory in a program with a current annual budget of some $27 million. Under memorable coaches like Barnhill, Broyles, Holtz, Hatfield, Ford, Nutt, Petrino and Bielema, Arkansas has also produced young men who have themselves gone on to greatness in the sport. In short, there is a great athletic tradition at the University of Arkansas, a tradition which Brandon ached to be a part of.

With high school graduation staring him in the face, Brandon turned his thoughts seriously toward what he would do about college. Since his birthday was in September, Brandon would be just 17 when he graduated from Harrison High. Of course, every high school athlete lives for a phone call from a college coach expressing interest in him as a player, and Brandon was no different in that regard. But the University of Arkansas was not calling, and this was a crushing disappointment to Brandon. Though he stood out as a high school player in his own small town, neither the Razorbacks nor other big schools considered Brandon Division 1 material. Knowing that less than 12 months separated him from college, the Burlsworths began thinking early about where Brandon would attend college and hopefully play ball.

There had been a letter from The United States Military Academy at West Point (Army) offering him the chance to "be all he could be" on their football team, and Marty wondered out loud if this might be the best choice. No one, from his coach to his family, was even remotely dreaming about the NFL, so two to four years in the military after college seemed a viable option in exchange for college tuition.

"Mom, you know how regimented Bran is," Marty argued. "He does everything by a schedule and routine. They do the same thing every day in the military, just like him. Maybe the Army experience would be the perfect fit for his personality."

Barbara however was thinking on an entirely different level. "Where is Army? New York? Oh my goodness! Are you kidding? We'd never see him again. Forget it!"

And that was that.

Barbara Burlsworth wasn't about to ship her baby boy that far away from home. After all, he was only 17, and theirs was a close-knit family. Besides, having Brandon so far away would mean Barbara would hardly see her son for at least four years. Combining that with required service in the Army meant he could likely be sent anywhere in the world. That may mean several years more time away from home. By that time, he would be in his late twenties. Nope. Army was not an option. Case closed. Next subject, please.

Smart enough not to argue with his mother's reasoning, Marty began to think about Brandon's college prospects a little closer to home. They visited Henderson State College and Ouachita Baptist University in Arkadelphia. Then the University of Central Arkansas began expressing some interest. Though these smaller schools seemed to want him, Brandon didn't actually get any serious offers. The only Division I school that was serious was Army, but Marty already knew that bringing that up again meant certain war in the Burlsworth household.

Then a friend of Marty's, Bud Walsh, offered a suggestion. Walsh managed the local Goodyear tire center in Harrison and was a close friend of the Burlsworths. Just about every member of the family, including Brandon, had brought their car to Bud countless times over the years for new tires, brake jobs, and oil changes. Bud reciprocated by showing an ongoing interest in Brandon and his football career. Like just about everybody else in Harrison, Walsh was a Goblin fan. It wasn't unusual to see his business marquee congratulating a Harrison High School team on a recent victory or accomplishment. In that regard, the marquee usually stayed pretty full as both the guys' and girls' athletic teams seemed to be constantly winning something. Bud and Marty had discussed Brandon's hopes for a football scholarship, with Marty expressing his frustration at how the University of Arkansas had failed to show much serious interest in his younger brother. The two were talking one day while Marty was having some work done on his car, when Bud made a suggestion. "Marty, why don't you give Harold Horton a call over there in Fayetteville?" Walsh asked. Being a member of the local Razorback Booster Club in Harrison, Bud knew the names of a few key people in the university's athletic department, and at the time Harold Horton was the recruiting director at the University of Arkansas. "Give him a call and tell him about Brandon. And be sure to tell Horton that Brandon is being pursued by some of these other schools. That might help him see that he is worth taking a look at," Bud suggested.

And that is exactly what the oldest Burlsworth brother did. Marty contacted Horton and made his best sales pitch on behalf of his brother. As a result, Horton invited the two of them to come over to the university for the upcoming game against Auburn. That sounded like a plan to Marty since Brandon and the Harrison High Goblins were playing in nearby Siloam Springs that Friday anyway. Having already scheduled a visit to the University of Central Arkansas in Conway for that weekend, Marty called and cancelled the visit in light of the current offer from Horton. Though Brandon was ecstatic at the prospect of a visit to the U of A, he didn't like the idea of canceling an existing appointment and was initially skeptical when Marty told him he had called off the meeting, expressing his lack of confidence in his big brother's decision.

"You really think we should have cancelled?" Brandon wondered out loud.

Though he had his share of disagreements with Marty over the years, Brandon trusted his big brother on just about any issue. But to him, it appeared that the eldest Burlsworth had missed the runway with this decision. Sensing his brother's skepticism, Marty tried to help him understand how critical the timing was in the situation. "Bran, I believe this is an opportunity we can't afford to turn down," Marty said convincingly. And that reassurance was good enough for the high school senior.

Brandon had been to Fayetteville several times before, attending his first Razorback game at age nine. He had also been present for the Hogs' first conference game against the University of Georgia. That was an exciting day as the Bulldogs' standout Garrison Hearst showed why he was hailed by sportswriters across the nation as a thoroughbred running back. Although to Brandon, it didn't matter what star athlete he saw just as long as the Hogs were playing. He enjoyed each and every trip he made to the university. However, it's one thing to be part of the faceless 50,000-plus screaming fans up in the stands and quite another to pay a personal visit inside the Razorback athletic facilities. If a prospective Arkansas high school football player were ever straddling the fence on whether to become a Razorback, a visit such as this would certainly go a long way in pushing him over the edge. For a 17-year-old athlete, this was the ultimate backstage pass — a pilgrimage to the "Mecca" of Arkansas athletics. Walking down on that playing field, peering inside the weight room and visiting the locker room was the holy grail of Hogdom. For Brandon, seeing those college players served as a self-induced premonition of what he might become … if he kept working hard and had a little help from above.

But convincing a recruiting director of your prospects as a major college player can be about as difficult as selling ice cubes to Eskimos. Recruiters are typically inundated with requests, letters, and phone calls from coaches, players, parents, relatives, and alumni requesting a special "look at our boy." But keep in mind the coaching staff gets paid to know who the best potential high school recruits are, especially in their own state. They take their job very seriously. Most football fans fail to recognize the huge leap in the caliber of play from high school to Division I college football, not to mention the mere size and strength of the players. They oftentimes mistakenly believe their hometown star athlete has what it takes to play with the big boys in college just because he was a high school standout. Unfortunately, their request letter soon ends up in File 13. In addition, that recruiter is cognizant that his recommendation goes a long way in a head coach's decision to offer a scholarship to a player. With the amount of scholarships limited, and considering the large value of the scholarship itself, it pays to be very picky in the recruiting business. Of course, none of these thoughts were in Brandon's mind at the moment. He was just glad to be on campus.

But no matter how excited Brandon was, there was a big difference between how the Arkansas coaching staff looked at the other recruits visiting that day and how they looked at Brandon. The kid from Harrison was at this time only six feet tall and weighed about 240 pounds. "High school size," they told him. Brandon just did not stack up physically against the much taller three hundred pound monsters that were being actively recruited around him. He was too small for D-1, and that was all there was to it. This material reality would have been accepted for what it was by most people. But Brandon Burlsworth wasn't most people. If he could not be considered for a spot on the team unless he got bigger then the only thing to do was to get bigger, even if he had to force his bones to expand through sheer application of will. Undeterred, he started ramping up his eating immediately.

Despite the lack of interest from the coaches, visiting the Razorbacks that day only helped to further whet Brandon's appetite, causing him to hunger even more for a chance to play at the university. Marty's mind, however, was shrewdly weighing the situation. Rather than savoring the moment like his brother, his thoughts turned to the future, pondering ways to help increase Brandon's worth as a potential player. A few months later, at the invitation of Harold Horton, the pair went up to Fayetteville again, this time to see the Razorback basketball team play. During that visit, Marty spotted Horton across the way.

"Bran, look over there. It's Coach Horton." Drawing Brandon's attention to Horton, Marty began thinking of a way to enlarge the probability that Horton and Coach Ford would give the wannabe Hog a serious second glance. At the same time, Marty was trying to come up with a way to avoid appearing too obvious or eager. Overplaying their hand could hurt their chances. Being a professional photographer in Harrison, Marty had achieved quite a reputation for taking excellent portraits of families and individuals. His numerous awards being testimony to his skills in the studio, Marty photographed nearly every high school senior who walked across the graduation platform at Harrison High School. And when he wasn't in his studio, he was roaming the sidelines at Razorback games, shooting for his hometown newspaper. With his expertise at capturing a precise look in the studio or a moment during a game, Marty knew that the perfect shot doesn't always come with the first click of the shutter. He was well aware that a single shot or angle rarely produces the portrait he's looking for, so he tries other approaches until he gets the picture he wants. At the Hogs' basketball game that day, Marty decided to load in a different speed of film and employ a new tactic in helping his brother achieve his goal. Landing Brandon a shot to play for Arkansas would require several different angles.

Standing there, Marty elbowed his brother, giving him a suggestion. "Bran, go over there and stand beside Coach Horton. Look as tall and big as you can, but don't make it too obvious." Obliging without a word, Brandon made his way over to Horton and took his place beside him. Having already both grown a bit and gained some weight by this time due to his massive caloric consumption, Brandon did his best to show off his newfound girth. Silently standing there erect as a statue, chin out and staring straight ahead, Brandon looked more like a sentry at Buckingham Palace or a Secret Service bodyguard than he did a prospective football player.

Watching all this from a distance and attempting to contain his amusement at how stiff his kid brother appeared, Marty nonchalantly strolled over to where Brandon and Coach Horton were standing. Re-introducing himself to Horton in a way he hoped would seem as spontaneous as possible, Marty nodded his head toward Brandon. "He's still growing, Coach." For a split second, the coach wondered who Marty was referring to, but then quickly clued in, turning to look at the statue-like figure beside him. "Oh, he is growing, isn't he?" Horton agreed. Their plan had worked as they had made another minor investment toward Brandon's stock as a future Razorback.

Brandon would eventually grow three inches during his senior year, topping out at 6'3" by the summer. Even so, he always wanted to be bigger. He aspired to be 6'5" or at least 6'4". Just an inch or two can make a difference when a recruiter or scout looks at you on paper. Once, during his later tenure with the Hogs, Brandon actually did measure 6'4", but that's because he was measured in the morning when you are at your tallest after a night's sleep. But regardless of the difference in size, Brandon had only managed to make a small difference in Horton's opinion of him. Unfortunately, it wasn't enough of an impression to warrant a scholarship, as the Razorback coaching staff already had their eyes set on their recruits for the next year.

Marty called Horton in February of 1994 and was told the Hogs were not going to be able to give Brandon a scholarship. Disappointed but unphased, Marty and Brandon pressed on with Plan B, thinking, *maybe if there isn't a scholarship available now, there will be by the time next fall rolls around. Maybe somebody will drop off the team.* As a result, any time Marty read in the paper that someone had left the team for any reason, he immediately dialed Horton's number and asked, "Do you have a scholarship now?" Horton repeatedly and firmly told him the university was already committed on all their scholarships. Still, Marty watched the paper like a hawk for any signs of hope.

According to Marty Burlsworth's understanding, the football team had 25 scholarships to give, but what confused him was that, as far as he could ascertain, they were only using 24 at the time. Were all the scholarships really taken or was their insistence on there being no more room just a form of polite rejection? Being a realist, Marty was also trying to increase Brandon's chances at other schools concurrent with his pursuit of Arkansas in the event things didn't work out there. He sent out videotapes of Brandon's high school performances, newspaper clippings, and photographs — anything that might cause a Division I school to give him serious consideration for a scholarship. He knew if Arkansas didn't come through, Brandon would need somewhere else to go. That sparked a letter-writing campaign, with information about the Harrison football player sent to the University of Alabama, Clemson, SMU, LSU, Texas, Oklahoma, OSU, and virtually every big Division I program in the region. Though he received numerous polite responses, none showed any real interest in offering Brandon a scholarship. To a school, they were only open to him coming to the team as a walk-on. The problem in that scenario, though, is that there is always the risk he wouldn't make the team, and that would be a double loss — no scholarship and no football team. The Burlsworths simply were not in a financial position to support such a scenario.

Meanwhile, over in Fayetteville, Coach Horton remembered Brandon and endeavored to help the young man any way he could. Not wanting Brandon to be discouraged,

Horton suggested they try Southwest Missouri State University in Springfield. Since Arkansas couldn't scholarship him, perhaps they would instead. But to the Burlsworth boys, with their hearts set on the big school in their home state, that was akin to being turned down by a beautiful girl for the senior prom, only to be offered a chance at dating her younger (and less beautiful) sister. It was not the response they were looking for, but in deference to Horton, Marty called the school anyway. Upon doing so, he discovered they didn't even offer full scholarships in their football program, only partial ones. For Marty and Brandon, such news was actually more of a relief than a disappointment, given they didn't want to go there in the first place. Later, the school claimed the reason they never offered Brandon any scholarship money was because they were under the impression he was already committed to another school, which, in reality, he technically was at the time.

What happened was that Harrison Coach Tommy Tice had consulted with Brandon and Marty, recommending the boy go ahead and sign a letter of intent with Arkansas Tech University in Russellville. Tice knew Brandon as a player and as a person and wanted to help provide a way to protect him from being left out in the autumn cold come football season. It's not completely uncommon for an athlete to sign a letter of intent with one school, only to end up at another. Coach Tice told his friends at Tech not to count on Brandon staying with them, as Burlsworth was seeking a spot on a major college team. So Brandon went ahead and signed with Arkansas Tech, but nonetheless remained restless within. Something deep inside him was still unsatisfied. For a high school football player, just knowing he is going to play college football is enough, but not for Brandon. He wanted to be a Razorback. Coach Horton said it was pride that kept Brandon holding out for a chance to play at the University of Arkansas, and perhaps he was partly right. Marty, however, suggested it was just the way Brandon was, to fixate on a goal and not give up until he achieved it. And he was partly right, too.

For Brandon's part, all he wanted to do was to stand up on graduation day at Harrison High and have it announced that he was attending the University of Arkansas. He wanted everyone in his hometown to know he was going to be a Razorback football player. For a small town boy from Harrison, Arkansas to play for the Hogs was more than just a dream come true — it was the fulfillment of a fantasy, the culmination of a high school athlete's ultimate aspiration. High school players in Arkansas don't dream of playing in the NFL. They dream of playing at Arkansas. The Razorbacks are the professional football team as far as they're concerned. With all due respect for the other Arkansas colleges and universities, in Brandon's mind there was no greater thrill than to wear Razorback red. However, on graduation day, Coach Tice stood and announced Burlsworth had a scholarship to Arkansas Tech. For Brandon, it was like getting the silver medal instead of the gold. Instead of feeling like the champion he knew he was, he felt more like the runner-up.

To make matters worse, Danny Ford's staff still wasn't convinced Brandon could actually play at the major college level. Brandon had gotten big … very big. But size alone wasn't the litmus test. Besides, all that eating had given Brandon more weight than true strength. They weren't about to bring on a player just because he weighs over 300 pounds. Division I football is not charity football. It's about winning, and winning big. After all, Ford had already won a national championship at Clemson in 1981, and the pressure was on him to bring that caliber of football program to Fayetteville. He was not afforded the luxury of taking on a player he wasn't convinced had the skills necessary to compete with competence and win. All this in spite of the fact Tommy Tice had called Ford more than once in an attempt to persuade him concerning Brandon. "Coach Ford," Tice said, "I have never called anyone twice concerning a player, and I don't know you well. But as time goes by you'll learn I am a straight shooter and won't lie to you about my players. This kid Burlsworth is special. Trust me." But special or not, the door at Arkansas seemed to be slamming in Brandon's face. And with the fall fast approaching, it wouldn't be long before that door would be securely bolted shut.

But the Razorback coaching staff didn't yet know something Marty and Brandon's family knew. They didn't know what Tommy Tice knew or even what the town of Harrison knew. Most of all, they weren't privy to what Brandon himself knew. The as-of-yet undiscovered secret was that the young man wearing #54 for the Goblins did indeed have everything necessary within him to play competitive Division I college football. The only thing he really lacked was a chance - an opportunity to prove himself worthy of being on the team. He needed someone to give him a break, allowing him to demonstrate he would do whatever it took to become the kind of player deserving a spot on the roster. He needed just one chance to earn the right to occupy a space in the Razorback locker room. But he was not being offered a scholarship. It soon became crystal clear to Brandon that if he were ever going to have a chance to play for the Hogs, he would have to risk trying to make the team as a walk-on. Even though he had no idea how he could afford it, this seemed to be the only option open to him regarding the University of Arkansas.

At the time, Brandon's dad, Leo and brother Grady thought he ought to take the full-ride scholarship to Arkansas Tech. Grady, in particular, had been a spiritual guide for Brandon, and he trusted his godly wisdom. But ultimately it was Brandon's decision to decide between taking a scholarship at Tech or walking on at Fayetteville. The decision lay in his lap, so he did what he always did when he faced problems. He prayed about it, taking his request to God. He knew that after weighing all the options realistically, it would be a matter of

God's Spirit communicating to his. Since childhood he had believed that God's way is always the best way, even when it conflicted with his own desires. More than anything, he wanted what God wanted and prayed for His will to prevail. Brandon would do whatever He asked him to do, even if that meant going to a smaller school. So after much prayer and thought, the consensus between Brandon's mind and his heart was that God wanted him to try and walk on to the team, with no guarantees of making the squad or getting a scholarship. "I wanna be a Razorback," he said again. Like his mom, Brandon was confident after he had thought out his decisions. And he had been thinking about this one for several years. He was going to Fayetteville.

And that was that.

Apparently God began working in others as well, as around this time Danny Ford sent word to officially invite Brandon to come and try walking on the team. With this invitation, he would be considered an "invited" walk-on.

Marty was confident that once at the university, Brandon would literally run through a brick wall for his coaches, doing anything and everything they asked of him and even more. He knew that if given the chance, Brandon would eventually prove his worth to the team, putting other players to shame with his relentless work ethic. But all that was yet to be seen by the Razorback coaching staff. For now, Brandon would be a potential walk-on. And that meant he had to try out with all the other young athletes who aspired to wear a helmet stickered with a charging Hog. There would be no promises. No guarantees. No security. And no scholarship. It simply meant Ford and his coaches had an open mind concerning Brandon. Brandon was ready to press on to something greater, and that something was almost here as the Razorback football team was gearing up for another season.

But achieving this goal would require a whole new level of discipline for Brandon. He would have to lose weight, and lots of it. He would have to greatly increase his speed, agility, and strength. In short, he would have to go from a plucky, small town stand-out to an elite athlete if he were to be able to line up toe to toe with the best players in the country. And nothing could be allowed to hinder that pursuit if he was to play for the Hogs. Accomplishing this feat would be one of the greatest challenges of his young life. It was a challenge Brandon would welcome with open arms.

Brandon celebrates both a big win at Alabama and his birthday with Vickie, Joe Don, and Barbara — September 20, 1997.

NINE

A New Football Player

As mentioned before, when Brandon had first visited with the Razorback coaches, he was told he wasn't big enough to play D-1 ball. So during his senior year in high school he went from 210 to 311 pounds in a matter of months, growing three inches in the process. But his size increase was not the kind of weight a coach would desire, coming in large part from cheesecake and junk food.

Visiting with Tommy Tice that fall, the high school coach told him, "Brandon, you're not gonna make it, son. You're way overweight now."

"No, Coach," Brandon protested. "They told me I had to get my weight up." Typical for Brandon, he did exactly what his coach had told him to do, he had only done it in a misguided way. This mistake would prove to be a costly one for the future walk-on, but it would also set the stage for one of his greatest triumphs.

From the first day he stepped onto the practice field, Harold Horton and the Razorback coaching staff could see the dedication and serious single-mindedness of the walk-on from

Harrison. Despite all the extra weight, during those first practices Brandon played with exceptional intensity, driving linebackers backward even after the whistle had blown. Between one of those plays he told Marty, who was there observing, "Maybe I drove him too far back." Evidently so, because on the very next play from scrimmage Brandon felt a deafening blow to the ear hole of his helmet from the forearm of a frustrated linebacker. With his bell still ringing (and stinging) from the hit, Brandon was met by an intense glare from the upperclassman player that seemed to say, "Welcome to college football, Burlsworth."

"He had no business hitting me there," Brandon later jokingly said to Marty.

But that didn't dampen Brandon's aggressive playing style. He kept on blocking with the same level of intensity. But though he was a hard-hitting player, Brandon still struggled with his speed. In a previous tryout at Henderson State University he had run the 40-yard dash, but it took place indoors in a restricted area so tight that he finished by running through an open doorway. His time was clocked at 5.2 seconds, not good enough to match speed with the highly conditioned defensive lineman of the Southeastern Conference. All that extra cargo he had gained slowed him down and hindered his strength, since the weight was more fat than muscle. The Razorback conditioning coach considered his size "soft weight," and that simply wouldn't cut it at this level. Something would have to be done. A radical change would be necessary to build Brandon into the kind of player who could competitively play at the Division I level, and it was not something he could pull off on his own.

But just as with many other times in his life, a mentor would step in and provide Brandon with just what he needed.

For decades, the Green Bay Packers were perhaps the quintessential professional football club. With the infamous Lambeau Field as the venue for countless victories, some of pro football's greatest heroes made their mark in a time when every team played on natural grass (or in Green Bay's occasional case, ice!). No pro football fan will ever forget the image of the legendary Vince Lombardi being carried off the field on the shoulders of his players after that first-ever Super Bowl, beating the Kansas City Chiefs 35-10 on January 15, 1967. The Packers also played what many consider to be the greatest game in NFL history, the "Ice Bowl." With temperatures as low as 13 degrees and a wind chill of minus 46, quarterback Bart Starr scored a winning touchdown from the one-yard line with 13 seconds remaining, sealing a hard-fought victory against the Dallas Cowboys.

With Lombardi at the helm, the Packers made football history, creating in the process what would later become a bona-fide dynasty. They were the original "tough guy team" of the National Football League. One of those tough guys was offensive lineman and Hall of Famer Forrest Gregg, who was also one of those players carrying Lombardi off the field after Super Bowl I. The renowned Lombardi once called Gregg the "finest player I have ever coached." Perhaps this is why later Gregg would be asked to return and coach his former team, surrounding himself with a staff that, with any luck, would bring back the gridiron glory once so celebrated in Green Bay.

Gregg was committed to building strong, tough football players. He knew that the stronger you were as a player and the better shape you were in, the greater the chances were of dominating your opponent. Believing this, Forrest Gregg recruited Virgil Knight to become the Packers' strength and conditioning coach, with the added responsibility of directing the tight ends as well. Knight was a rugged individual, a "man's man" with a commanding presence. He was just the kind of fellow you needed to coach (and sometimes intimidate and back down) the oversized bodies and inflated egos of professional football players. Having enjoyed a short stint with the Pittsburgh Steelers as a player, Virgil understood the game on two levels. Coach Knight demanded a great deal from his players' physical conditioning, knowing that each week they would face another pro team who had been training just as hard. In many ways it's a struggle involving the survival of the fittest. Knight pushed his men, riding them hard to help them achieve their ultimate potential as professional athletes. And his proficiency at his job earned him eight years with the Packers, an uncharacteristically long tenure considering the revolving coaching door in the NFL.

So when Danny Ford took over the head coaching duties at the University of Arkansas one of his first hires was a strength and conditioning coach. Ford was committed to the physical training of his players and was determined to snag a proven winner. When Ford called on Knight, the Clarksville, Arkansas, native was happy to return to his home state and join the Razorback coaching staff. His primary duty was responsibility for the overall physical conditioning of the athletes, beginning his new job the same fall that saw Brandon step onto the Razorback field. His philosophy was that players and teams were made in practice and polished on the field. He believed that physical conditioning helps a player feel good about himself and that confidence is shown on the playing field. He also knew from experience that somebody else can push you in conditioning far better than you can yourself. The physical shape and conditioning of players was, in his mind, 50 percent of the team's big picture. With that as a working philosophy, Knight geared up to mold the Razorbacks into championship caliber condition.

That meant running mile runs as well as sprints, jumping rope, doing agility drills and weight room training. Experience had shown that some athletes would do as little as possible just to get by and keep their status on the team or in the starting lineup. Others are fence-straddlers who can go either way, thus needing an extra push from someone else to help them achieve their goals. Part of Knight's conditioning also meant helping athletes lose or gain weight when necessary. And that's where Coach Knight was first introduced to Brandon. Knight knew Tommy Tice and trusted him as a friend. Earlier, Tice had called, telling Knight, "Brandon will be the first one at practice and the last one to leave," giving Virgil an initial good impression of the walk-on lineman.

On the first day of practice, Knight saw Brandon across the field and initially thought, *Who is this fat kid?* It didn't take him long to find out, as Brandon immediately walked over to Knight and said, "Coach Tice told me to tell you hello. I'm Brandon Burlsworth." Virgil could tell right away that Brandon was respectful and somewhat shy. He could also tell that Burlsworth had some athletic ability, but it was overshadowed by a high school mentality that "bigger is always better," therefore explaining why Brandon had gained so much weight.

First he wasn't big enough to play, and now Coach Knight was telling him he was too big to play. This confused Brandon until Knight explained to him that size is only an asset when it is accompanied by conditioning and muscle. Calling him into his office, Coach Knight gave him the game plan.

"Brandon, you have athletic ability. There's no doubt about that. But we have to get this weight off of you."

"Yes sir," Brandon said. "What do we need to do, Coach? I'll do anything you want me to do."

Knight immediately put the over-300-pound freshman on a strict diet. Walking him over to the athlete's cafeteria, he asked the ladies there to give Brandon a special meal.

"How much am I gonna lose, Coach?" inquired Burlsworth.

"I don't know yet, Brandon," replied Knight. "I'll let you know when we get there."

For several months Brandon went to that cafeteria eating only the foods coach Knight had prescribed for him, never wavering from his disciplined eating regimen. He then pushed himself to the absolute physical limit to achieve his goal. Day after day, Brandon developed an incessant routine. Get up. Work out. Go to class. Eat the right foods. Take the right supplements. Drink a Diet Coke. Work out in the weight room. Weigh in. Run. Practice your agility drills. Study. Recopy all your notes from class. Go to bed and pass out into a deep slumber. Then get back up early the next morning and do it all again. No matter what.

No. Matter. What.

Considering he was in his freshman year at college, this disciplined lifestyle was considered an anomaly, a kind of anachronistic wonder in a world where thousands of teenagers and young adults are partying on any given night of the week. Typically, the immaturity of youth carries with it the propensity to mishandle their newly found freedom from home. And nowhere is that tendency more literally "fleshed out" than on college campuses all across the country.

The large percentage of college students who choose to major in extracurricular activities and minor in education may do so in spite of a healthy family upbringing. The truth is, being away at college is a test, only not the kind that is administered in the classroom. It's a stewardship to be given your own life to do with as you please. Go where you want and with whom you want. Date whom you choose. Drink or smoke what you please. Study what you wish and when you wish. Eat what you want. Stay up as late as you desire. Come back to your dorm when you want, or not come back at all. Join a fraternity or sorority. Run for student government. Join a campus organization. Catch a few z's on a back couch in the library. Play intramural sports. Manage your own money. Keep up with your possessions and clean your own room.

These are but a few of the choices that face the average college student. The bottom line is that it's your life to live and it's a badge of honor to handle it wisely. It's the freedom you've always longed for, but many soon discover it's easier to get than it is to manage. And with the foolishness of youth often comes excess. Most college students recover from their time frolicking in the field of wild oats just in time for graduation. Some just get by while others actually excel both academically and spiritually. Some flourish in their personal growth and leadership skills, feeling prepared to confidently face the job market after four (or five or six) years pursuing their college degree.

Unlike some students, Brandon wasn't easily distracted with activities outside his self-prescribed routine. Being a task-oriented person, he had developed over the previous few years an acute sense of focus that enabled him to work and play with greater intensity. He had an acquired the skill of concentrating ferociously on an assignment, whether it was in the classroom, on the field, or in the weight room. He was deliberate, converging his thoughts and energy on a single mission. Continuing his workout strategy, he came home on weekends, heading out to the Harrison High track on Friday nights to run at 11 p.m., sometimes even in the rain. In Brandon's mind, however, it wasn't raining. His mental focus was as clear as a summer's day. Running his mile, he turned it up a notch in the last quarter, kicking it in for a strong finish all the way to the end. It wasn't good enough for him unless he exceeded what he was supposed to do.

Between his senior year in high school and the time he began at Fayetteville, Brandon spent the entire summer working out at the Harrison fitness center from seven to eight a.m., five days a week. Marty, who was getting ready for play in the local softball league, worked out with him, the two spotting each other on the bench. But mainly those hometown workouts were designed to help Brandon get ready for grueling two-a-days. Now he was using that same gym on weekends to get where his coach needed him to be.

This commitment to excellence began to apply to everything for Brandon – including his academic and personal life.

He definitely stuck out from his peers and it wasn't long before they started to take notice.

Brandon didn't like to have his stuff moved, his locker messed up, or his room trashed. Once, fellow linemen Grant Garrett and Russell Brown visited Brandon in his room, just to "mess with him a little." Upon entering, they spotted Brandon at his desk copying some notes.

"Burls, whose notes you copying?" Garrett asked.

"Mine," came Brandon's short reply.

Garrett and Brown looked at each other in amazement, with Grant responding, "Now why would you want to do that?"

"Cause they're too messy," was his curt reply.

That prompted Garrett and Brown to begin kidding him about his bare walls as Garrett took the wrapper from a piece of candy he had just popped in his mouth and threw it into the wastebasket. Brandon got up from his seat and retrieved the wrapper out of the trashcan and threw it into a wastebasket in the hallway. "You guys are dirtying up my room," he complained.

Over that first semester, Brandon and his unique ways grew on his teammates. As their friendship developed it seemed there was always some kind of brotherly conflict between Brandon, Grant and Russell. When the three oversized football players rode in Garrett's pickup truck, Brandon would sit in the middle, legs spread in a relaxing position. Because he demanded so much legroom and refused to budge an inch, Garrett and Brown nicknamed him "Mr. Rude," a title they brought up whenever they rode in the truck. "You don't have to have all the room in the pickup, do you, Burls?" they would say. But it wasn't just in the truck where Burlsworth vied for space. On the team bus riding from the airport to the hotel, Grant made the mistake of sitting behind Burls. To relax, Brandon leaned his seat back, all but crushing Garrett's knees. More than slightly annoyed, Garrett pushed the seat back up and off of him. This prompted Brandon to lean back again, and again Garrett pushed it back, this time with more force. This back and forth kept on until Grant, frustrated and worn down, finally just got up and moved to another seat.

It bothered Brandon if he was given too many details about a task. He liked being in college because his job was simple — going to school and playing football. And he did them both really well. Girlfriends were optional, and because he was so focused on his faith, family, and football, romance would have to wait. Brandon tended toward shyness around girls anyway, preferring to be with his family or friends. For now, Brandon's love interest would be football.

So while teammates were hanging out or going on dates, enjoying their newfound collegiate freedom, Brandon was either hitting the weights or hitting the books. Gradually, the weight fell away, and his strength increased dramatically. In just a few months of this monastic lifestyle, Brandon had dropped nearly 60 pounds of unnecessary weight, prompting Coach Knight to once again call Burlsworth into his office.

"Brandon, you're at 256 pounds and you're stronger now than when you were 300 pounds. Now we're going to go the other way. We'll put the weight back on slower and harder."

A widening grin emerged on Brandon's face. "Does this mean I can quit eating green labels, Coach?"

"Green labels? What do you mean?" asked Knight.

"Well, sir. Below all the foods in the cafeteria line are these colored labels. Ever since I've been on this diet, they only let me eat the green labels. Can I stop eating the green labels now?"

Laughing to himself, Knight gave the trimmed-down Burlsworth permission to eat what he wanted.

With the proper weight training and diet, Brandon began beefing himself back up to what would eventually be a muscular 308-pound frame. This was a far cry from the days back in high school when he served as a 165-pound "practice dummy" for upperclassmen on the Harrison Goblins team. Brandon was aware that because of his age and status as a walk-on, he would have to prove himself in the weight room and on the practice field if he was ever to see any playing time in a game. So he set out to do whatever it took to show himself worthy of both a scholarship and a spot on the Razorback football team. Years earlier, Coach Tice had taught Brandon and his high school teammates a principle that had stayed with Burlsworth. He would say to his team, "Guys, it doesn't matter what anybody else thinks, it only matters what you think." When the coach had tried to persuade Brandon to take the scholarship offers from smaller schools and to go get an education, Brandon responded, "But Coach, I wanna be a Razorback. Remember, it doesn't matter what anybody else thinks. It only matters what I think, right? Didn't you say that?"

"You're right, Brandon," said Tice, realizing Brandon had trapped him in his own reasoning.

As a result of his weight loss and improving physical shape, his only real injury came as he got his knee twisted during his red-shirt freshman year. Again, it was Coach Knight's belief that if you were in good shape and physical condition, you would be less likely to sustain injuries. Brandon had seen a single play weaken his good friend Ed Robinson's college football career, and he was determined to prevent the same thing from happening to him if at all possible.

Combined with Knight's physical conditioning program was offensive line Coach Mike Bender's influence on Brandon, both as a player and as a person. Though he was just getting to know Bender at this point, Brandon would later list him as one of the men he admired the most in his life. Though some men and women have the ability to influence from a distance, the most powerful impact made in a person's life is frequently made from up close. Whether it's a teacher, coach, pastor, or friend, influence and relationship go hand in hand. And it's the kind of influence that has depth to it. It's more than just inspiration, for inspiration tends to be top-heavy with emotion, which is typically short-lived. Relationship influence is a "life-to-life" thing that often lasts for the long haul. Mike Bender had that with the shy boy from Harrison.

Like Brandon, Bender's personality fell into the "strong-but-silent" category. Put a cowboy outfit on him and mount him on a horse and you might mistake him for a John Wayne stand-in. A large man with rugged looks, Bender had logged plenty of yardage, coaching for various teams ranging from high school to college and the pros. Danny Ford was acquainted with Bender when he was at Clemson, and Mike was on Joe Morrison's staff at South Carolina. When Ford came to Arkansas, he located Bender, who was coaching up in the Canadian Football League, and called on him to join the Razorback staff.

Brandon soon grew to love and appreciate Bender's style of coaching, which was detailed and precise, leaving little room for error. Brandon would refer to their way of working out on the field as "doing our Bender steps." Coach Bender strove for perfection with his offensive line, and he all but got it out of his players. Mike gave Brandon all the attention a developing lineman needed. But he only had to tell him once what he was supposed to do. Brandon's obsessive approach to the game proved to be a coach's dream.

Late in the fall of Brandon's freshman year, Marty called Horton and was pleased to hear the coach say he had some good news.

"Brandon doesn't know it yet, Marty, but he is getting a scholarship today that will take effect in January," then adding, "He's gonna be a three-year starter for us." Marty was ecstatic and couldn't wait to pass the good news to Brandon, Barbara, and brother Grady. Apparently Brandon's relentless work ethic and willingness to pay any price necessary had earned him the respect of the administration and coaching staff. Danny Ford later reflected on not seeing Brandon's scholarship potential from the beginning, commenting, "Well, we missed that one."

By January, Brandon did indeed have a full scholarship to the University of Arkansas. But all that made no difference to Brandon. He had resolutely determined that his new mission was to show the Arkansas Razorback coaching staff they had just made the best decision of their lives.

Brandon was a popular target of autograph seekers; shown here after a game at Little Rock.

TEN

Calling the Hogs

There is a certain magic to game day in Fayetteville. It's a unique event comparable to nothing else in college football, with its packed parking lots and pre-game tailgate parties. Purists listen to the play-by-play on transistor radios during the game. Faces are painted with images of razorbacks and fanatic fans wear "Hog hats." Pennants and pompons wave in the hands of aspiring female cheerleaders. They drive from all over the state, sometimes fending off the bite of the Ozark mountain air, covering themselves with blankets, usually red ones. At the burst of a rain cloud, red umbrellas are unfolded and red ponchos are unpacked. Programs, seat cushions, and just about anything within arm's reach become fair game for staying dry in a north Arkansas rain.

And like every other college team in America, Arkansas has its share of self-programmed "gridiron geniuses" who second-guess every other called play on the field. This is an interesting phenomenon about college football. It seems every stadium has its own sort of eerie effect on certain people. It's the bizarre game day occurrence that causes normally mild-mannered fans to be magically transformed into seasoned strategists. Upon passing through the stadium gate, these select fans acquire supernatural vision, enabling them to suddenly see from 70 yards away more accurately than the officials can just seven feet from the play. In their minds, they pass better than the quarterback when he misjudges a throw and call plays better than the coaches who do this for a living. This miraculous conversion from ordinary fan to football mastermind is a mystery that no one has yet to explain. Yet it continues every fall Saturday in every college stadium across America. Imagine the potential if every one of these pigskin prodigies could be gathered up to form one coaching staff! Go figure.

But far beyond the annoyance of the few fans who think they actually invented the sport, a Razorback game is a great experience, a festival-like atmosphere, even a way of life for some. Some men dedicate a season to hunt, disappearing into the deer woods on successive weekends, their wives and children adjusting to Dad's hunting habit. For others, it's a Razorback addiction, and everything else is put on hold for three months in the fall. It's not unusual for a family to shell out hundreds of dollars for hotels, travel, meals, tickets, and souvenirs in a typical football weekend. But for those fans who are hog-wild about their Razorbacks, it's an experience they will argue is well worth the expense.

During a typical season in Northwest Arkansas, the Ozark Mountains add fluorescent colors to their repertoire, seemingly painting their leaves just in time for kickoff. Present at every game are overweight and out-of-shape men vicariously living out their football fantasies through their younger, more svelte counterparts. And then there's the smell of the game — hot dogs, nachos, cotton candy, burgers, peanuts, and popcorn, which may explain, to some degree, the overweight men. And don't forget the female contingency of Razorback fans who can be just as passionate about the game as any man. Throw in some screaming, cheering, booing, calling the hogs, and a competitive college football contest, and you have yourself quite a Saturday outing in Fayetteville.

After red-shirting for a year in 1994, his freshman year saw Brandon serve in the role of backup guard as the Razorbacks won the SEC Western Division Title. That year he played in all 11 games as a reserve guard, primarily with field goal and placement units. But in 1996 he saw action in all 11 games again, this time as starting right guard where he recorded 50 knockdowns and was named to the SEC Academic Honor Roll for the second time, an honor he achieved every remaining year of his college career. After moving into the starting lineup in his sophomore year, Brandon would remain there until graduation. He was starting to make his mark.

But Brandon wasn't only a stand-out on the field. His unique personality and odd quirks drew attention from coaches and fellow players alike. Brandon simply had his own way of doing things, and his peculiar habits and idiosyncrasies proved to be a constant source of comedic relief and sometimes irritation to his closest college buddies. While initially driving his teammates crazy, these eccentricities later became a beloved part of the Burlsworth mystique.

As a freshman, Brandon had picked out a parking space for his 1993 white Subaru outside the Broyles Complex. It was an obscure spot far in the corner and Burlsworth, true to his repetitive nature, parked there every day without fail for five years. Stuffing his muscular 300-plus-pound frame into the tiny automobile, Brandon looked like a gorilla on roller skates. But aside from a little obvious discomfort, appearance didn't matter to Burls, only function.

Being a no-frills kind of guy explains why his dorm room was so bare, some would even say barren. While most college students enjoy decorating their rooms with posters, furniture, and stereo equipment, Burlsworth was content with a bed, a chair, a computer, a small TV, and bare cinderblock walls. Typically, guys are slobs when it comes to their dorm rooms. Disorganized and disheveled, there is no telling what you might uncover under the dirty laundry that rises like Mount

Kilimanjaro in the far corner of a guy's room. Empty pizza boxes containing remnants of crust require carbon-dating to determine age.

Not so for Burlsworth. Everything in his room was clean and had its place, and the quarters remained neat at all times. The room was fundamental and basic. Just like Brandon. After all, this was a temporary dwelling, not his real home. This was a glorified hotel room to him, and who hung pictures in a hotel room? When many of his upperclassmen teammates had moved into their own apartments, Burls remained in the dorm every year until graduation.

A fierce creature of habit, Brandon was committed to routine. He liked things in order, in their place. This brought consistency and security, with no surprises along the way. Like his car and room, Brandon was more concerned with function than with form.

As part of his obsessive nature, Brandon was not one to cut corners … literally. As Brandon and his teammates came out of the cafeteria during two-a-days, with their legs already tired and an uphill climb staring them in the face, the guys would regularly cut across the grass to the parking lot. But not Burls. He would stay on the sidewalk, following the original path prescribed by the architect of the building and grounds. This, of course, meant it would take him twice as long to get back to the dorm, taking him some 50 yards out of the way. Being way ahead of him, the other players joked and kidded him about it, prompting Burls to shake his head with disgust. "You guys just wouldn't understand." And they didn't. They also never understood why Brandon never spent his road-game per-diem money, stuffing it instead into the glove compartment of his car. "Burls, you're ignorant," teammate Russ Brown would say. "You've got a bank in your car!"

"I'm saving it to buy some Wal-Mart stock," Brandon explained. Instead of cashing the checks to buy food, Brandon would accompany his teammates at mealtime. Sitting beside them, he would eye their food and ask, "Hey, you gonna eat that chicken?"

They didn't understand why he rarely ever threw anything away either, keeping a 1995 NFL calendar long after the year had expired. He kept it on his dresser, right up there with his clock radio. Also on the dresser was an old dried up, half-used bar of soap. Perhaps you know the kind, hardened like cement, with a deep crevice running the length of the bar. That pitiful-looking bar of soap hadn't seen a drop of water in months. Though he used other soap, this bar just sat on the dresser month after month, strategically placed there as if it was a lamp or decoration, like it belonged there. During the summer before his senior year, the athletic dorms were being used to house delegates for a convention being held at the university. As a result, Brandon was forced to find temporary digs, landing a spot at the apartment of friends Jeremiah Washburn and Joe Dean Davenport. Because Washburn was gone home to his parents for several weeks, Brandon moved into his upstairs bedroom while he was away. And with him came the soap. Jeremiah would return for a day or two, and rather than reclaim his bedroom, he just crashed on the downstairs couch. During one of these return visits, Brandon had gone home to Harrison for the weekend. During that time, Washburn and Davenport discovered they had completely run out of soap in the bathroom. Too cheap and perhaps a little too lazy to run to the store, they debated as to what they should do.

"You know, Wash, Burls has that old ratty bar of soap upstairs," Joe Dean said. "It still works."

"Are you kidding?" Jeremiah protested. "If we use his soap he'll kill us both!"

"Okay, fine," Davenport challenged him. "Then you go buy us some soap."

"I'm broke. You buy it," Washburn argued.

"I'm not buying it," Joe Dean retorted.

There is a certain unavoidable humor in picturing the two huge college football players, 6’6” and 6’7” respectively, engaging in a verbal wrestling match over a three-inch bar of dried soap.

After several minutes of debate punctuated with long pauses, Jeremiah looked at Joe Dean and concluded, “I guess Burls won’t miss it that much … you think?”

Davenport agreed. “Naaah, he won’t care. Go up and get it.”

“I’m not going up there. You go get it,” Washburn said. And with that, the soap literally bit the dust. They completely used it up, with not so much as a sliver left behind as evidence of the crime. Later that weekend, Brandon returned to the apartment, where he immediately headed upstairs to unpack his stuff. Washburn and Joe Dean were downstairs, silently looking sideways at each other. After only a moment, a loud voice pierced the silence.

“WHAT HAPPENED TO MY SOAP?!” Brandon yelled from upstairs.

Panicking, Joe Dean cried out, “Wash did it!”

“Joe Dean made me do it, Burls!” Jeremiah chimed in.

“Sorry Burls. We had to use it. We were out of soap,” Davenport explained.

With that they heard the bedroom door slam shut. Some time passed, and Jeremiah, feeling a little guilty, went up to the bedroom to reconcile with his friend. Knocking on the door, he opened it and found Brandon lying on his bed, staring in silence at the ceiling.

“Burls,” Washburn meekly pleaded with his buddy, “it’s just a bar of soap.”

Brandon slowly looked over at his friend. “Yeah, I guess so … but you still shouldn’t have used it.” And with that, it became a dead issue.

Washburn and Davenport found it odd that while Brandon loved playing practical jokes on his teammates, he hated to be the recipient of them. When teammate Chris Chalmers instigated a practical joke on him, Brandon's custom was to say, "Chris, let me see your driver's license." After the 5'10" Chalmers surrendered the license, Brandon pointed to the picture and said, "You know what that is right there? That's a smart aleck!" Then just as quickly, Burls would be ready to play a joke on one of the other guys, saying to Chris. "Hey, let's go mess with Wash. I'll start; then you come and finish it." They'd then kid Washburn about being from North Carolina or play some kind of prank on him.

On road games, the Hogs were given per-diem money to eat, and some guys would use some of the money to go to the movies. Because he saved his money in his glove compartment, Brandon never bought any popcorn or drinks at the theater. But after sitting down it wouldn't take long until he said, "Hey, Grant, give me some of your popcorn." Then after about five or six large handfuls of popcorn, he'd say, "Hey let me have a sip of your Coke. I need to wash this down." He would then whip out a straw he had been concealing for the right moment.

Brandon resisted any temptation or diversion. He was meticulous about his routine. Same daily schedule. Same route to class. Same way he folded up his knee braces after practice. Same way he fixed his shoelaces. Same pre-game ritual. Same workout. He always walked through the freshman locker room to get to the varsity locker room. Always. Everything had a place. Everything was in order. Everything had purpose. He was systematic and deliberate. Nothing was arbitrary. Nothing random. Nothing wasted. Every day for five years, Brandon had his ankles taped on the same table in the Razorback training room. That first table is normally reserved for the freshman players, whose ankles are generally taped by graduate assistants. Then, as players become upperclassmen, they move down to a table at the other end of the room where a more experienced trainer tapes them, men like Kevin Pitts and

Dean Weber. Those guys can do things with tape that would make a player feel like he's wearing another sock. But Burls refused to move, year after year, choosing instead to remain at the same table. This forced the trainers to leave their station and go to the other end of the room just for Brandon each time. But Burls figured that since that table had worked for him in the beginning, why move?

Later, before his last home game for the Hogs, there was a concerted effort to get him to move down to the end table to be taped by the seniors. One trainer, out of desperation, got down on his knees. "Burls, I'm begging you," he pleaded, "Just once let us tape you over there with the other seniors."

"Nope. This is my table," came his confident reply.

They may as well have asked the earth to reverse its rotation, so immovable was Brandon in his routine. And it was that very routine that others loved to kid him about. After class, when Burls arrived each day at the training room to be taped, carrying a notebook, two pencils, his keys, and student ID card, he meticulously placed them in the same spot on the inside window ledge. Same spot. Every day. And he would know if they had been touched or moved, getting especially upset when the jokesters hid them from him. His methodical routines were his way of remaining focused on the task that lay before him. He even wore the same pair of shoes in practice for five years. Like the Children of Israel who wandered in the desert for 40 years wearing the same sandals, those shoes also amazingly never wore out. Go figure.

Russell Brown joked with him that you would have to be a genius just to remember all the things he did every day. But what was complicated to others came as natural as breathing to Brandon. Burls liked routine, being neither bored nor stifled by it. In fact, he thrived on it. It fit his personality and temperament. And his personal prosperity was energized by it.

Though the Hogs played with a lot of heart over Brandon's sophomore and junior years, those two seasons produced disappointing losing records, including two merciless beatings at the hands of the Florida Gators. That meant practices had to be more intense for the team, and nobody was more committed to correcting their mistakes than Brandon. All his coach had to do was say the word and Brandon would do it. Burlsworth wanted to please his coach and do the job right, and the majority of the time he did. In fact, Brandon's practice and game performance became nearly flawless. This prompted some of the other Razorback linemen to issue periodic protests to Coach Bender.

"Coach, you never yell at Burlsworth like you do at us when we make mistakes," they complained.

"That's because he rarely ever makes any," Bender replied. "Now if you work like he does, maybe I won't yell at you either!"

It wasn't that Bender had never jumped on Brandon's case; it's just that the coach studied his players and knew, like with your own children, what communicates with one may not necessarily communicate with another. Case in point: One afternoon prior to his junior year, the Hogs' offensive line was going through some key drills. Bender had given them specific instructions on how the play was to be executed and what each of their roles was to be, including detailed footwork. Brandon, perhaps feeling a bit over-confident, decided to improvise a bit using a different step than the one previously prescribed by Bender. Blowing the whistle signaling the end of the play, the offensive line coach made a beeline for Brandon and proceeded to use the next few minutes to harshly rebuke him for "doing his own thing" instead of sticking to the specifics of the play. After verbally raking him over the coals, Bender peered through Brandon's facemask and recognized a huge teardrop streaking down the 300-pound lineman's cheek. That public reprimand proved to be the only motivation Burlsworth would ever need. "Right then and there," Bender recalled later, "I knew I would never do that to him again. There would be other, more effective ways to teach Brandon and to build him as a player." And he was right, as Brandon all but drove his future mistakes into extinction.

Bender kept pushing, and the Hogs' o-line became more impenetrable as time went on. He told them, "Men, if you get your butt kicked out there on the field, then I'll get mine kicked, too. Whatever happens to you happens to me, good or bad." Listening intently were Chad Abernathy, Russ Brown, Grant Garrett, Burlsworth, and Bobby Williams, who together comprised "Bender's Bunch," a moving wall of muscle and motivation weighing over 1,500 pounds. And though Mike Bender is naturally a soft-spoken individual one-on-one, you didn't want to miss too many blocks or blow an assignment in a practice or especially in a game. Like Coach Ford, he graded tough and expected big results out of his players.

Brandon's deep respect for Coach Bender also spawned great admiration for him as a person. Perhaps it was the coach's humility that he looked up to. Or it could have been the fact that Bender also became a friend to Brandon, periodically inviting him and other players over to his house for dinner. Brandon also struck up a friendship with Mike's son, Brent. Like Brandon, Brent had a penchant for memorizing facts. Whether it was sports or history, the two young men shared a natural love for trivia and were both considered factual "lifelines" by their respective families. But beyond that, they were also genuine friends. Because Brent worked at the university, it became convenient for the two to enjoy an occasional lunch together.

One day Danny Ford was overseeing a scrimmage for the team. Beyond merely practicing formations or running through line drills, scrimmages put the team in game situations as a way of simulating reality. Brandon looked forward to these practice games, mentally and physically exerting himself as if it was a real contest. He didn't want to experience another loss the next Saturday. But as it turned out, his loss would come even sooner. Only this time it wouldn't be on the football field, but rather in his family.

At the outset of that team scrimmage in 1997, word came to Coach Ford on the sidelines that Brandon's dad, Leo, had passed away. Having been diagnosed only three months earlier with lung cancer, Leo had been given every treatment available, but still the disease spread rapidly, ultimately claiming his life. Leo had made a successful ten-year recovery from his earlier battle with alcohol, but nearly a lifetime of smoking had taken a deadly toll on his body. He would defeat alcohol, but cancer was an enemy that proved unbeatable.

Brandon's name was called from the sidelines and the big offensive lineman compliantly trotted over. Once there, he was gently told of his dad's passing. Coach Bender recommended he immediately leave the scrimmage, shower and head on home to Harrison, but Brandon balked at the idea, preferring to stay and finish the scrimmage first. Leo Burlsworth had as healthy of a relationship with his son as one might expect, considering he had been divorced from Brandon's mom all those years. The two did see each other periodically and Leo even attended some Razorback games to watch his son play. Even so, there wasn't the same closeness between the two that Brandon shared with his mom. After all, she had raised him. This, combined with his obsessive dedication to his team, caused Brandon to resist his coach's suggestion he drive home. But after some sideline debate, Bender was able to persuade Brandon to return to Harrison. Bender reminded him that whether or not he thought he should go, it was his family who needed his support right now. Reluctantly, Brandon agreed, showered and made the 90-minute trip back home for the funeral. Once there, it became clear to Burlsworth that his coaches were right and that he had made a wise decision. It was times like that when it paid to have older and wiser men watching over your son while at college. Danny Ford and his coaches had pledged to Barbara they would look after Brandon, and this incident proved they passed the test with flying colors.

Brandon was home and with his immediate family. For that, he was glad. There was nowhere more dear to his heart than Harrison and home. But this was a homecoming of a different kind, with Leo being the one going home to heaven. Standing near the casket that day, Brandon said goodbye to the man he wished he could have known better. He had hoped somehow things could have been different, that they could have been closer, together somehow. Yet in spite of his shortcomings, Brandon knew his dad had finished life well, having begun a relationship with God before his passing. For the younger Burlsworth, it was the closing of one chapter in life and the beginning of another. And though he was saying goodbye, Brandon was confident he would see his dad again. His Bible, which he knew well, told him of a day when all believers in Christ would be together. On that day there would be no periodic visits, no separations, no divorce, and no heartache. There would be a family reunion one day in heaven, and then everything would be perfect … forever. Knowing this truth was a comfort that helped Brandon grieve and deal with his loss. Another thing that helped was to refocus back on Fayetteville and football.

Somewhere along the way a coach had told Brandon a good lineman was one who had strong legs, and that was all it took as he began working intensely on his leg strength. As in all his weight station duties, he always completed all his reps, never cheating or cutting corners. Brandon was convinced that those times in the weight room would pay off on the field. Helping to convince him was Virgil Knight and Assistant Strength Coach Don Decker. Decker, who would later assume Knight's role after his departure, immediately noticed Brandon's diligence in the weight room. Burls was determined to be the first one in the weight room and the last to leave. Even if he had completed his workout, he would find something else to do. And he would do it by the book every time.

But despite his "whatever it takes" attitude, even Burls got into a slump every now and then. This only caused him to work harder, so hard in fact that Decker had to kick him out of the weight room on several occasions. Triceps. Biceps. Pectorals. Calves. Thighs. No muscle group was left undeveloped. If anything, he overtrained in some areas. But when he trained, he did it on the same weight bench, using the same pulleys with the same weights. Though his upper body was not as developed as a few of the other linemen, Burls still possessed a big chest supported by his tree-trunk legs and long arms. Decker remembers Brandon's elation at mastering 400 pounds on the bench for the first time and 700 pounds on the clean and jerk. Little did he know it at the time, but the kid from Harrison was setting a standard for work ethic for Razorback football. Long after Brandon's tenure, Coach Decker on rare occasion referred to a player as having a "Burlsworth work ethic." He only ever said that of a few players.

But it wasn't just the weight room where Burlsworth excelled. Part of the linemen's conditioning requires they each complete four 400-yard runs under a certain time. Without much time to rest in between, those hot August runs were experiences so intense Chris Chalmers used to say that they made you "see visions of Elvis." Almost surreal, those runs invoked even more than that — vomiting, hyperventilating, and when you could manage to spare a breath to speak, an intermittent prayer of desperation. Burlsworth weighed over 300 pounds and was "smoking guys who were 250," Jeremiah Washburn remembers. And Wash would know. On the last day of those runs, the media was invited to take a look at the team. So Jeremiah decided on that day he would beat Burls. It was hot August and just before two-a-days began, Washburn found himself right behind Burls on the fourth lap. Making their turn on the final curve, Jeremiah turned on the afterburners and blew past Brandon. *Ahh, sweet victory*, Jeremiah thought to himself, already basking in the satisfaction of winning the race. Then all of a sudden, Washburn saw Burls streak past him like he had been shot out of a cannon, beating him by 30 yards at the finish. Burls wasn't about to let anybody beat him, let alone his buddy Jeremiah. "Burls had guts and heart," Washburn recalls. "He was always better."

And his ability to concentrate was admirable. Almost in a game-day trance, nothing diverted Burlsworth's attention from his mission. "If the team bus ever blew up," center Grant Garrett joked, "Burls would walk out on fire to where the ball is." His sense of focus was almost otherworldly and brings to mind the words of legendary coach John Wooden, who said, "For an athlete to function properly, he must be intent. There has to be definite purpose and goal if you are to progress. If you are not intent about what you are doing, you aren't able to resist the temptation to do something else that might be more fun at the moment."

During his junior year, the Hogs played host to the Auburn Tigers at Fayetteville. Coming into that game the Razorbacks were 3-3 and desperately needed a win to save a sense of self-respect. It was homecoming and fans everywhere were hoping the Hogs would somehow pull out a win. However, after a hard-fought battle as the game clock read 00:00, Danny Ford's offense had managed just 21 points to Auburn's 28. It was a defeat that sent the Hogs' win-loss margin to below 50 percent, producing a post-game locker room mood which was unusually somber.

Harrison coach Tommy Tice attended that Auburn game. In fact, he drove over to attend as many games as he could. But though Tice was always seen there, he never saw much of the actual games themselves, except of course when the Razorbacks were on defense. The majority of his time was spent looking through a pair of binoculars, focused on what #77 was doing on each play. His sideline surveillance of Brandon had become somewhat of a hobby Tice had developed ever since he saw the scrawny adolescent stumbling onto the field way back in junior high. Having coached Brandon and helped guide him through his recruitment, Tice felt a kind of personal responsibility for the young man. Besides, the two remained close friends, as Brandon would drop by the high school to visit when he was home. There was a special bond between Brandon and his coach. Tice was also a family friend who could not have been more proud of the former Goblin lineman.

Whenever possible, following each home game, Tice would stroll down to the Razorback athletic facility and into the locker room where he would pay a quick visit to Brandon. Entering the dressing room that afternoon, Coach Tice immediately recognized the all-too-familiar odor of sweaty men, mud, dirt, and grass-stained uniforms. Except for the sounds of multiple showers running, however, Tice didn't hear a whole lot of post-game chatter. Spotting Brandon from across the room, Coach Tice paused for a moment. There, sitting in his corner locker with head down and blood running from his nose, was Burlsworth. His jersey and uniform pants were soaked from a rainy Saturday afternoon downpour in Fayetteville. It was quite a sight for Tice to see a fighter and competitor like Brandon so dejected and defeated. He knew Burls didn't take to losing very well, and that day it showed. He also knew there was a good chance the Razorback lineman was sitting there replaying game film in his head, reviewing plays and mentally beating himself up for his mistakes or what he might have done better. Standing there, Tice's mind began to reflect on the past.

Seeing Brandon from across the Razorback locker room that Saturday, Tice felt in his heart it was time to re-institute an old custom. Burlsworth, who had been staring at the floor the whole time, sensed someone was looking at him and slowly lifted his head, catching Tice's gaze. Immediately rising to his feet, the 308-pound right guard started walking across the room. As he drew closer, Tommy noticed big tears were welling up in Brandon's eyes. Extending a mud-stained hand, Brandon offered his old coach a firm handshake. That's when Tice broke the silence.

"I'm afraid that's not going to be good enough today, Brandon." Throwing his arms around the young man half his age but twice his size, Tommy Tice gave his friend an affirming bear hug, and Burlsworth responded in like manner. Following that locker room embrace, Tice looked up at Burlsworth's still sweaty face, matter-of-factly stating, "Brandon, have I told you I loved you lately?" By this time there were tears in both their eyes. "No, Coach," Brandon said quietly, "but I sure could use it today."

"Well, Brandon. I love you."

"Coach, I love you, too."

Not much more needed to be said after that. Though it didn't take away the sting of losing, receiving a reassuring hug from a trusted hometown friend and mentor sure meant a lot at a time when he needed it the most. It didn't matter that despite losing that game, Brandon was having a good year, eventually recording 52 knockdown blocks in the Razorback's 11 games. You tend to forget the good things when caught in an emotional raincloud of defeat. That's why all athletes need a regular reality check, giving them a sense of balance between sports and life. They need to be told again that life is for living and sports are for playing. One you do the whole time you're here on the planet, and the other you only do for a few short years. There's a big difference between the two, though the boundary lines are not marked with the same white paint found on the field. Perspective in sports is tantamount to longevity and success. Effectively dealing with tough losses demands that an athlete re-align himself often. Brandon Burlsworth was no different. That brief locker room visit from Coach Tice was a tangible reminder to a competitive 21-year-old that there are some things in life a lot more important than winning football games.

Brandon opposite future NFL teammate Peyton Manning; coin toss of the 1997 Tennessee game at Little Rock.

ELEVEN

Going "Nutts"

If there's any truth to the old saying, "A change will do you good," then it certainly applied to the Razorback football program prior to the 1998 season. Following back-to-back losing seasons (4-7, 4-7), Danny Ford saw the handwriting on the wall and was asked to step down from his position as head coach. After five years of coaching the Razorbacks (1993–97), the former national championship winner retired to his farm in South Carolina.

It was a bittersweet exit for both Ford and his players. The coach's departure spelled a measure of uncertainty concerning the future of the Razorback football team, particularly for the senior classmen. These young men had been scouted and recruited by Ford and learned under him. And though they didn't always appreciate his demeanor and hard-nosed, old-fashioned approach to conditioning, they had developed a terrific respect for the tobacco-spitting Alabama native. Ford, along with his assistant coaches, had hammered into these players' minds the disciplines and skills necessary to become champions. But he had also been the man who had given them the chance to wear a Razorback jersey. That in itself inspired a degree of loyalty and gratitude. Unfortunately, the team failed to come together in a way that brought enough winning seasons to Fayetteville, and Ford was asked to leave.

For Brandon, losing Coach Ford was also an experience filled with mixed emotions. It was Ford who had officially invited Brandon to try and walk on the team. It was Ford who kept his word to the Burlsworth family, promising Brandon every opportunity for him to earn a potential scholarship. He had given his pledge to take care of Barbara Burlsworth's youngest son. It was a pledge he took seriously, and one he more than fulfilled. Some fans may not appreciate his win-loss record or coaching style, but Danny Ford will always be fondly remembered by the Burlsworth family as the man who made it possible for #77 to take the field.

On a more personal level, Brandon was also upset because Ford's exit meant his assistant coaches were leaving as well. And that meant losing offensive line coach and friend Mike Bender. For Brandon, it was more than a loss to the team. It was a personal issue. Following the announcement of Ford's firing, Brandon and some of the offensive linemen gathered together, bringing a verbal petition to Frank Broyles' office. Their hope was that somehow the athletic director would allow Coach Bender to stay. Broyles, in the gentlemanly spirit for which he is famous, graciously listened to the athletes' concerns and request. With a grandfatherly tone and heavy southern drawl, the long-time athletic director explained to the anxious young men that a key to the Razorback's historic success was to allow the new head coach to choose his own coaching staff. That was a part of "the Razorback way." This was not what the players wanted to hear, but they partially understood and reluctantly nodded their heads in agreement with the man who has become somewhat of an NCAA icon and elder statesman in the sports tradition of Arkansas. But in their hearts, Brandon and his fellow athletes grieved over having to say goodbye to Bender, a man they had grown to both admire and love.

In December of 1997, Broyles announced the new Hog head coach was going to be Houston Nutt. Nutt was a Little Rock native who had been a Razorback fan from childhood. Himself a product of a sports-oriented family, athletics had occupied a chief spot in Houston's life, having played reserve quarterback under Lou Holtz one year at Arkansas before transferring to Oklahoma State. OSU proved to be a better offensive fit for Houston, who preferred passing to running the option. After graduation, Nutt became an assistant to then coach Jimmy Johnson. Returning to Arkansas in 1983, he joined Lou Holtz as a graduate assistant. Following six seasons back at OSU as receivers' coach, Houston found the desire to be a head coach too strong to resist. He subsequently accepted the lead role in the football program at Murray State, leading the team to the Division I-AA playoffs two straight years. This success brought him to the head-coaching job at Boise State, where he stayed for a year before being offered the helm at Arkansas.

Nutt's reputation as a motivator and player's coach fueled in part Broyles' willingness to bring the Arkansas native on board. College athletes are men and women who are typically highly motivated, passionate, and often driven people. They require a proven leader who has the ability to inspire the will to win and the positive attitude needed to pull it off. Being from Arkansas, Nutt was well aware of not only the high expectations Hog fans demand from their coaches, but also of the Razorback tradition and mystique. Houston brought to the Razorback program his own brand of experience and savvy, having learned his craft from some of college football's finest — Frank Broyles, Lou Holtz, and Jimmy Johnson.

Nutt's style of coaching varied from Ford's, though. While Ford was more of an old-school disciplinarian, Nutt had added to that the spirit of a cheerleader. He also had the advantage of having grown up in Arkansas and playing briefly for the Razorbacks. As a result, he knew well how to drill deep into the spirit of Hogmania, tapping a gusher of Razorback pride that soon pipelined itself to more homes in Arkansas than cable television. Anyone who dared to "call the Hogs" waited to see what the new coach would do. Nutt brought to the table an enthusiasm combined with calculated optimism.

The Razorbacks' veteran offensive line waited with semi-skepticism as the new coaching regime moved into their offices in the Broyles' athletic complex. One of the first things Houston Nutt did was to call a meeting involving Brandon and his fellow senior players.

"Guys, I want you to know that this is your football team. What do you want?" Nutt's initial overture to the young men was met with a deafening silence, with not one of the senior players speaking a word.

Finally, after an awkward pause that seemed to last several minutes, Burlsworth rose to his feet, assuming leadership. "Coach," the senior guard spoke softly and with a tone of reverence, "you're gonna be my second head coach, and this is my last year as a Razorback." His voice then grew more confident as he declared, "We'll do anything you want us to do. But would you please not use the word 'rebuild' … ever? Not this season."

The Hogs had been last in their Division for two straight years and were picked to be last again that coming season. The Razorback running offense had ranked 112th the previous year — dead last in all of Division I. But Brandon thought that if the team really came together and pushed themselves they could win this year. He reasoned it was far too late for the current team to restructure everything they had built up to this point. In their minds, Houston Nutt was somewhat on trial at that meeting. His next move would be critical in establishing trust with his inherited team's leadership. As the wheels turned in the coach's mind, he contemplated the crossroads he faced. Because first impressions can be lasting ones, Nutt's response would go a long way in setting the tone for the entire next year. It would also determine to some degree his relationship with the very men who carried the weightiest influence with the team. Nutt had built a reputation of being the kind of coach who was as committed to his players as he was dedicated to winning football games.

Finally, Houston broke the silence and spoke, granting Brandon his request and affirming his men with a smile and nod of the head. Inwardly, Nutt was desperately trying to contain his emotion. Dismissing his players, Houston went directly to his coaching staff and announced, "Men, we've got something very special here with these seniors. We have guys who are willing to go as far as we want to take them. They are so hungry for success they will do whatever it takes to achieve it. And I believe Brandon Burlsworth will lead us there." Choosing to avoid immediate radical change, Nutt would opt instead for gradual adjustments over time made through relationship, influence, and earned respect.

That day marked a milestone for Nutt and the Razorback football team. It was also a beginning point of a new tradition as he began seeing Brandon every morning at 6:00 a.m. in the training room, doing something "a little extra" in his conditioning to gain the added advantage needed to win. He wouldn't stop there.

Brandon knew he was always at his best when he was working toward a goal. So he set a new goal for himself that year: become an All-American. This meant he was shooting for the ultra-elite — to be recognized as the very best player in the nation at his position. Being as single-minded as he was, Brandon was determined not to be distracted from his football focus. Consequently, he had asked Marty to take care of other details regarding his career, allowing Brandon to do what he did best. Brandon had told his big brother, "I'll take care of things on the field and you take care of things off the field." And that's exactly what Marty did, beginning a campaign of e-mailing football writers, plugging and promoting his not-so-little brother as an All-American candidate. Aware that players were judged on team record, level of competition, and individual performance, the senior Burlsworth brother was determined to get the word out about Brandon, including pictures of him wearing "the glasses." But due to the past few losing seasons the Razorbacks had recorded, Brandon wasn't receiving a whole lot of recognition. It certainly wasn't the acknowledgment his brother thought he deserved. Following his junior year, Brandon never even made the Outland Trophy list. The brothers attributed this oversight in part to the team's last place 4-7 record the past two seasons. That meant this final season would have to be an extraordinary one for the Razorbacks if Burls had a chance at making All-American. Brandon would do everything he could to make sure that extraordinary season came to pass.

That summer, Burlsworth lived with Washburn and free safety Chris Chalmers, staying at their apartment. It was around 3:00 a.m. when Washburn was unexpectedly awakened by Brandon. "Wash! Wake up. I've got something to show you." said Burlsworth. Dragging the 6'6" lineman out of bed still in his underwear, Brandon led him outside to the grass where he proceeded to demonstrate some new blocking steps he had developed for the o-line. A backup guard at the time, Washburn had not anticipated pre-dawn practice drills as a part of earning his scholarship. But for Burlsworth, this was the kind of thing you could expect. He told Houston Nutt they didn't need to rebuild, that they could win this coming year, and he meant to do everything he could to make good on his end of the bargain. With this commitment to excellence, it was no surprise Brandon won more awards than any Razorback that year.

Burlsworth's attitude further carried itself onto the practice field, too. During the team's first scrimmage under Nutt, things weren't going well as the offense struggled to get in sync. As the coaches watched with furrowed brows and folded arms, they heard Brandon's voice cry out from within the huddle, "How bad do ya'll want it?" For a guy who never said very much, Brandon commanded attention when he spoke. His 6'3", 308-pound body housed a growing leader who was awakened when the team needed an extra boost. His words inspired the Razorback coaches and jump-started the offense back into gear. Something was happening....

Not too long after this scrimmage, Houston Nutt called a meeting and told his players about the importance of being responsible people. "Good people do the little things, like picking up a gum wrapper to help keep the campus clean," was a sample of what Nutt said at that meeting. On the way back to the dorm, teammates Garrett and Brown spotted Brandon coming around the corner, carrying two huge handfuls of trash. "I found this on the grass" was his greeting to them. Realizing he had taken what Coach Nutt had said literally, the two men knew no piece of campus trash would be safe now that Burlsworth had taken up the banner. They shook their heads in amazement as Brandon continued down the path, picking up trash along the way.

Brandon had an emerging quality missing in many athletes today — the desire and ability to influence others. Nutt admits it wasn't something he imparted to Burlsworth or anything for which the coach could take credit. This desire to influence others began way back with his mom's godly influence in his life, continuing throughout his childhood and teenage years. It seemed that when one influence ended, another began in his life almost as if the whole thing was pre-planned. Like a baton being handed off to the next runner, Brandon's life became a stewardship of sorts to his ever-increasing list of mentors. And whether on or off the turf, he was determined to lead others as well.

Still, there was an adjustment to make for Brandon. And another impending alteration in his life would be to learn under a new offensive line coach. Mike Markuson would be that coach, and as expected, it was a slow adjustment for the mostly senior offensive line. In fact, the entire offense was getting used to a new coaching style, and to some degree, Brandon initially found it an unwelcome challenge. Markuson was markedly different from Bender. Not only did he have a different approach to blocking, he was also from "up north," being a Minnesota native. For a small town southern boy who had rarely crossed the Mason-Dixon Line, it was another hurdle to overcome. Besides, it was difficult for the linemen to change in a matter of weeks what they had been taught for the past three or four years. Brandon privately conferred with Marty, "Everything I know about blocking I learned from Coach Bender. I don't want to change now." Though Brandon would remain close to the Bender family, Danny Ford's firing had meant there would be no more Coach Bender at practice or on the sidelines. This was one change that took some getting used to, especially for a young man who had betrothed himself to "Bender's way" of doing things.

The new coach's blocking technique was different, with Markuson bringing back zone blocking, a method proven to be successful with the team in years past. But for the offensive line, some of the new footwork and steps caused a difference of opinion between coach and players. They were forced to work harder, smarter, and faster if they were to adjust to the new plays and be ready for the season. And though their relationship was initially awkward, time on the practice field meant time spent together, and ultimately Markuson gained the players' respect as well as their allegiance.

The result was that despite his former insecurity concerning the team's future, Brandon's Christian approach of believing the best in people combined with Nutt's wise approach caused the senior's suspicions to quickly fade. Brandon soon began publicly heralding the praises of Coach Nutt, calling him "a very good motivator, one of the best I've ever seen." Nutt's positive perspective gave the players a renewed self-confidence. They began believing in themselves and what they could do on the field. During one of those legendary two-a-day practices, with players gasping for air in the sweltering heat and humidity, Coach Nutt unexpectedly blew the whistle, ordering every player off the field. Confused but grateful for a chance to catch their breath, the team was then led over to the campus pool where they were ordered to jump in and cool off with a swim. The Hogs expressed their gratitude by throwing every coach, including Nutt, into the water. The coach's strategy was working off the field, too, as he and other coaches involved themselves in players' lives, dropping by their dorm rooms and apartments to check on them or just to hang out or chat. It looked like a new day was dawning over the Ozark Mountain town of Fayetteville, and a whole state would ready itself to bask in its rays. Though no games had been played as of yet, the change was starting to do them good.

All emotion and positive motivation aside though, Nutt was keenly aware of the serious nature of his new responsibility. With a multi-million dollar annual budget, he knew you couldn't keep your day job by delivering inspirational pregame speeches. There was a mountain for him to climb in the Ozarks, and unless he made significant progress toward the summit, another "climber" would soon take his place. A football coach begins his tenure somewhat on "death row," with consistent wins being the only currency purchasing his pardon to freedom. For a head football coach at the major college level, winning seasons also mean higher salaries, powerful associations, professional perks, celebrity status, and ultimately having your name and image enshrined in history with other past legendary gridiron coaching greats. Losing seasons, however are a different story. As the pigskin proverb goes, "There are only two kinds of college coaches: those who have been fired and those who are going to be." In this business, you're generally known as either a winner or a loser. There is seldom any tolerance for those men caught on the middle ground. No compromisers, backsliders, or lukewarm believers. It's an all-or-nothing occupation.

No surprise then that college football in Arkansas has become just shy of being officially recognized as another religion in some folks' minds. Saturdays are Sundays in this particular faith. The stadium is the sanctuary. The band is the orchestra. The cheerleaders are the choir and the game day program is the hymnbook. The coach is the preacher who calls the plays for the flock and the team members are the leadership who run those plays. It's largely a spectator religion where the "professionals" do the real work. The congregation, or fans, primarily watch and eat. They are the ones who possess enough zeal on Saturday to shame any hand-raising, foot-stomping congregation shouting "hallelujah" on Sunday. They also pad the offering plate through ticket sales, concessions, and officially sanctioned merchandise. There was no doubt the university was looking for a miracle, and with Houston Nutt as new resident evangelist, it looked like a Razorback revival was coming to town.

Athletic Director Frank Broyles privately figured it would take a few wins before the state would warm up to the new coach, but fans immediately responded to his zeal and enthusiasm as ticket sales began shooting through the roof. This not only meant higher morale for the fans, but it also ensured Nutt a longer-than-expected honeymoon period. Like the infamous King Henry VIII, Razorback fans were accustomed to disposing of "unproductive brides." But as ticket sales began increasing, Broyles added fuel to the fervor by announcing plans to expand Razorback Stadium in Fayetteville, adding some 20,000 seats to the structure. The stage was being set for Nutt, and he would either be hailed or hung on it. Nevertheless, the promise of a bright future looked good, and Nutt was riding a wave of positive pre-season press. The real test would come with those first few contests.

That day came soon enough as the Hogs played host to Southwest Louisiana State in Fayetteville on September 5, 1998. You couldn't have jackhammered a toothpick into Razorback Stadium, so packed was the arena. But an even greater presence than the fans themselves was the unseen spirit of anticipation and excitement filling the venue to the brim. It was time once again to call the Hogs, and the resulting cheers reverberated throughout the hills and valleys of Northwest Arkansas. By kickoff, sororities and fraternities had finished their mid-morning brunches. Tailgaters had completed their own version of the pre-game meal. Alumni had walked around Old Main, the university's landmark structure, searching for their name carved in stone on the infamous Senior Walk. The Razorback marching band had taken its place in the stands and Razorback red overwhelmingly blanketed the 50,000-plus seat stadium.

The first game captures more of the purity of college football than perhaps any other time during the season. Everything is new. The slate is clean as each team has a fresh start for another year. Like his fellow teammates gathered in the tunnel that day, Brandon's heart was beating faster than normal. "Opening day jitters," they call it. Butterflies are filling every stomach, with most athletes silently praying and hoping they just fly in formation for the day.

Brandon was elected as a team captain for this, his senior year. He was one of four, joining defensive end Ryan Hale, center Grant Garrett and tailback Madre Hill. It was an honor that recognized Burlsworth's leadership on the team, his example on campus, and his service in the community. With their new coach leading the charge, the team galloped onto the field like the "wild band of razorback hogs" for which they are named. The crowd rose to its feet, literally going "Nutts," and a season was born in decisive fashion as the Hog whipped Southwest Louisiana 38-17.

The following week the Razorbacks snapped a three-game SMU losing streak, riding the Ponies hard for a 44-17 win. The game began with Nutt calling a play that resulted in an 87-yard touchdown pass from Clint Stoerner to Anthony Lucas, tying the record for the longest reception in school history. But the key to the play's success was a cut block by Burlsworth on Mustang defender Luke Johnson, enabling Stoerner ample time to get his pass in the air.

Next was Alabama, with Nutt aware that beating the Crimson Tide was never a given. On the Wednesday before the game, the Razorbacks had a terrible practice. Hardly anything went according to plan. Failed blocks, missed tackles, and poorly-executed plays all added up to a dismal day in pads, and things weren't looking good for Saturday.

Coach Nutt met with his staff that night to discuss the game plan against the Tide. They needed an advantage that would keep the winning streak alive and with it gain even greater momentum. After the meeting, Nutt walked out of the room and was startled by a noise he heard. At first he couldn't discern what it was, but then it became clear — it was the sound of shoes moving on turf.... Sliding. Shuffling sounds. Rapid footsteps. Then more shuffling. Curiously peering around the corner, Nutt squinted in the darkness and made the outline of a man's frame. Walking closer, he recognized it was Brandon. "Burls, what are you doing?" Nutt asked.

Momentarily startled, Brandon replied, "Coach, we didn't have too good of a day today did we?"

"No we didn't, Burls. Not at all," was the Coach's reply.

Brandon explained. "Well, I was just over here making sure I got all of my plays down."

Though the room was still dark, the stadium lights suddenly flipped on in the coach's head as it dawned on him what was happening. Brandon, realizing the team had had a poor practice, was going through his role on every single offensive play so as to avoid a mistake come Saturday. He had assumed personal responsibility for the bad practice, so much did he care about the team's performance. Realizing what he had been doing there all along and away from the spotlight, Nutt smiled at his senior guard, placing a hand on his shoulder.

"Brandon," he counseled, "it's 10:30 at night, son. Go on home and get to bed. We're going to be just fine come Saturday, Okay?"

A faint grin emerged on the corner of Brandon's mouth. "You know what, Coach? We are gonna be fine, aren't we? We're gonna beat Alabama on Saturday."

Houston Nutt went to bed that night feeling better than he had felt all week, just knowing he had a team captain so concerned about a bad practice, so dedicated to doing "something extra" about it. And that feeling was present three days later. With renewed team energy and growing fan support, the Razorbacks executed a 42-6 slaughter of the #22 Alabama Crimson Tide. It was the Alabama's worst defeat in 30 years and marked the 1,000th victory in the history of the Arkansas football program. Brandon made six knockdown blocks in the fourth quarter alone, blasting through aggressive 300-pound defenders, driving them into the turf.

Something was happening....

A camaraderie was forming on this team, stronger than ever before, with each player determined to do his part. As for Brandon, he would do his job to ensure he gave his best effort on every play of every game.

By this time, Brandon had also developed a physical trademark in the oversized black glasses he wore each game day. One day in the previous season, Brandon approached Head Trainer Dean Weber concerning his eyes. For three years, Brandon had found that with the intense heat generated under his helmet, sweat was pouring down into his eyes, at times making it difficult for him to see. This, combined with the fact that he had some difficulty focusing, prompted him to seek to improve his vision. As a result, Weber gave Brandon a catalog and told him to pick out any pair of glasses he wanted.

Flipping through that catalog for several minutes, Burls' eyes finally landed on a page.

Pointing to a picture, Brandon said, "I want these."

The glasses were ordered and soon delivered, and Brandon took them to the locker room where a group of players were suiting up for practice. Now he was ready to unveil them to his teammates.

"I have something to show you," he announced to the group, "if you promise not to laugh."

Slipping on the glasses, Burls looked up at his fellow players, who immediately burst into uncontrollable laughter. This went on for some time and was accompanied by occasional one-liners. As they pointed and guffawed, Brandon just shook his head.

"I knew you'd laugh. I knew it."

"Naturally," teammate Russ Brown recalls, "he picked out the cheapest and ugliest frames. That's Brandon."

Fellow lineman Grant Garrett ribbed him even further. "You deliberately wanted to get the ugliest pair of glasses you could possibly find, didn't you, Burls?"

Brandon's only defense was, "I just wanna be able to see what I'm hitting out there." Soon the nicknames began rolling in. Drew Carey. Kurt Rambis. Clark Kent. It wasn't long before the media picked up on the glasses. Newspaper articles and sports columns, even ESPN eventually reported the Drew Carey comparison. But the glasses gave Brandon persona. They made him more recognizable and soon became a trademark. And he took all the kidding in stride. "I didn't want anything flashy," Burls later said. "I like them because they're easy to take on and off."

Due to the hard-hitting intensity that takes place on the line of scrimmage, the odds were that at some point in practice or during a game, Brandon would have the glasses cracked, snapped in half, or at least have a lens poked out by the swiping finger of a defensive end. So the Arkansas trainers decided to keep a backup pair of those glasses just in case.

Not long after obtaining his new spectacles, the Razorbacks were enjoying a practice scrimmage in preparation for an upcoming game. Quarterback Clint Stoerner returned from the sidelines, calling the offense into the Hogs' huddle. As he was giving the team the next play, he looked at each one of them and they began snickering. Burls, who had his head down listening to the called play, lifted his eyes briefly only to be met by Stoerner's gazing back at him through an identical set of glasses. That sent the whole team breaking up with laughter, including Brandon, who grinned a smile as big as his heart. These were his teammates, and he knew that behind the kidding and underneath the pads were friends who really loved and respected #77. But the ribbing he took from those glasses wasn't confined to the light-hearted jabs thrown by his Razorback teammates. Brandon's defensive opponents also gave him a hard time. Only they weren't trying to be funny. Their purpose was to insult and injure with their words. They wanted to throw him off his rhythm, confusing him and causing him to jump off sides and be penalized. They made a concerted effort to "rattle his cage," to divert his mind and concentration which would give them that fraction of a second advantage needed to gain the upper hand on the play. Taking his position at the line of scrimmage in the first quarter of a game, the trash talk began.

"Hey four-eyes!" "What's up, Drew Carey?" were some of the usual jabs, accompanied by sometimes off-color comments meant to demean Burls and question his masculinity. Brandon's eyes remained focused as he reminded himself, *It doesn't really matter. I don't have to look good to play good.* He was right too. His disciplined mental attitude sent a command to the rest of his body, turning his resolve up another notch. By the fourth quarter those very same opponents had become strangely silent, their lips seemingly sewn shut as

Burlsworth dominated them with his outstanding play. Funny what being consistently driven back and knocked to the ground time after time will do for your speech. Coach Nutt would tell his boys, "Hit them hard! Help them up and tell them you'll see them again in 25 seconds." More effective than if he had washed their mouths out with soap, Brandon was teaching them lessons on how to treat your fellow man with respect. By the time class was dismissed at game's end, they got the message.

The next victims in the Hogs' stampede were the Kentucky Wildcats, playing their first-ever game against the Hogs. Another game. Another victory. Arkansas was now 4-0. But following that win, Nutt decided to bring a new tradition to the team. In a game against Memphis, Nutt surprised his players, introducing red pants, replacing the usual white ones. The whole team was emotionally pumped about the change. That is, everyone except Brandon. Half protesting, half joking, Brandon quipped, "Y'all could have told me about this beforehand." A ferocious creature of habit, Brandon was caught off guard by the uniform change and, to be honest, never cared much for them. In fact, he didn't want to wear them at all. Even so, his performance wasn't affected as the Hogs beat Memphis like a drum. This fifth victory in a row caused coaches and sportswriters alike to begin taking notice, finally ranking Arkansas the 20th best team in the nation.

The Gamecocks of South Carolina then faced the momentum of the Razorbacks, coming away with a 41-28 loss. At one point in the game it looked as though Carolina had the winning edge, but a 24-point 3rd quarter performance nailed their chances and sealed the victory for Arkansas.

Hogmania was sweeping the state, and the whole country was taking notice of what the Razorbacks were doing week in, week out. Their surprise comeback season, after two years in the cellar, became one of the top sports stories of the year. Nutt never said the word "rebuild." Brandon Burlsworth and the rest of the Razorbacks did everything they could to assure he never had to.

Being his road-game roommate, Jeremiah Washburn was privy to Brandon's obsessive attention to detail, particularly when it came to his role on the team. Brandon had developed a ritual of sorts before games. It began the night before as he geared his mind toward the following day. But the closer to kickoff, the quieter he became. Most players had their own version of the "game day face". Many even had their own rituals and superstitions. And considering Brandon never had much to say anyway, his silence was not as noticeable as you might expect. But his teammates could tell the wheels were turning in his mind. He was thinking about the game ahead, and in particular his role in that game.

Before the game, when most players rested and watched TV, Brandon's routine involved lying back on his bed, closing his eyes, and placing a pillow over his head. Then, as Washburn describes, "You would see his feet twitching, moving back and forth and from side to side, going through the entire game in his mind, rehearsing every step of every possible play." Brandon studied his role as right guard carefully, playing his position over and over in his mind like a video loop before he ever set foot on the field. Washburn knew better than to talk out loud or interrupt the senior guard as Burls closed his eyes, retreating into his own world. With mantra-like meditation, Brandon mentally chanted those plays until they became second nature to him. When it was time to go to the stadium, Jeremiah's job was to say, "Burls, it's time to go now." Without a word, Brandon would rise from his bed, take the elevator down and catch the team bus. This ritual never altered one bit the entire season. It was his way of preparing and it certainly worked as he recorded 61 knockdown blocks during his senior year, being penalized only one time.

During road trips, on the night before the game, Coach Nutt would have the usual team meeting with his players.

Between that team meeting and lights out was a grand total of 30 minutes. Grant and Russell, road game roommates, asked Brandon, "Hey, Burls, come up to our room and visit with us."

"No, I can't," Brandon said.

"Aw, come on, Burls. Just for a few minutes," Brown persisted, eventually wearing him down.

"Okay, I'll come up for a few minutes," Brandon conceded.

The Razorbacks won the game the next day, which caused Brandon to visit Grant and Russell's room just before bedtime on the night before every remaining game. Burls had adopted a new ritual, and his teammates just left the door open for him.

Though Nutt never used the word, the 1998 football season was proving to be a rebuilding year after all for Brandon and the Razorback football team. Coach Nutt had not only reconstructed their record, but had also rebuilt their spirits. He had inspired them to play with a fresh energy and unity they had lost, or at least misplaced for the past few seasons. It felt good to hear fans scream and yell in triumph instead of in contempt. It felt good to bodysurf a victory wave into the locker room after each game. It felt good to see stadiums full again. It felt good to work out and practice during the week, looking forward with eager anticipation to Saturday. It just felt good to win again.

And the whole state of Arkansas was feeling it.

While it may or may not "take a village" to raise a child, it certainly does take an entire team to win football games. And in that '98 season, every Razorback football player was doing his job to help put another number in the win column. Everybody wanted it. Everybody was playing to win. Everybody faced forward with expectation and desire. But perhaps nobody wanted it more than Brandon. Marty told him if he really wanted to make All-American, then he would have to exhibit an exceptional performance during the year. The brothers had an inside phrase they used whenever the moment called for Brandon to reach deep within and play above and beyond his normal level. Now was that time for Brandon to "turn up the nasty," as he would say. He would really have to play full throttle this season if he was to reach his goal of becoming an all-SEC and All-American football player.

Marty scheduled an appointment, approaching Athletic Director Frank Broyles and Sports Information Director Rick Schaffer about promoting Brandon as an All-American candidate. Though it took longer to respond than Marty had hoped, eventually the university did issue press kits touting Brandon's abilities and past achievements. But all press releases aside, it was Burls' consistent competitive play on the field that garnered him the most attention.

The Hogs' next opponent was a tough team from Auburn University. The last five times the two teams met, the Tigers had walked away the victors in four of the contests. Auburn was a tough SEC school with an established reputation. Brandon recalled that in previous years, if the Hogs were down by seven points, you would see coaches with heads down on the sidelines, shoulders slumped. That attitude ultimately had a trickle-down effect on the players. But this was a team reborn, and when Auburn scored two quick touchdowns against the Hogs, putting the Tigers up 21-17 in the third quarter, Coach Nutt wore a face that exuded unwavering confidence in both his strategy and in his team. "That's one thing about this team," Brandon said. "We believe."

There are times to do more than just believe, though. You have to show people what you believe. With 3:28 left in the game, and Arkansas trailing, Burlsworth roll-blocked and leveled Auburn linebacker Ryan Taylor, allowing Eric Branch to score the Hogs' game-winning touchdown on a 14-yard run. The enthusiastic Razorbacks carried their fervor into the subsequent game against Ole Miss, blowing them out by a score of 34-0. It was homecoming at Fayetteville, and that day Brandon earned the Crip Hall Award, recognizing the most outstanding senior Razorback.

It was the team's first 8-0 start since 1988, when Arkansas was still in the now-defunct Southwestern Conference. Now they were playing in the SEC — the toughest conference in college football — and the Hogs were undefeated. The collegiate sports world intensified their watch of the Razorback's meteoric rise in the rankings. Plenty of eyes were also carefully scouting #77 and his extraordinary play, game after game.

During each game of that senior year, Brandon was intently focused on his job and role as a player. With each contest and every play, he converged his thoughts onto a single mission. Nothing would divert his attention away from the task at hand. He went from the sidelines to the huddle, from the huddle to the line of scrimmage. From the line of scrimmage, he executed the play with every ounce of mental and physical energy his 308-pound body could muster. All the pistons fired at once. Every faculty of his person would have to be on optimum alert. No part of him was allowed to relax. The deafening roar of over 50,000 screaming fans became mere background noise to him. His ears were tuned to a different frequency, one with no static interference. While on the field, Burls heard the voice of his quarterback as he called the play and shouted his cadence. But he also heard another voice as well. This one came not from a uniformed player, but rather from within. It was the voice of his conscience, dictating to him that with every play he should "honor God by doing your best." Those two voices, one shouting and the other whispering, became his marching orders. And fortunately for the Razorbacks, Brandon was a good listener. So concentrated was his focus that Marty concluded, "Of all the nice stadiums he's played in, I don't think he ever saw a one of them."

Being a professional photographer who also volunteered for his hometown newspaper, Marty became part of the media crew that roamed the sidelines of Razorback football games, snapping frame after frame. His weekend assignment for the Harrison Daily Times newspaper conveniently allowed him a unique vantage point from which to view every Razorback game. It also meant he could be near his brother. Marty, Vickie, their oldest son Joe Don, and Barbara Burlsworth traveled to every one of Brandon's games, home or away. From the stands, Barbara and Vickie sat tense, following Bran each play, making sure he was okay, then playing "catch up," trying to find the ball in play.

These games, of course, meant some long trips and exhausting drives, not to mention dropping quite a chunk of change paying for lodging, meals, and other travel expenses. Sometimes they would drive all night from a road game on Saturday so they could arrive back in Harrison by Sunday morning. Baggy-eyed and tired, they often had but an hour or two of sleep before church services began. More than once, Brandon arrived back in Fayetteville on the team's chartered flight at one or two in the morning, whereupon he would hop in his car and drive the 90-minute trip home. That way, he and his mom could go to church … together. For the Burlsworth family, this was a sacrifice they were more than willing to make. There was little thought about cost. It only mattered that they see Brandon do what he loved doing more than anything — play football. Now, he was in his senior year, his last as a Razorback, and every game was even more special to them. In fact, many players' families traveled to those road games, and the Burlsworths felt as if they had found an extended family in them.

Because he already had his camera in hand, Marty had a year earlier initiated a post-game tradition of sorts. Following each Southeastern Conference game he gathered together Brandon, Ryan Hale, and Chad Abernathy. Assembling at midfield, Marty took their picture with the scoreboard in the background. This would serve as a visual record of the outcome of those winning games, as well as a memorable pictorial of three friends. Naturally for Brandon, doing something once meant he was going to do it again and again. Every time. The same way. Same players. Same shot. Every game.

However, following the Auburn game that year, several other players gathered with them for the picture. Chad Abernathy, anxious for a refreshing shower after two hours of nose-to-nose fighting against Auburn's offensive linemen, headed for the locker room right after the picture was taken. Thinking he had fulfilled his post-game obligation, he was startled a few minutes later to see Brandon come running into the locker room. "Chad, what are you trying to do, jinx us? We need a picture of just the three of us out on the field right now." Seeing his teammate standing there, still sweating from the contest, Chad knew Burls was serious and would not let it go until another photograph was taken. So, breathing a sigh of resignation, Abernathy walked back out on the field, grabbing the nearest Razorback helmet he could find, and posed for the picture. Somewhat of a minor hassle at the time, all three players were later glad they took the time for the portraits. Today, those photographs have been enlarged and framed, and hang proudly and prominently in the offices of Hale and Abernathy.

Of course every coach and his team understands that the most important game of any season is always the next one. Never was this truer than it was for Arkansas' next contest, facing the number-one-ranked team in the country, the Tennessee Volunteers. This was to be the "Battle of the Unbeatens," with the winner very likely to be later vying for a national championship. This Razorback team, who had earlier been picked to be last in their division, was now within striking distance of playing for the big prize. As one announcer said before kickoff, "Everything … everything is riding on this game." Neither that announcer nor anyone else could have known that this game would later go down as one of the most exciting and infamous in college football history.

Going against the Hogs was the fact that the game would be at Neyland Stadium in Knoxville. The Hogs knew orange would outnumber red that day, but none fully realized that by kickoff on November 14, 1998, they would be playing before 106,365 fans, the largest attendance in Razorback football history.

As expected, the two teams waged war from the start, with most of the battle taking place in the trenches amid a constant rainfall. Brandon had mentally prepared for this game like no other. Having watched game film the week prior, working out in the weight room and conditioning on the track, the only thing left before game time was to mentally prepare.

The whole Hog football team was postured with like mind, and came on strong, amassing a 21–3 lead over the #1 ranked team in the nation. Brandon was having an outstanding game as well. If the Razorbacks beat Tennessee, the possibility of a national championship game berth seemed all but assured. Arkansas fans hadn't won one of those since 1964 and should it happen in Nutt's first season as coach, he would write himself into the history books, assured a permanent place in the folklore of college football. Heck, they might even rename the state after him.

However, the Volunteers were doing everything in their power to keep their place at the top of the hill and began a concerted comeback, which by the fourth quarter had trimmed the Razorbacks' lead to 24–22. Tennessee almost scored again when the Vol's Al Wilson picked up a blocked Arkansas field goal and began racing down the sidelines in the driving rain with nothing but broad daylight between him and the end zone. The touchdown was narrowly prevented by Burlsworth, who galloped after the defender 40 yards downfield, outrunning his own teammates and knocking Wilson soundly out of bounds at the 36-yard line. The driving rain had failed to extinguish the fire to win in Brandon's heart.

Fast-forward now to late in the game. With a paper-thin two-point lead, Arkansas had both the ball and the clock on its side, with just over a minute left to go. It was second down, and the Razorbacks had the ball on their own 41-yard line. Eighty-six seconds were all that separated Nutt gaining added momentum to an already perfect season. It looked as though an Ozark tailwind had made its way to Knoxville, and was now blowing the Hogs to victory. All they had to do was play smart and hold onto the football. Some Tennessee fans were leaving the stadium in despair, trying to beat the post-game rush. Radio announcers were proclaiming the Hogs were about to go back to Fayetteville undefeated at 9-0. Brandon and his team's incredible hard work and dedication seemed to have paid off as the Razorbacks were only seconds away from dethroning the number one team in the nation on their home turf. They would make sports headlines all across the country and probably even be featured on the cover of Sports Illustrated while finding themselves only one two more games away from playing for the national championship.

What happened next has become one of the most replayed and regretted moments in Arkansas football history, as well as one of the most infamous moments in college football lore. Some Razorback faithful even go so far as to rank it only second in ignominy to the heartbreaking loss to Texas for the national championship in 1969. But no matter where you place it, you can't forget it, despite coaches' and players' concerted efforts to do so.

The Razorback offense broke their huddle and trotted to the line of scrimmage. The rain continued to pour down, further soaking the field, the fans, and the football. But of the over-106,000 fans there that November day, only a minority had left their seats and retreated to the safety and shelter of their cars where they listened to the final seconds of the game on the radio. Concession stands were deserted and every sideline player for both teams had found a vantage point from which to see the end of the game. Players on the Tennessee sidelines were wearing a beaten look. If you weren't on your feet somewhere in Neyland Stadium, you were about to be. Razorback fans at home watching on television mentally began preparing victory celebrations.

On the field, the tension mounted as 22 drenched, game-weary athletes geared up for the next play. Quarterback Clint Stoerner began his cadence and took the snap from center Grant Garrett. It looked as though it would be simply a clock-burning safe call. Then unexpectedly, disaster struck. Tripping as he stepped back and turned, Stoerner lost his balance and fell, the wet football slipping from his hands. Instinctively, a defender dove for the leather. In a few seconds, the Razorbacks' charging momentum spun 180 degrees. It was now Tennessee's ball, and they were dangerously close to scoring position.

A closer look reveals it was Burlworth's man who recovered the fumble for the Volunteers, and Brandon, quickly responding, was the first man to jump on him, downing the ball. Both sidelines erupted, one in celebration and the other in utter disbelief. Five plays later Tennessee scored a game-winning one-yard touchdown. The Volunteers handed the Hogs a demoralizing 28-24 defeat following that infamous fumble, proving golf is not the only game of inches.

The Razorbacks, with the game all but in the bag, had seemed to just give it away at the last second. Their national championship hopes were over because Clint Stoerner put the ball on the ground … or so it seemed.

In the locker room after the game Burlsworth approached Stoerner. He had come to apologize to Clint because it was his leg that tripped up the quarterback, leading to the fumble. In a review of the game film, it at first appears Brandon's defender drove the 300-pound lineman backwards, throwing him off balance for just a fraction of a second and causing his leg to catch Stoerner's, sending the quarterback wildly to the ground. Others argue Brandon was merely taking a pre-planned inside drop step back exactly as he had been taught to do on the play.

Either way, the fact remains that at that precise time, Brandon's leg tangled up with Stoerner's foot, leading to one of the most unforgettable moments in the chronicles of college football. "How ironic," some would later ponder, "that a player like Burlsworth, so religious about his footwork, would make the smallest mistake. Others blamed Stoerner for the mishap which ultimately cost them the game. Regardless, Brandon wanted his friend to know the quarterback shouldn't carry the blame on his shoulders.

It's at a time like that when fans and players alike are reminded that sports, like life, often bring unpredictable upsets and setbacks. Someone has said the test of a person's character is not whether he fails, but rather how he handles that failure. If that is true, then Clint Stoerner demonstrated unusual character after the Tennessee loss. Facing the media as well as his team and coaches, Stoerner accepted full responsibility for the pivotal fumble that ultimately cost the Razorbacks the game and potentially a run at a national championship. Even though Brandon stepped on his foot and caused him to "stumble and fumble," as the famous play call put it, Clint Stoerner never mentioned Burlsworth's name. He put it all on himself.

Ask any player who was there that day, and to a man, they will say it was "nobody's fault." Things like that are just a part of the sport. A freak occurrence. Busted plays, unscripted and unplanned, simply happen, and there's no use trying to analyze or explain them. For sure, there was no blame game being played in the Razorback locker room that wet Saturday in Knoxville. These young men had played as a team, scored as a team, and made mistakes as a team. Win or lose, they did it as a team.

Unfortunately, a play like that did happen, occurring in a critical game at a crucial moment, and with heartbreaking results. Rebounding from a loss like this, with so much promise within their reach, would take a lot more than a motivational speech from first-season Coach Houston Nutt. The

Hogs would have just six days to recover and turn their spirits around for the next game. But unexpectedly, lightning struck twice. For the second week in a row Arkansas' opponent managed a game-winning score with less than a minute to play. And it was yet another defeat on a rain-soaked field, this time to the Mississippi State Bulldogs. What was promising to be a dream season for Brandon and the Razorback football team was now beginning to seem more like a nightmare.

Road roommates — Jeremiah Washburn and Brandon relax in their hotel the night before a game.

TWELVE

ALL-AMERICAN

After being picked to finish last in the SEC Western Division, the Arkansas Razorbacks had recorded an unbelievable 8-0 start, their best in ten years, and had drawn the football team and the university into the national spotlight. As a result, their ranking in the polls steadily climbed, reaching number eight in the country. But in college football, rankings change faster than the weather. After the frustrating loss to Tennessee and the defeat by Mississippi State with only seven seconds to play, the Hogs were reeling from the one-two punch. Both of those losses, in the eyes of most people, came down to one play and were decided by a matter of feet and seconds.

How odd that in sports, a win, even a season or a national championship, can be traced back to one key play. Danny Ford was right. It's the little things that matter. Those two defeats temporarily knocked the breath out of the team, greatly affecting their growing momentum, not to mention their ranking in the polls. Ironically, both losses occurred on the road. Both came during a driving rain and both were decided within the last minute of the game. But while those setbacks were tough pills to swallow, the pride and spirit of the Razorback football team was not broken. This was the team Danny Ford had conditioned and originally developed, and Houston

Nutt effectively built upon that foundation. Nutt had instilled within his men a sense of destiny, causing the Razorbacks to believe that within them lay both the athletic and emotional ability to overcome those losses and bounce back. After all, many of these athletes had played side by side for three years. They knew each other and had grown together as a team. They had lost before and learned hard lessons from their defeats.

In their 11th game of the season, against a tough LSU football team, the Hogs proved they were tired of losing close games in the last minute of the contest. The Razorbacks waged war that post-Thanksgiving November day at War Memorial Stadium, smoking the Tigers 41-14. It wasn't even close. In that game, Brandon recovered a blocked field goal that set up a one-yard touchdown run by Chrys Chukwuma. Raising the ball high in the air, the Hogs and the stadium erupted into an ovation. With that final regular-season win Arkansas felt the wind once again at their backs. They were just thankful it didn't rain! For Brandon, it marked his 33rd consecutive game to start at right guard, and his last game at home. That meant his college career was coming to an all-too-imminent conclusion. It was the close of one chapter of his life and the beginning of another, yet unwritten episode. There had been many special Razorback memories for the chubby kid from Harrison, and some of those memories included friends from his hometown.

Few people were more proud of #77 than was Grant Williams, Brandon's high school business teacher. At the very start of Burls' last season, Grant and son Austin (who idolized the Razorback lineman) wrote Brandon a letter letting him know they were watching him every chance they could, and that they were trying their best to make it to Fayetteville to see him in a game or two during his last season. As you might expect, tickets to Razorback games were not so easy to get. But "if we can find a couple of tickets, we'll be there," Williams wrote. Eventually the Williamses did manage to obtain tickets, seeing

Brandon play two games in his final year at Fayetteville. One of those games was against Ole Miss in Razorback Stadium. Just before kickoff, Brandon and some of his teammates were in the end zone warming up when Grant Williams snuck down onto the field and inched up behind Brandon, tickling the lineman's ribs.

"Surprise! We made it to see you," Williams said.

"Mr. Williams? Wha … what are you doing here? How did you get down onto the field? How did you get past security?" Brandon was understandably caught off guard, as fans weren't allowed on the playing field, especially just prior to kickoff.

Williams laughed, "I don't know. I just did it."

The last person Brandon expected to encounter in the Razorback end zone was his old teacher and arm-wrestling buddy. Here was the diminutive-looking Williams surrounded by a herd of oversized SEC linemen. Like an overalled farmer at a black-tie dinner, Williams was out of place on the field and soon might be out of the stadium unless Brandon did something about it. Trying not to draw too much attention to the situation, Burls thought quickly and said, "Mr. Williams, I want to see you after the game, so don't leave, okay? Come down and see me after the game." And with that, Williams returned to his seat in the stands.

Though he had initially been a little nervous about Williams being down on the field, that visit really meant a lot to Brandon. It proved to be a hectic day for Brandon as the media was vying for his attention. He would soon be whisked away and given the Crip Hall Award for his outstanding play, but nothing could keep him from a promise made to an old mentor and friend.

Burls knew well that the mania and media attention of college football was, for the most part, short-lived and fairly superficial. Over time, people forget who won what award and who was interviewed after which game. Those things are the icing on the cake for a college player and it's a very satisfying experience to be recognized for a job well done. But newspaper articles grow yellow with age and the shine on trophies fades. Another year will follow this one, and another story will have to be written, another award given. All the attention and hype emanating from the flash of the photographer's camera becomes old news as the next newspaper hits the front porch. But the ones who really matter are the people who "knew you when," who love you for who you are, not for what you have accomplished.

The Hogs finished the regular season with a highly respected 9-2 record and a ranking of number 11 in the national polls, at one point being ranked number 7. This earned them a bid to the Citrus Bowl where they would face defending National Champion Michigan State on New Year's Day in Orlando before 70,000 fans.

The evening before the game, Michigan coach Lloyd Carr bumped into Brandon at a Citrus Bowl charity event. The Wolverine coach nervously joked with him, expressing some concern at the prospects of Brandon's performance during the game. And the Michigan coach had good reason to be concerned. Prior to that bowl game, the Hogs' offensive line, led by Burlsworth, had allowed 23 fewer sacks than the previous season, second fewest in the conference. This allowed Clint Stoerner to break his own school passing records for most yardage and touchdowns. No one ever asked, "Where's the beef?" that year as the charging linemen cleared a downfield path for the Razorback's running game, which was averaging nearly 100 yards per contest. With the dramatic turnaround season the Arkansas team was enjoying, it came as little surprise that the *Football News* named Coach Houston Nutt the National Coach of the Year. Nutt was also a finalist for the acclaimed Bear Bryant Award.

With all this going for them, the Hogs brought quite a bit of momentum into Orlando on the first day of 1999. With

18,000 loyal Razorback fans making the trip to provide the background noise, the Hogs took the field. Led by tailback Madre Hill, who wisely followed behind the awesome blocking of the Razorback's offensive line, Arkansas' running game galloped for 348 yards in that Citrus Bowl game. But in spite of the high scoring contest, the 15th-ranked and defending-national-champion Wolverines handed the Razorbacks their third loss of the season. Final score: Michigan 45, Arkansas 31. The Hogs finished 9-3 and headed to the locker room. But Coach Nutt encouraged his team in one of his now famous post-game locker room talks, telling his players this was no time for them to hang their heads in shame. Because of their dedicated play that season, the Razorbacks enjoyed their first top-20 finish in nine seasons, ending up 16th in the country.

Brandon's Razorback playing days were now officially over. And so was his education. In his five years at Arkansas, he had earned a B.A. in marketing management (1997) and an M.B.A. (1998). Following that New Year's Day loss to Michigan, University of Arkansas Chancellor John White walked through the Razorback locker room, consoling players and congratulating them on a fine season. Pausing for a moment, he publicly commended Brandon to the group for being the first player in the school's history to receive a master's degree before playing in his final football game. There was some smattering of applause as Brandon, unaware of the rarity of his achievement, raised his eyebrows and responded by simply saying, "Really?"

By this time Burlsworth had become a four-time member of the SEC all-Academic honor roll. He had started in 34 consecutive Razorback football games, grading better than 90 percent in all 11 regular season games. He finished the season with 62 knockdown blocks, leading the team in that category. Being the near-perfect player, he was penalized just once his senior year. But even then it wasn't a personal foul call, but rather an illegal procedure penalty typical of linemen anxious to get the play moving. Because of his attention and alertness on virtually every play, he and the other Razorback linemen recorded the second fewest quarterback sacks in the SEC. Brandon had had an incredible year and led his team to a dramatic comeback season, but would it be enough for him to reach his goal?

Ultimately, it was. The Burlsworth family, the people of Harrison, and citizens all across the state of Arkansas were elated when the new broke that Brandon Burlsworth had been voted all-SEC and first team All-American by the *Football News*. He had done it.

Brandon Burlsworth, the overweight walk-on player from tiny Harrison, Arkansas, became the first Razorback football player to earn the coveted All-American status since Jim Mabry did it back in 1989. Considering the select group of athletes on that year's All-American team, this was quite an honor. It's a mark of distinction only a microscopic percentage of college athletes ever have the privilege of enjoying — All-American. It meant you were the best at your position. It signified that, out of all the athletes in the country, you set the standard at your position, playing it better than anyone else.

But all that was now past success to Brandon. The person he was dictated that he set new goals for his immediate future.

Now that he had achieved All-American status, everybody wanted to know if the National Football League was the next stop for Burlsworth. The NFL draft was on its way. "It has been a dream I have always had," Brandon said, responding to the question. "The last few years I have seen it could become a reality, and I am going to take every opportunity to see that I accomplish that goal." Unlike those who had previously questioned his potential, this time there was little doubt that he could achieve such a lofty goal.

It appeared his fierce work ethic was paying off, as Brandon would have two final opportunities to showcase his talents and athletic ability. The first would occur when he played in

Brandon, just 21 months old, on his way to weighing 308 pounds and bench pressing 450.

At three years old with his new wagon.

Brandon with his grandfather, "Slim" Long

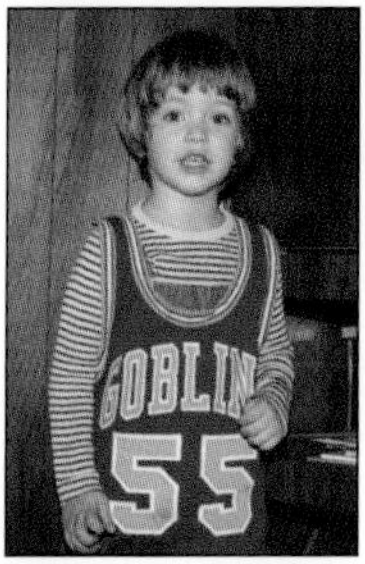

Already destined to be a Goblin

Soccer anyone?

The Early Years

Brandon, age ten, takes a dip with his nephew, Joe Don.

The Burlsworth men (L-R): brother Grady, Brandon, father Leo, brother Marty, and nephew Joe Don.

Brandon (closest to the wall) meets Brooks Robinson (seated) at a national baseball tournament in Wyoming.

As a sophomore in 1992, Brandon pitched for the Harrison Goblins.

Brandon, as a freshman, begins to learn the game of football.

Big brother Marty helps Brandon with a high school science fair project. Marty, 16 years older than Brandon, was an important role model.

With his mom, Barbara — his biggest fan.

Senior lineman for the Harrison Goblins

Arkansas state all-star team pick

Homecoming Escort

High School Senior Year 1993-94

1994-1999
The University of Arkansas

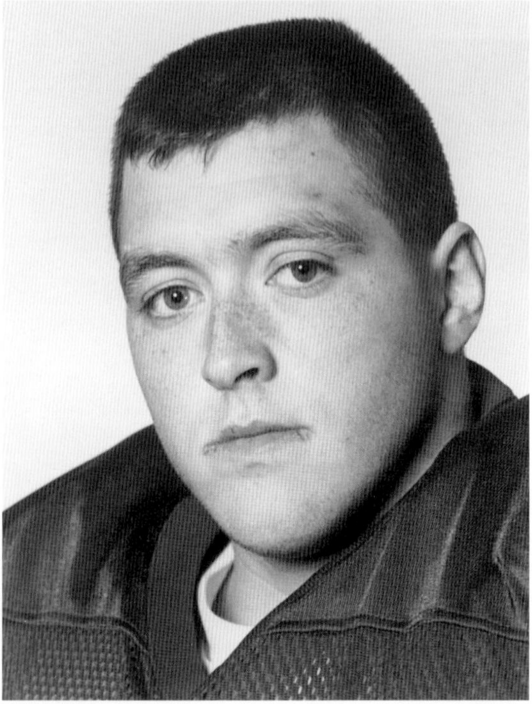

A pensive shot reflecting the determinattion and desire to excel as an Arkansas Razorback.

The road crew: Barbara, Joe Don, Vickie, and Marty. In Brandon's four years of playing for the Razorbacks, the road crew never missed a game — home or away.

Coach Danny Ford was the one who gave Brandon the opportunity to prove himself as a walk-on with the Razorback team.

#77 • 6' 3" • 308 pounds
#54 • 6' 3" • 287 pounds
#60 • 6' 0" • 284 pounds

The horsepower in the middle: #77 Brandon Burlsworth (right guard), #54 Grant Garrett (center), and #60 Russell Brown (left guard) held the Razorback line for four years.

After every win, Marty would take a picture of Brandon, Ryan Hale, and Chad Abernathy. The scoreboard in the background told the story every time.

Quarterback Clint Stoerner takes a break with the guys that protect him. (L-R) Bobby Williams, Brandon, Stoerner, Russell Brown, and Chad Abernathy.

Coach Nutt and the Razorbacks celebrate a victory by singing the Razorback fight song.

A shot from Brandon's senior year shows him in action against LSU.

Brandon protects quarterback Clint Stoerner against Memphis.

Through the Eyes of a Champion

This was Brandon's last college game, played against Michigan, January 1, 1999 in the Florida Citrus Bowl.

Brandon talks with Coach Nutt before boarding the team bus after the South Carolina game.

A devoted Hog fan is shown with his favorite Razorback's jersey painted on his bare back.

Brandon with his mom at Razorback stadium in Fayetteville

Vickie declares herself the winner of the best legs contest.

What a great smile!

Brandon with two of his nephews, Brady and Joe Don.

Brandon as a Razorback presents a game jersey to his former high school coach, Tommy Tice.

Brandon speaks with his old high school football team after a game.

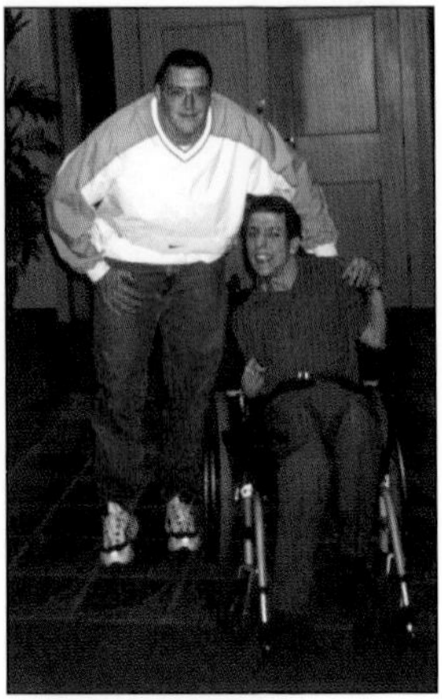

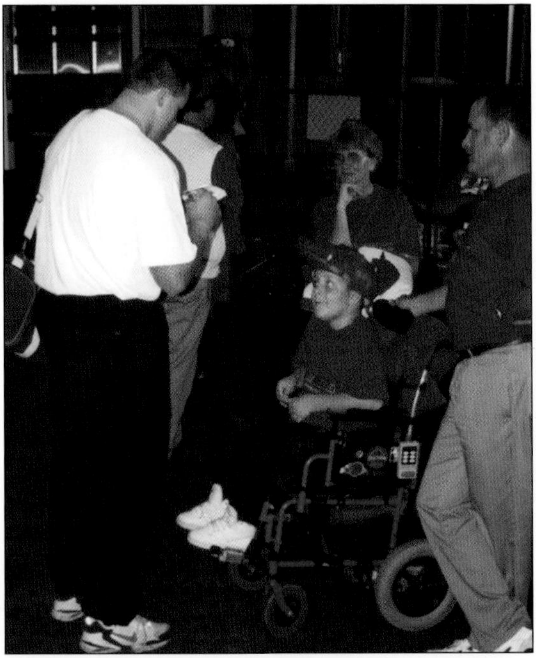

Making Time For Others

Barbara poses with her three sons, Marty, Grady, and Brandon.

What a gift God gave Brandon in his friend, Ed Robinson.

With his close friend and teammate, Nathan Norman.

People that matter most: friends and family

Offensive line coach Mike Bender gives some pointers to Brandon during the Alabama game in 1997.

Brandon, Grant Garrett, and Russell Brown with Coach Mike Bender and his son, Brent (center). Brandon once said, "Coach Bender taught me everything I know about college-level play."

Marty and Brandon talk with Nathan Cole, Brandon's suite mate.

Brandon, Barbara, and Marty show their elation just a few minutes after the congratulatory phone call from Indianapolis Colts' president Bill Polian. It was a moment that Brandon had been working toward for a long time.

Drafted By The Colts

No one will ever use locker #247 again.

The locker Brandon used for four years is now encased in glass. His helment, jersey, practice shoes, and famous glasses are on permanent display.

(l-r) Grady, Jeannie, Barbara, Joe Don, Marty, Vickie, and Louis Campbell retire Razorback #77.
November 20, 1999, War Memorial Stadium, Little Rock

In Memory

The Movie

It was perhaps inevitable that a movie would someday be made about Brandon Burlsworth's remarkable life. The film, set to be released in late Summer 2016, is appropriately titled "Greater". Chris Severio stars as Brandon Burlsworth in the film.

Mike and The Farmer battle for Marty's soul during a tense scene from Greater. From left to right, Todd Julian as Mike, Nick Searcy as The Farmer, and Neal McDonough as Brandon's brother Marty.

On location at Donald W. Reynold's Razorback Stadium, director David Hunt discusses a scene with Chris Severio and Connor Antico (right), who plays Arkansas quarterback Clint Stoerner in Greater.

Brandon smashes into a defender during a high school line drill in a scene from the movie Greater. The unfortunate player being lifted off his feet and driven back several yards by a wallop from Chris Severio is none other than Brady Burlsworth, Marty's real life son. Brady was glad to have a cameo in the movie made about his uncle Bran, even if he had to feel the consequences of his performance for a few days afterward.

The Blindside's own Quinton Aaron (center) clowns around during a break in the filming of Greater. Aaron plays a coach during a scene at the mini-camp which Brandon attended after being drafted by the Indianapolis Colts. Aaron is joined by Patrick Duff (left), who portrays Indianapolis line coach Howard Mudd during a key thematic moment in the film.

Star Neal McDonough (left) rehearses a scene with Ethan Waller (right). Waller was a classmate of Producer Brian Reindl's daughter when the 13-year-old landed the coveted role of young Brandon Burlsworth in Greater. Waller was described as one of the filmmakers' best finds. "A total natural," director David Hunt said of Waller. "He had never acted before, but he stole every scene where he appeared and he was great to work with. Ethan is one to watch."

The Volunteers' monster offensive line rounds the corner on a pulling play during the legendary 1998 Arkansas vs. Tennessee game as portrayed in Greater. This "Battle of the Unbeatens" had national championship implications and featured one of the most notorious endings in college football history.

The Burlsworths trust. Barbara (Leslie Easterbrook), Marty (Neal McDonough) and Vickie (Cassie Self) during the rousing finale of Greater.

the annual Senior Bowl, held each year in Mobile, Alabama. It was the 50th anniversary of the all-star event, pitting players from the North against the South. As they do each year, the Fellowship of Christian Athletes held a dinner in honor of the senior players. The event had gained a local reputation as selected players were asked to participate, with some giving their personal testimonies concerning their faith in Christ.

With well over 2,000 in attendance, the dinner was held in the Mobile Convention Center. It was a who's-who crowd with players, coaches, NFL scouts, local media personalities, and even the current America's Junior Miss in attendance. The event doubled as a fundraiser for various ministry, churches, families, teams, businesses, and individuals. The guest speaker that year was Tampa Bay Buccaneer Head Coach Tony Dungee. The NFL coach spoke of how his Christian faith saw him through some rough seasons and how it motivated him to press on to victory. Among the over-2,000 who heard Dungee that night was the Arkansas Razorback's star offensive guard. Listening attentively, Brandon heard the coach's testimony of how the Christian faith and a fierce will to win were not mutually exclusive concepts. Hard work, toughness, and aggressiveness were welcome traits in the life of a Christian athlete. And so was character. This was further confirmation to Brandon that he was exactly where God wanted him to be. Bringing those two worlds together — faith and football — just seemed so right to him. To do what he enjoyed more than anything while bringing joy to the One he loved more than anyone brought an unusual sense of contentment to Brandon. It felt good to play football for God. And it felt good to be honored for doing so as each of the senior players at the FCA dinner, including Burlsworth, was introduced and asked to stand. This prompted a rousing ovation for the Razorback, even from fans of SEC opponents Auburn and Alabama.

Later that week, Brandon would join the other outstanding college football seniors in practice. All of these athletes were being watched carefully and critically by NFL scouts that week. In the course of the game-week practice exercises, offensive linemen were matched up one-on-one against a defensive end, and the two would go through line drills in full pads. These match-ups were videotaped for interested scouting NFL teams. When it came Brandon's turn, he and his challenger met face to face at the imaginary line of scrimmage. On the first couple of plays the defensive player shot past him with very little effort, even causing Brandon to lose his balance and fall to the ground. The rest of the players stood by and watched, some applauding and encouraging as they waited for their own chance to prove themselves.

There was a tremendous peer pressure of sorts during those drills for Brandon, with his fellow college seniors all gathered around to see who was going to beat whom. Unfortunately, Brandon was the one who was getting beat. That's when he reached for the knob in his brain labeled "turn up the nasty," dialing it up to ten. Burlsworth, with mounting frustration at being schooled in plain sight of the best players in college football, experienced a dramatic reversal in his level of performance. On the following mock play scenario, Brandon met his defender head on, pound for pound, muscle for muscle, standing him up and impeding his progress. On the following play, he grabbed the defensive lineman and drove him hard into the turf. And every practice play after that, he dominated him with that same will to win that had earned him a spot on that roster.

But Brandon would have to go beyond practice and do that in the game, too. He would have to demonstrate the same competitive spirit combined with athletic precision. In other words, he would have to be his usual self, fixated on each play. That anxious determination displayed itself in many ways to those who saw Burlsworth play that year. Brandon often did a unique thing with his hands while he was in the huddle, a sign of his restless, nervous energy. It was a little habit he used to get psyched. With his arms straight down at his sides, he opened and closed his hands rapidly, sort of a flexing exercise for his hands and forearms.

This "trademark" was combined with another habit of his, one which occurred while down in his stance at the line of scrimmage. Staring straight ahead into the eyes of the defender, Brandon would take a look to his right and left, with a quick turn of his head, almost as a final way of using his body language to communicate to his teammates, "Are you guys ready? ARE YOU READY?" Then just as quickly, he focused straight ahead again, ready to thrust himself into his opponent like a rocket punching through the atmosphere. Bringing together former opponents like Charles Dorsey of Auburn and Anthony McFarland of LSU, Burlsworth got the chance to play with the defensive linemen this time instead of against them for a change. It always matters how you play, especially when you know somebody important is watching you. And Brandon and his South-squad teammates played like somebody was watching that day as the South beat the North 21-16.

It had been an exciting year; one Brandon would never forget. And no one would forget him, either. Two of his senior year goals were to make the all-SEC and All-American teams. He had accomplished both of them. He had met and exceeded his strength goals in the weight room. (Do you have any idea how much strength you need to knock down a 290-pound, muscle-bound, angry defensive lineman?) As a result, he became one of the strongest players in the Southeastern Conference. And while his inner strength was quiet, his on-the-field strength spoke in ear-piercing decibels. Aside from his traditional red zone call of "How bad do you want it?" Brandon wasn't much of a vocal leader on the Razorback squad. He led more by example, showing his peers how to do the job and do it right. Ever since the day Barbara Burlsworth entrusted her somewhat overweight biscuit-eater into the care of a coach wearing a Razorback shirt, Brandon had shown anybody who was watching that it took more than natural ability to be a real champion. Hard work. Sacrifice. Sweat. Pain. Repetition. Focus. Perseverance. That's what it took to be a winner. Great athletes are made in such ways. Champions are made in such ways. He demonstrated in his college career that sports not only build character, but that they also reveal it. And fans nationwide liked what they saw in him.

Now Brandon's college days were a part of his personal history, a closed chapter in his life story. The memories he packed into his suitcase upon cleaning out his locker at the Razorback athletic facility were too numerous to recount. Triumphant victories and demoralizing defeats. Bible studies, buffets, and best friends. Weight rooms and locker rooms. Mentors and mental toughness. His Razorback memories were permanently stored in an invisible cardboard box somewhere in the attic of his brain, a box he planned on reopening many times in the future.

Earlier in the 1996 football season, prior to the start of a road game against Tennessee, coaches Harold Horton and Virgil Knight were standing at midfield, conferring with some "men in suits," … "pigskin power-brokers," if you will. You know the type. They're among the elite few who have the clout to stand at midfield and shoot the breeze just before such a huge game. Motioning Marty Burlsworth to come over from the sidelines, Horton pointed to him, commenting to his suit-clad colleagues, "This guy right here was the only one who thought Burlsworth could play." Marty just smiled with an inner sense of self-satisfaction. How ironic yet appropriate for a comment like that to be made at the center spot in the stadium that would see one of the most significant games in Razorback history. It was a moment to enjoy, even relish, and Marty mentally milked it for all it was worth.

A few days later he related the comment to a friend from Harrison who responded, "No, you weren't the only one, Marty. There was a whole town of people here who knew he could play." Sometimes men in suits should listen more to small-town folk.

That an obscure kid from Harrison, Arkansas, should rise to achieve such success is newsworthy to be sure. But the way in which he did it is the real story. Being so goal-oriented kept Brandon on track every step of his college career. He refused to allow himself to be derailed by anything or anyone. He knew where he wanted to go and how best to get there. Keeping his objectives before his eyes at all times, Burlsworth reminded himself daily of his purpose and mission. If he were to be the best he could be at his position, everything else of lesser importance would have to be secondary. Vision. See the goal. Focus. Target yourself like an arrow released toward its mark. And never stop trying. Never.

Through those Drew Carey-like glasses Brandon saw the world a little differently than the rest of us. His unique perspective on life was more than just a way to view how or why things happened. It caused him to actually *make* things happen. Unless you had ever been three inches from Brandon's face while he wore his game-day spectacles, you would have never noticed it. But the manufacturer had engraved something on the thick bridge of those bulky black glasses. Two words, barely visible and yet profoundly prophetic. Those two words were … All-American.

Signing autographs after the Senior Bowl in Mobile, Alabama, January 23, 1999.

THIRTEEN

Behind the Glasses

Brandon had become a football legend. Bleacher Report would later name him "the greatest walk-on in the history of college football." But behind those famous glasses and his rhinoceros-like charging on the field lived a regular guy. Behind the scenes, Brandon was an ordinary person with his own set of faults and failures.

During Brandon's senior year, while driving his little Subaru, he had a minor "fender bender," having rear-ended another car. The outcome for Burls was that his front bumper was slightly dented. Of course, Brandon was well aware that at the first sign of any weakness or slip-up, his buddies would pounce on him like a lion on prey. And so, in uncharacteristic fashion, he parked his car in the back of the administration building instead of his usual spot in front of the athletic complex. It was the only time he ever altered his parking lot routine. Grant Garrett was walking to class and by chance spotted Brandon's car parked out of its usual parking place, as if in hiding. Telling Russell Brown about it, they strolled over to Burlsworth's locker later on that day.

"Hey, Burls. You have a wreck or something?" teased Brown. Then they pulled out all the stops, kidding him about it for several minutes.

"Yeah, I was just wondering which one of you guys was gonna break it out on me. I parked it up there so you wouldn't see it. But go on, make fun of me," Brandon said.

And they did.

But again, though Brandon loved to play pranks on his friends, he hated for the same to be done to him. In fact, aside from getting so mad he wouldn't talk to you, Burls had a more favorite and effective way of getting back at his buddies for their pranks. His punishment of choice was to take his big fingers and drill them into their hipbones. "Gosh, that always hurt," said Garrett, and it became his most effective method of retribution. Though it was always done in good fun, Burls made darn sure it hurt.

But all that energy used to play practical jokes and playfully battle with your teammates soon causes one to work up quite an appetite. And make no mistake about it, Brandon could work up an appetite. He wasn't much for regular restaurants, though. Brandon was partial to those select establishments who offered their clientele the luxury of a buffet experience. Whether it was Shoney's for breakfast or Ryan's Steak House for dinner, Burlsworth and buffets became a familiar combination. Imagine the horrified look on a restaurant manager's face upon seeing five Razorback football players, each weighing 280 to 300 pounds walking through his door. You can be sure he lost money every time they came, as each player walked away with multiple plates and servings.

The rare exception to this buffet binge was a periodic outing across the Oklahoma border to a steak place called "Phil's." Hog's Quarterback Coach Joe Ferguson knew the owner of the establishment and had recommended it to the guys. Once there, Burls would soundly consume a 56-ounce steak. Not too partial to vegetables, Brandon was a meat-and-potatoes-only kind of man. He loved it when he got invited to a player's home for dinner or a birthday meal. Each fall, Joe Dean Davenport's mom invited several of the players out for Davenport's birthday dinner. Because the Davenports raised cattle in nearby Tontitown, the oversized athletes feasted on huge steaks, baked potatoes, and corn on the cob, followed by a healthy dessert portion. Nobody walked away hungry after a dinner at the Davenports, especially Burlsworth. He loved to eat, and needed to in order to fuel his massive physique. But just to keep on each other's case, the boys occasionally pointed at each other and said, "Hey, you're getting FAT!" Comments like that prompted an ever-escalating barrage of light-hearted insults.

At team meetings in the Broyle's Athletic Complex, Brandon sat in the same seat every year. Once, a freshman player unknowingly sat in Brandon's seat. Standing silently and without saying a word, Brandon would rather stand than change his favorite seat. Finally, one of the other senior players castigated the lowly freshman. "Hey, you're in Burls' seat. Get up!" And he did, after which Brandon quietly reclaimed his spot.

On a more personal note, Brandon had many of the same likes and dislikes as others in his generation. His favorite movie was *Star Wars*, and he even had the movie soundtrack on CD. Like hero Luke Skywalker, Brandon also reminded himself to "stay on target." Brandon's glasses may as well have had crosshairs inserted in the lenses, so fixed and focused was his vision and work ethic. Quitting was not an option, though countless times his body, being on empty, screamed for it. In his heart was a resolve greater than the pain.

No rap or hip hop music for Burls. He'd just frown and shake his head at such noise. Give him some Christian music, some Eagles, a little Garth Brooks, and a "Totally 80s" CD, and he was a happy man.

That was Burlsworth to a T. And although he wasn't the biggest, fastest, or strongest player on the Razorback team, his determination was symbolized by the fact that when he walked out of the locker room with chinstrap buckled, he did not unbuckle it again until he returned to his locker. Coaches and players alike agree that Brandon had limitations as far as his natural abilities were concerned, but he was a natural at working hard, and as a result nobody in America could touch him his senior year.

But that final year in college saw growth in other areas of Brandon's life as well, particularly in his spiritual life. A year earlier Coach Decker was approached by Arkansas Athlete's Outreach to inaugurate a Bible study for Razorback football players. Decker, as strength coach, sought to build up his men both physically and spiritually. He agreed to facilitate the Bible study provided that his pastor, Darren Rogers, could teach it.

That first meeting saw eight guys initially make the weekly commitment to attend, including Burlsworth, Ryan Hale, Grant Garrett, Russell Brown, Chris Chalmers, Jeremiah Washburn, Anthony Lucas, and Clint Stoerner. Those eight players comprised much of the Razorbacks' offense. The first study was at Decker's house, and Pastor "D" asked the men what they would like to study. A couple of the guys mentioned that they had missed out on the chance to attend Sunday school growing up and suggested they just start from the beginning. It seemed like a good idea to the rest of the group, so that's where they began — in Genesis. Pastor Rogers hit the high points of each book as they began walking their way through the Bible.

For Brandon, he enjoyed the interaction with the other guys discussing spiritual things together. Having been raised in both a godly home and a good church, Burls was familiar with the basic stories of Scripture but desired a deeper knowledge and experience. Oddly, he carried a paperback Bible whose cover was distinctively pink. The guys snickered privately but didn't dare say a word to Burls about it. Brandon had apparently had the Bible for years as it was worn and frazzled from long-time use. That Bible had served him faithfully as he thumbed through it day after day in his personal reading.

At the end of the teaching time, the guys would turn to Burlsworth and ask, "Brandon, is that right?" checking the pastor for accuracy. Burls would say, "Yep. He told you straight."

But beyond the biblical facts and knowledge imparted in that weekly study was the special camaraderie that developed between the guys. They were more than just teammates. The young men were becoming spiritual brothers. As they did on the field, they met in that Bible study for a common goal and united purpose: that purpose being a Person. What drew them together every Thursday night was a calling greater than playing football for the Arkansas Razorbacks. There was something spiritual there, something eternal. Something that would bond them together in the years to come, far beyond wearing a common uniform. There was a Christian partnership between them and a unifying spirit. While on the field, they were expected to be strong at all times. Weakness is associated with losing. But in that small group, they shared concerns and struggles, revealing their Achilles heels to one another. They prayed for one another's spiritual walk with God and for their football injuries. Many times they saw God restore a player physically, just in time to play in the game. Some of those same players were interviewed on TV after the game and gave glory to God for making them healthy enough to play.

Players came together in that Thursday study, black and white. Color didn't matter as their common faith in Christ tore down racial barriers. In the small group, hearts were being forged as genuine fellowship was born. With that fellowship came the freedom to let down their guard, to be real and honest. That small study began to outgrow Coach Decker's house, moving to a room at Rogers' church, then eventually relocating to the Razorback Club to accommodate the 50 or so who soon attended faithfully. By the time the '98 season began, those men had more to draw on than just practice scrimmages and time together in the weight room. Like another group of eleven, 2,000 years ago, they had a power beyond themselves.

The outcome was that several players attributed much of that season's success to the unity and brotherhood developed between the men during those Thursday night meetings. That Bible study continued to grow and minister to players long after the 1998 season.

It was the most natural thing in the world for Brandon to join that Bible study. Since childhood he had cultivated a deep desire to know God and a strong understanding of His Word. That desire was first planted in his heart by his mother. The old adage claims the apple doesn't fall far from the tree, and in this case it's true to the core. Every person's perspective in life is influenced by his or her upbringing and family background. Along with her other sons, Barbara Burlsworth had instilled within Brandon an early reverence for God and a respect for others. On a University of Arkansas information form, Brandon had listed his mom as the greatest influence in his life, because as he put it, "she is willing to help with anything." She modeled a lifestyle that was passed down both by design and by default to her sons. Perhaps that's the greatest thing we can leave our kids. Isn't it interesting how parents indelibly influence their children simply by being themselves? Like a soul tattoo, the mark a mom or dad leaves on their sons and daughters goes beneath the skin, yet is visible to all.

To Brandon, family was more than just a word used to describe relatives living in the same house. "Family" are those people who have been with you from the beginning. They're the ones who know the worst things about you yet love you anyway. "Unconditional love," they call it. Families fight, but they also forgive. Because he was far from perfect, Brandon had a lot for which he needed forgiveness within his own family, such as times when he got mad and held a grudge. Like the day brother Grady was visiting and unknowingly tread on part of Brandon's sacred ground.... Marty's wife Vickie had a tradition of baking a dessert of some sort for Brandon when he would return home. Grady was walking through the Burlsworth kitchen, spotted a cake, and decided to partake of a few pieces. Upon discovering his older brother had eaten most of his cake, Brandon furrowed his brow and held it against Grady for a few days. But that was part of his immaturity as a young man and still-growing Christian.

Notwithstanding his faults and imperfections, Brandon was able to focus his life through the lens of Scripture. The way he saw it, he was put on this earth for a purpose. Instead of being born randomly, he believed God had a plan, a blueprint for his life. Like pieces of a puzzle coming together, Brandon gradually understood more of that plan as he matured, though he kept it simple. Love God. Go to church. Read your Bible. Pray. Live right. Work hard. Do your best. He was convinced that character was more important than convenience, and part of that character was learned in church. That's why he made the trip back home to Harrison every weekend to attend church with his mom. Don't ask him to do anything on the weekend because he was going home no matter what. That small winding two-lane highway that weaves its way through the Ozarks became as familiar to Brandon as his own neighborhood, so often did he drive it. Piling up thousands of miles on that route, each Friday Burls was like a nag headed to the barn. Home. Family. Church. Friends. Familiarity. All these contributed to the developing character of the 22-year-old young man. As a result, those who knew Burls were more than convinced there was something extraordinary behind those glasses. All Clark Kent comparisons aside, Brandon didn't need a phone booth to change personas because he was the same person with or without the specs. And it was through those lenses that he saw life from a unique perspective.

You never heard a curse word come from his mouth. He was one offensive lineman who was never offensive. He never drank a beer, though one was handed to him once as he walked through the door at a reception prior to the Carquest Bowl in Miami. Brandon politely took the drink from the fellow and walked around for two hours with it warming in his hand. Upon leaving, he handed it back untouched to the server who had given it to him, saying, "Thank you."

The only time he ever drank alcohol was purely unintentional. On a spring evening in '98 a group of players, some with wives, decided to go eat at the Outback Steakhouse. There were about 15 of them, Grant Garrett and Russell Brown included. Brandon was eating a hefty portion of food and washing it down with his always-standard Diet Coke. Ever the prankster, Grant whispered to Russell, "Watch this." Turning to Brandon, Garrett said, "Hey, Burls, you want a strawberry drink?" To which Burlsworth compliantly replied, "Sure," whereupon Grant bellied up to the bar and ordered a strawberry daiquiri with double the usual amount of alcohol. Bringing it back to the table, he set it before Brandon and the big offensive lineman worked the drink into his rotation, unaware of the real contents. After a couple of those daiquiris, all compliments of Garrett, the group left the restaurant. Realizing at that point the trick that had been played on him, Burlsworth looked at Grant, promising, "I'll get you."

Garrett was unaware his prank had upset Brandon so much until later. Brandon returned to his apartment in a simmering anger. Walking past Nathan Norman, Burls went straight to his room, put on his sweats and left. Disappearing for two solid hours, he returned soaking wet from head to toe. Sweat was dripping off his nose, chin, and fingertips, pouring down his back. "They tried to trick me," was all he said as he headed for the shower. He wanted all that alcohol out of his body so badly he had run non-stop for two hours in an attempt to sweat it out.

Brandon's pursuit of physical purity led him to a life of moral purity as well. Brandon believed God was right when He said sex was best when kept within the marriage relationship. And that guiding principle served as a moral compass for him as he began occasionally dating.

Though he carried himself with a quiet demeanor, underneath was a fierce competitive spirit on the football field. That almost perfect play masked a young man who was as human as the rest of us. Mistakes and missteps dotted the landscape of his character as they do the rest of us. But Brandon was never one to look back for long. He had better things to do. There was another prize ahead to claim, another goal to meet. He knew he wasn't a perfect person. But he also knew God had already promised He would never give up on him, but rather continue working in his life every day until He took him from earth to heaven (Phil. 1:6). That truth became an undeniable source of hope that drove the man behind the glasses.

The Razorbacks add to their trophy collection: bringing "the Boot" back to Fayetteville following a big win over LSU.

FOURTEEN

Upward Draft!

Virtually every young boy growing up has a hero, and for most it's usually a sports hero. Mantle or Mays, Starr or Staubach, Abdul-Jabbar or Jordan, these superstars set the standard for aspiring adolescent athletes. They inspire dreams of greatness and fantasies of heroic finishes. What kid hasn't imagined playing the game in the arena of his mind, heightening the scenario to dramatic proportions? It's the final game of the World Series, full count, bottom of the ninth, last pitch. It's fourth down and goal, down by five with time left for only one play. It's six seconds left, you get the ball out of bounds at mid-court and you're down by one. And, oh yes, the crowd is on its feet. Can you hear the roar? Deafening, isn't it?

And this fantasy also comes with its own play-by-play announcer. He's the best there is, though oddly enough, he sounds strikingly similar to the voice of the player himself. There's a slight tingle down the spine as the anticipation builds toward the climactic moment. In that highlight film, which plays repeated loops exclusively in the IMAX theater of the head, a 12-year-old boy is the main character. Here comes the pitch. The shot is off. The snap is taken. You know the rest. Our hero scores the winning touchdown, nails the last-second buzzer-beating shot, and slams a blistering line-drive homer into the left-field bleachers. Game over! We win! Fans are jumping up and down. Players are pouring out onto the field. Arms are lifted high in triumph. You can hear the sportscaster marking the occasion with a history-making broadcast. "Ladies and gentlemen, in all my years of sports announcing, I've never seen a finish like this. One man has just written himself into the record books. Oh my, my! This game is over! Just listen to this crowd."

It is traditionally at this point when the announcer's call is drowned out by a pre-emptive female voice heralding from a broadcasting booth located in the kitchen, "Okay, everybody. Dinner is ready." Suddenly the transmission signal is lost, and the brain's screen goes blank. But that's okay. It's a movie he can watch anytime he wants. No need for a DVD player to see this cinema classic. In this theater he has on-demand inspiration even after lights out, which is a great time for dreaming anyway.

As a young boy, Brandon was no different from other kids who dreamed of one day being great in athletics. Only his hero didn't play offensive line. For Brandon, his sports idol was St. Louis Cardinal shortstop Ozzie Smith. The "Wizard of Oz" they called him. He earned the name "because of the wonderful things he does," or did, at his position. He waved his glove around that part of the diamond like a magician's wand, to the amazement of spectators and opposing players alike. A spectacular leaping ability combined with cat-like reflexes caused batters to mentally give up after hitting the ball towards shortstop. They knew that ball's chances were slim-to-none of making it past Smith. He had glue in that glove. With his signature back flip, he mesmerized major league baseball. He was one of the great ones.

Just looking at the oversized poster of Ozzie that hung in his bedroom helped nurture a budding desire for something more in Brandon. That's what heroes are supposed to do. They inspire others to achieve their maximum potential, helping them to achieve peak performance. For a boy, this performance happens more in the head than on the field. But as he grows physically and becomes a young man, his inspiration turns to perspiration, which in turn, leads to success. That's what Burls had seen happening in his life. He had grown spiritually and physically, matured socially, and now sought to further himself professionally. But like everything else he had accomplished, it certainly wouldn't come easy. If Brandon were to make it in the NFL, it would require a heroic effort on his part — more of his focus and work than previous goals. Every day he had looked at his outdated 1995 NFL calendar. And every day he reminded himself that nobody struts into the National Football League. Even high draft picks still have to earn the chance to play. The level and caliber of play in professional football compared to college was greater than the jump from high school to college. Players were markedly faster and stronger. The game was quicker. And the margin for error was much narrower. On average, an NFL player's career doesn't even last as long as it did in college. Salaries are high but so are the expectations. And with the intensity of the game, an athlete's playing days can be cut short with a single tackle.

How would Brandon measure up against the best of the very best? Players who not only worked hard but also had far more natural ability than he did?

Being selected in the NFL draft is a dream of almost unreal proportions for a college football player. But once a player is fairly well convinced he will be taken in the draft there is another level to shoot for. Being drafted is one thing, but to go high in the draft is much better. The higher you are as a draft pick, the more valuable you are to the team, thus giving you more leverage and bargaining power when it comes to negotiating your contract.

Either way, a good rule of thumb was that in order to be drafted and increase your stock in that draft, a good performance at the NFL combine was a must. Having a good showing at this event, held annually at the RCA Dome in Indianapolis, would go a long way in determining your immediate future in the NFL. There, head scouts and coaches from every professional team are in attendance. They come equipped with stopwatches, clipboards, video cameras, and a discerning spirit. It is their job, along with the head coach, to come to a critical consensus concerning their team's greatest position needs and to decide who would best meet those needs. Of course, those professionals have been observing the top college prospects for some time. It's a science of sorts, a deliberately calculated decision that carries with it great weight. A player has been studied for years prior to this day. Pro teams have monitored his college career, kept game statistics and graded him along the way. They have kept a watchful eye on injuries sustained during that time, however minor or severe. They've noted how long it took to rehabilitate and bounce back from injury. They've looked at his overall health record to see if there have been any recurring illnesses. They've listened to his college coaches to pick up insight on his work ethic, his ability to learn, and his mental fortitude. They want to know what kind of athlete he is, how much talent he possesses, and whether or not he has already reached his potential. If a player peaks in college, there is no room for improvement and this disqualifies him as far as professional football is concerned.

Make no mistake about it, a draft pick represents an important investment on the part of a professional football club. It's a financial investment to be sure, an initial gamble on the part of the team owner, sometimes involving millions of dollars. Millions. It's a capital business venture, in some ways no different from opening up another store location. The intended hope is that this one will make you money and not cause you to go belly up. It has a minor resemblance to the stock market, with all the buying and selling that occurs. And while players are not stocks or stores, they can be assets or liabilities. Assets most often have their contracts renewed. Liabilities are traded like unwanted baseball cards. Some would say like cattle. And if there is any truth to that, the combine serves as the equivalent of the Ft. Worth stockyards, where hundreds of hopeful athletes await their turn to showcase their skills and impress the men who make the decisions on such matters.

The rookie combine affords the teams one last look and evaluation of the potential draftees. Draft picks are traded and shuffled around some, but for the most part, a team gets only one pick per round come draft day. Traditionally, the team that finishes with the worst record the previous year gets the number one pick. That's so the teams can remain relatively balanced and competitive (in theory, anyway). Realists know it's a matter of smart management and wise coaching that ultimately give a team a fighting chance to win championships. After that, it's conditioning and consistency that take a team to victory.

Brandon and Marty had discussed the combine months ahead of time and they knew what would take place there. They were aware there would be no second chances. No gimmes. They realized a stellar college career can be somewhat overshadowed by a lousy showing in Indianapolis. There was no doubt in Brandon's mind that he would have to make a very good impression. With the event fast approaching, there were several specifics on which he would have to focus. First, he had to keep his weight up to a true 300 pounds. Pro scouts had suggested they wanted Burlsworth to play at 315 pounds and yet not lose any speed. That meant continued development of his short yardage agility skills. But Brandon also was aware that at the combine players were tested, timed, and scrutinized on many different physical levels and exercises. He would be analyzed on his repetitions on the bench press, timed in the 40-yard dash, line drills, "shuttle runs," judged in the squat and the vertical jump. All this spelled an ongoing conditioning and weight program for Brandon.

Just because he had finished his education at the university and his tenure with the Razorbacks, there would be no time for slacking off for #77. This was not a time for relaxing until the phone hopefully rang on draft day. All across the country, athletes were conditioning themselves in anticipation of the NFL combine and draft. Running. Lifting. Abstaining from certain foods. Taking supplements. Sacrificing. Working hard. Some of those athletes would be vying for Brandon's spot in the draft, and he knew it. To him, this was another competition, another chance to stand out from the crowd, an opportunity to prove himself better than the rest. This was a time for increased discipline, not a time to rest on his laurels.

To facilitate his goal, Brandon moved in with teammates and friends Joe Dean Davenport and Jeremiah Washburn in Fayetteville for a few months, which would afford him easy access to the Razorback weight room. In everyone else's mind, Burlsworth was a certain top NFL draft pick, destined to become famous and make millions. For those reasons and many more, Brandon had become a mentor and model to younger athletes who observed his work ethic and lifestyle.

Freshman Josh Melton was one of those observing athletes. Like many new red-shirts, Josh was somewhat in awe of his new status as a Razorback. He was just getting to know his way around the athletic complex when he first sensed Burlsworth's presence in the weight room. As a recruited lineman himself, Josh studied Brandon's ferocious resolve during his weight-lifting workout. He made special mental note that Brandon never cut corners, always lifting the bar with arms fully extended instead of three-fourths of the way. Because Brandon was such a visualizer, he always saw the end result before he even began. Like an Arkansas farm cow repetitiously chewing the cud, his days were filled with rhythmic long hours in the weight room, over and over again, extra drills, saying no to other things that might distract him from his goal. Fellow senior lineman Grant Garrett confessed, "Some of us have lives outside of football, like hunting or fishing. Not Brandon. He likes to lift weights." Brandon was confident that God would reward his efforts. For him, the joy was not just in reaching his destination. It was also in the journey itself. This is not to say his workouts were painless, but they were flawless. You could set your clock by them. And the proof was in the product those workouts produced. As he watched, Josh Melton was impressed with Brandon. But beyond that, he was convicted and motivated to become all that God wanted him to be as well.

Living up in Fayetteville those few months afforded Burls the opportunity to specify his workout, tailor-making it with a view to the upcoming rookie combine. He focused on the bench press, striving for as many reps as possible at 225 pounds. Then he piled the weights on to see what was the maximum he could bench press. He practiced his vertical leap, the NFL shuttle run, and the 40-yard dash, among others. On days when he was not conditioning, Brandon drove home to Harrison. There he spent time hanging out with family and friends, like his former high school teacher, Grant Williams.

Earlier that year, the region had experienced some ice and snow, making travel hazardous on the rural mountain roads. Williams called Brandon and asked if he wanted to ride out with him to feed his cattle. It was a freezing afternoon as Grant drove up to the Burlsworth home. Climbing in, Burls headed out to the country in Williams' truck, where the teacher turned and asked him, "So, Brandon, do you like the new coach?" referring to Nutt.

Brandon typically spoke with hardly a pause between sentences or words. It was a trait which grew, in part, out of his shy persona. In quick fashion he responded, "My old line coach, Coach Bender, taught me everything I know about my position. He taught me how to block." Though he had adapted to his new line coach well, Brandon was still loyal in his heart to the man who had taught him everything he knew about how to play his position. Burlsworth went on to say that he really respected Coach Nutt for his ability to motivate the guys and "pull the team together," but Mike Bender would remain one of the most influential people in Brandon's life. The two would continue to exchange e-mails, keeping each other updated on their lives.

Traveling from Burls' house to the Williams' farm that cold January afternoon, the two were approaching an intersection when suddenly Grant realized the truck wasn't stopping. Pumping the brakes, they went into a skid on the ice that covered the rural road. Sliding into the crossroads, the truck began turning sideways. No matter which way Williams turned the steering wheel, there was no effect as the vehicle was out of control. At that precise moment another car whizzed past them, narrowly missing the truck. Skidding to a stop, and with both their hearts nearly matching the rpm's of the truck's engine, Brandon and Grant breathed a sigh of relief and a prayer of thanks.

Finally, the time came to travel to the RCA Dome in downtown Indianapolis. By the time Marty and Brandon arrived, the youngest Burlsworth brother was as prepared as he possibly could have been — and his performance proved it. After media interviews which kept him up until midnight, Burlsworth rose at 5:30 a.m. for mandatory drug tests. Then it was on to physical exams where doctors poked, pried, and pulled on arms, shoulders, and legs looking for weak spots or injuries. Though artificial turf is generally slower, he ran the fastest 40-yard dash ever for a lineman at the combine, clocking a time of 4.88 seconds. The best time the year before was 4.93. He recorded a 33-and-a-half-inch vertical jump. (How many 308-pound men do you know who can do that?)

He also managed to max out on the bench press at around 450 pounds, while squatting over 700 pounds. Returning home from Indianapolis, Brandon and Marty both felt pretty good about Brandon's performance, believing it increased his value in the upcoming draft. Arkansas Head Coach Houston Nutt also thought Burls had a good chance to go in the first round or two of the draft, as he had been receiving numerous phone calls from pro teams regarding Brandon.

For the next eight weeks Brandon pretty much kept within his self-prescribed routine, commuting back and forth between Fayetteville and Harrison. It was during one of those trips to Harrison that Brandon decided to pay a visit to his old high school coach one night. It had been a while since he had talked with Coach Tommy Tice and Burls wanted to stop by and call on him. Actually, Brandon had ulterior motives for the visit. He wanted to work out in the Harrison High weight room, and Tice was the only man with the key.

Opening the front door of his home, the coach's face lit up upon seeing his former player again. "Brandon! Good to see you. Come on in and sit down. Let's visit for a few minutes." Brandon entered the Tice's den, promptly parking himself in a comfortable chair. The few minutes' visit turned into an hour as the two talked about this and that, mainly football and the future. There were some pauses in the conversation, as the TV was on, and Brandon was not fond of initiating useless chatter. Finally, Tice asked, "What do want to do in the NFL, Brandon?"

The face of Harrison's hometown hero lit up as if turned on by an unseen switch. "I wanna start my first year in the NFL," he said with a self-assured tone of voice. "It goes back to what I think," he said, referring back to an attitude Tice had instilled in him years ago. "And, Coach, I think I am as good as anybody there. I wanna make the all-Rookie team." It was clear that now, with just two weeks before the draft, Burlsworth had pro football on the brain. Soon it became evident the conversation was at an end as Brandon was anxious to get to the weight room. Taking the key from Tice, Brandon said goodbye on the porch and the coach watched his friend and former player stuff himself into the white Subaru, driving off into the night.

Finally, Saturday, April 17, came. Live from New York and Madison Square Garden, draft day had arrived. More like "destiny day" for scores of college athletes across America. Television sets were turned on and channels locked in. Living rooms were packed with relatives and close friends, anxiously anticipating the announcement of the draft picks.

Far from the concrete jungle of New York City, though, was the much smaller crowd that had gathered at the home of Marty and Vickie Burlsworth. The house was a second home to Brandon, and he would spend much of his weekend visits there. Driving home to Harrison on Friday afternoons, he would arrive in time to pick up Marty and Vickie's boys from school. Brandon loved spending time with the three boys. Brady, just five years old at this time, especially enjoyed hanging out with his favorite uncle. When the Burlsworths visited Brandon at school, some of the other players saw Burls' nephews running up to leap in his arms and whispered to one another, wondering if Brandon had a child he wasn't telling them about.

What made matters even more confusing was that initially some of the team also thought that, because of his 16-year age difference and intense involvement in Brandon's life, Marty was Burls' father. This confusion often persists even to this day, as much to his consternation, Marty is occasionally referred to by some as "Brandon's dad." Oblivious to all this, Brandon's nephews were just glad to see their uncle on those Friday afternoons, especially Brady. To him, "Uncle Bran" was a mountain of a man and there was nothing he couldn't do. Brady would climb on Brandon as if he were a set of monkey bars – just the kind of stuff you do when your uncle is a big, major college football player … and All-American. Occasionally, while riding in the car together, Brandon and Brady would join in and sing with the radio. Brady's favorite song to sing with Brandon was "We Are the Champions," as the two attempted to belt out the anthem, lifting their voices above those on the radio like dimestore Freddy Mercurys. Coming to the house, they would throw the football or play computer games until Vickie or Marty arrived home. Since they always used the back entrance as their main door, sometimes Vickie wouldn't know Brandon was there, and it surprised her several times to see him sitting silently in the kitchen, playing on the computer. The dialogue hardly ever diverted from week to week.

"Hey, Bran, you hungry?"

"Yeah," was his predictable reply.

And Vickie would fix him a snack.

Since Marty was playing out the role of official spokesman for the family and because their house could accommodate more people than Barbara's, they had decided the watch party on draft day would take place there. Originally Brandon had wanted just immediate family to gather for his special day. But there was another, newer extended "family member" he would have to get used to seeing — the media. As a result, TV crews had set up communications, complete with camera crews and reporters, at the Burlsworth home. Burlsworth was by this time a state hero and all the media outlets were covering his story. In addition, several friends had come over to share the excitement of the day. Marty sat in the living room, eyes glued to the television and ears raised like antennae listening for his little brother's name to be called in the draft. The selection process began and everyone waited as the names were read. One of the big stories of that Saturday at Madison Square Garden came when the Indianapolis Colts, having the fourth pick overall in the first round, shocked prognosticators by picking University of Miami running back Edgerrin James over Heisman Trophy winner Ricky Williams. The selections went on and the first round ended, and Brandon's name had yet to be called. Then the second round began, and they all waited on the edge of their chairs waiting to hear the Burlsworth name.

Tension was slowly building inside the 300-pounder. Being on the hot seat and in the limelight produced a level of discomfort in Brandon that made him feel claustrophobic and nervous. One minute he was outside on the porch, the next he was inside, pacing between rooms. Nervous energy shot through his body, making him feel like this was a bad day, not a good one. Needing some fresh air, Brandon walked out onto the big front porch that wraps part of the Burlsworth's turn-of-the-century home. Vickie Burlsworth followed her brother-in-law.

"You doing okay, Bran?" she asked. Having somewhat helped to raise Brandon, Vickie was crazy about her younger brother-in-law. She had watched him grow from an overactive preadolescent into the maturing man he had become. Once, when he was about six years old, Brandon had found a long wire in the yard and was whipping it around in a circle. Vickie, recently having been married to Marty, took it upon herself to tell Brandon to stop doing that before someone got hurt. About that time, the swirling wire caught her ankle, cutting the skin and sending a great deal of pain shooting through her leg. That was just the kind of impulsive behavior she had gladly and gratefully seen her little brother-in-law grow out of. But the memory of that stinging wire slap remains to this day … as does the scar it produced.

Vickie had become more of a big sister than a sister-in-law to Brandon. As a part of the Burlsworth's tight family circle, Brandon opened up to Vickie, allowing her to share in a part of him few others ever saw.

"I just hate all this," he said, confessing his nervousness over the attention he was receiving on that draft day. It didn't help that he had expected to be taken in the draft by this time. This day, to a large degree, would determine his future, and to anyone it would have been a stress-filled experience — how much more so to a 22-year-old who preferred his life to be in a neat, predictable order.

"Why don't we go somewhere and sit down for a bit," Vickie proposed.

"Okay," Brandon agreed. Walking over behind an old smokehouse located behind the house, the two found a couple of lawn chairs and took some weight off their feet for a while. Sitting out of sight from the crowd that was gathered for the big day, Brandon felt a temporary reprieve from the strain and nervous tension that had built up inside him. The two talked some, but mostly just quietly sat. It was a beautiful spring Saturday afternoon in Harrison, Arkansas. Brandon breathed a sigh of relief as the shade of that smokehouse sheltered him from the brightness of the sun, not to mention the glare of camera lights. It was a precious few moments of reflection for Vickie, as well. Looking at her husband's brother, she remembered a chubby little kid who at times annoyed the heck out of her during his boyhood years. But he was all grown up now. Very grown up. Physically and spiritually, she had watched his progress with great interest. She had cooked countless meals, even sending food back with him to Fayetteville on numerous Sunday afternoons. She, like anyone close to him, had endured some of his idiosyncrasies and personality quirks. But he was family and she accepted him just as he was, with the same unconditional love that characterized the close-knit clan.

Feeling somewhat temporarily relieved from the anxiety that had characterized most of the day, Brandon and Vickie made their way back toward the main house. Just then, Brandon's Uncle Leon came out of the house. "Hey Brandon. I'm gonna run up to Miller Hardware. Come with me."

Of course, to Brandon, this was just another excuse to dodge the attention he knew was waiting for him inside. Turning, he looked at Vickie and said, "I'm going." Vickie just shook her head as Brandon climbed into Leon's truck and backed out of the driveway. Driving to the top of the hill, the truck paused momentarily as Brandon turned around to discover Vickie still looking at him in disbelief. She was amazed that he was leaving at such an important time on draft day and thought for sure he would get out of the truck and walk back to the house. She then remembered Brandon had two microphones on him, placed there by television crews. She silently prayed, "I sure hope he has turned them off." And he had.

Returning inside the house, she stood at the edge of the living room and motioned for Marty. "Brandon just left to go to Miller Hardware with Uncle Leon," she whispered.

Pausing for a second, Marty responded, "Well, just don't tell anybody." Marty was hoping no one would notice that the person who was the main reason everyone had gathered together had just left the premises. Marty came back to his post in front of the television and watched for several minutes. By this time in the afternoon the draft had progressed. Vickie continued to pray. "Lord, let that child come back soon." About that time, out of the corner of her eye she caught a glimpse of Leon's truck pulling up. "Thank You, God," she silently said.

So as not to miss an incoming call from a team, Marty had several phones available at the house. Just then one of them rang. It was a representative from the Philadelphia Eagles calling. Brandon got on the phone and talked to him for several minutes, but the conversation wasn't centered around Brandon having been picked by the Eagles. Instead, the person on the other end of the line wanted to know what the weather was like there in Harrison. Small talk, mostly. Later, Brandon discovered they may have been trying to tie up the phone line so another team couldn't get through to him. But eventually another team did, on a secondary phone line. It was around six o'clock when the Indianapolis Colts selected Brandon the 63rd player taken overall and the first true offensive guard selected … one of the top 100 players in the draft. Then the phone rang again, only this time the caller wasn't interested in the weather.

"Brandon, this is Bill Polian, president of the Indianapolis Colts. Congratulations, you're an Indianapolis Colt!"

That March before the draft, Arkansas' offensive line Coach Mike Markuson, along with coaches Joe Ferguson and Danny Nutt, had traveled to the Colts' facility in Indianapolis to see about obtaining a screen play from them. While there, they met with the Colts' offensive line coach, Howard Mudd. The four of them were talking in the hallway outside Mudd's office as the Colts' coach related how he liked what the Hogs' coaches were doing on offense. After a few minutes Mudd brought up Burlsworth's name, expressing his admiration and interest in the young player. "I don't know if we can get him," Mudd said with a concerned tone of voice. But he was clear in communicating that they sure wanted him. As it turned out, they wanted him bad enough to forgo every other lineman in the draft to get him. Colts' coaches and scouts were conscious of the fact that Burlsworth was called by some "the most athletic guard in the draft," which was an enormous testament to Brandon's work ethic as, by all accounts, he was not nearly as naturally gifted as many of the other athletes. Later, after the draft and before the Colts' mini-camp, Coach Markuson told Brandon, "You're going to an organization and a line coach who really believe in you," knowing this made all the difference in the world for Burls. Confidence. Hope. Expectation. Excitement. For Brandon, all his dreams were converging into a single moment.

This was what he had waited and hoped for, the moment for which he had worked so hard for so many years. All that time in the weight room. All those two-a-days. All those times when he arrived early at practice and remained long after everyone else had left. Every drop of sweat. Every aching muscle. Every time he practiced in solitude when no one else was looking. The attention to detail, doing the "little things." Now it was all worth it. Now was the big payoff. In that brief moment, with a cell phone pressed up against his ear, his whole life's focus, as far as this world was concerned, came to a head, and everything that preceded it had played its part.... Playing tackle football at Superchurch. Meeting coach Tice at the weight room. Being kicked around as a high school sophomore. Being laughed at by SEC defensive linemen. All the hard work. The perseverance. The praying. It was all coming to fruition in that moment, the culmination of a boyhood fantasy imagined while lying on his bed staring upward into space. The realization of an overweight kid's ultimate dream was now beginning to sink in via that cell phone.

After receiving the news, the phones kept on ringing as newspapers, network affiliates, and radio stations were striving to get a soundbite quote from Brandon. Amid the screams, handshakes, high-fives, and hugs that filled the Burlsworth living room that day, Vickie grabbed a camera and took a snapshot, permanently capturing the moment on film. Gathering his mother and brother at his side, Brandon, glowing with pride, posed for a family portrait. In that single photograph a story was told. It was a story of a single mom who encouraged her son and of a brother who cared. But beyond that, it was also the story of a young man who never stopped believing. Nothing had sidetracked him from his passionate pursuit to be the best he could be. It was a moment to savor, and one to celebrate as well.

The poor, fatherless chubby kid who nobody believed in had walked-on to an SEC football team against all odds, lost 60 pounds in less than a semester, gained back fifty more pounds of muscle, earned a master's degree while still playing football, became known as the absolute gold-standard of work ethic and determination throughout all of college football, and ultimately became an unlikely All-American and now a high draft pick in the NFL. And he was only 22 years old.

Brandon Burlsworth had achieved pretty much everything he had set out to do up to that point in his life. Now it was time to turn to a new set of goals, both personal and professional. The sky was the limit.

Brian Stewart of the CBS Little Rock affiliate interviewing a new Indianapolis Colt on draft day.

FIFTEEN

An Impressive Start

The night of the draft was also prom night for Harrison High School, and Marty, being the city's premiere portrait photographer, had to dash off and photograph couples at the event. Meanwhile, Brandon told his mom, "Ed and I are going to celebrate," and Burls went to get pizza with his long-time friend and mentor. Riding in Ed Robinson's truck, the two talked about how exciting the NFL was going to be. Dwelling in Brandon's heart was a strong feeling of gratitude toward his hometown buddy. After all, it was Ed who had served as Brandon's first model and inspiration in both football and faith. His competitive play on the field and his humble demeanor off it had been a powerful example to Brandon, and one he had effectively followed … and surpassed. Ed was an undeniable link in the chain that connected a boy from north Arkansas to the National Football League. It wasn't hard to see, looking back, the hand of God working in Brandon's life over time, strategically placing the right people at the right time. Burls thanked God for Ed Robinson.

Returning home later in the evening, Marty and Vickie saw that Brandon was still there. The three of them sat up, talking a long time about what was going to happen next, the

NFL, and what it would be like to play and live in Indianapolis. Earlier Marty had called brother Grady to share the joy of the occasion. He and wife Jeannie were living in West Virginia at the time and though they regretted not being able to be there, the East Coast Burlsworths had filled a living room of their own with church members and friends who had come together to watch the draft and share the joy with them. Upon hearing the good news, Grady had opened an atlas and calculated the mileage between their town in West Virginia and Indianapolis. With only a five-hour drive between them, he and Jeannie would be closer now to Brandon than they had been in years. Because he had lived away from Harrison for some time, Grady had missed out on seeing Brandon and the family as much as he wished he could have. He had managed to make it to as many Razorback games as he could, including that rainy-day loss to Tennessee in Knoxville. Jeannie and a friend had also attended, but headed for the car when the rain got too much for them. Sitting in the stadium parking lot, they listened helplessly to the end of the game on the radio.

But Brandon had a special connection to Grady and Jeannie because of their Christian ministry. Brandon had asked Grady to coach him in the area of public speaking as he anticipated being asked to speak at churches, youth events, and civic organizations. His newly acquired status as an NFL football player would allow him as never before to use his platform to influence kids for Christ. On that draft day, after receiving congratulations from Grady, Brandon spoke to Jeannie, who told him how very proud she was of him. The conversation didn't last long, but it lasted long enough for Brandon to let Jeannie know that more than anything, now that he was an NFL football player, he had a new goal. "I'm looking forward to being a role model for kids," he said plainly.

Though they had yet to fully realize it, the Indianapolis Colts had just used their draft choice to select a first-class person. Brandon's first thought after being selected by an NFL team wasn't his recompense in finances but rather his potential role model in faith. Talking about being a good example was more preferable than talking about economic issues. Playing pro ball would mean a platform for Brandon from which he could expand his influence to thousands of kids across America.

Perhaps the Colts' horseshoe trademark really did symbolize good luck.

If there was one thought dancing around in Brandon Burlsworth's mind in the days following the NFL draft, it was just how fortunate he was. Considering his less than impressive beginnings, his soon-to-come orientation into professional football was preceded by a deep sense of personal gratitude to God for all He had done for him. From merely an external perspective, Brandon's rise to greatness in football was all his own doing. After all, it was his hard work in the weight room and on the practice field and running track that produced his strength and skill at his position. Those bone-jarring confrontations which took place each week on the line of scrimmage weren't made by some unseen angel on special assignment from heaven. His all-SEC academic status or his master's degree certainly wasn't handed to him during a church service. Brandon had earned those things.

It could be argued that being taken in the NFL draft was somewhat of a "no-brainer," given all that Brandon had accomplished. It may even be concluded that hard work and bulldogged determination got Burls where he was at this point in his life. But that's where a healthy dose of humility comes in handy. Brandon would be the first to admit that without the aforementioned things, he wouldn't have been planning an upcoming trip to the Colts' mini-camp. But looking a little deeper, you would discover that Brandon wasn't patting himself on the back, singing "How Great Thou Art" to his reflection in the bathroom mirror. The reason for Brandon's grateful heart was that he was smart enough to know that every good and perfect gift in life comes from God. Burlsworth firmly believed that his body, athletic abilities, desires, health, and even the very breath in his lungs were all gifts from God. It was God, he reasoned, who had given him everything he had. So, being the logical thinker he was, it only made sense for God to get the ultimate credit for the fact that he would soon board a plane to Indianapolis.

It's estimated that only the top one percent of college football athletes ever make it to the professional level. That being the case, it serves as a commentary regarding the caliber of play at that level. Only the fittest of competitors play here. Of all professional sports, football produces, perhaps, the best physical specimens. There aren't a whole lot of high school "walk-ons" at this level. Not many coasting in on past glory. These are professional athletes. Their job is to be in the best possible physical shape, knowing that their competition is striving for the same goal. A fraction of a second's difference in foot speed or a minor weakness in strength often determines a touchdown, a playoff, a championship, or a Super Bowl. Much is expected of these athletes as the degree of required competence reaches its highest peak. That's why you'll see pro players up at 7:30 in the off-season working out and lifting weights, seeking that ever-so-slim edge needed to gain the advantage and outplay their opponent. They concentrate on different muscle groups for each position, increasing size and strength in muscles most of us don't know exist. These men are thoroughbreds, and their team's front office is betting on them to perform and to win. At stake are tens of millions of invested dollars. Some argue that professional athletes are way overpaid and that today's salaries are out of control. Owners justify their multimillion contract expenditures, citing that a particular player will more than pay for himself through the draw he provides at the ticket counter as well as through licensed merchandising. The debate will continue, but one thing is for sure — though these athletes may become black and blue from playing on the field, they will never earn blue-collar wages.

Further escalating the argument are the lifestyles of some pro athletes. When a 22-year-old is suddenly handed a few million in cash, it tends to disorient his senses. Immediately, the world is at your fingertips. You can have virtually anything you desire. Sports cars. Dream homes. Fishing boats. Jewelry. Recording studios. Designer clothes. Electronic equipment. Country club memberships. A playboy's lifestyle. And if you have a family, this includes what you can now buy for your wife and kids. But with this new world of unfamiliar wealth comes a new set of unique challenges and near-irresistible temptations. Long lost acquaintances and relatives emerge from the shadows, creating parasitical friendships. Charities and non-profit organizations begin soliciting for tax-deductible donations. Uncle Sam eagerly awaits his portion of your income. Sports agents and attorneys get a slice of the pie as well. Money managers and financial consultants also make up part of the people on your new payroll. Strange as it may seem, some athletes' fortunes can be gradually eaten away like meat on a chicken leg in just a few short years. On the other hand, a player can mistakenly fool himself into imagining his income will always remain at this level. As a result, he foolishly mismanages and squanders his earnings in a very short time. Then, when he's released by the team because of an injury or poor performance, he finds himself pawning personal memorabilia from his brief career just to get by financially. Thankfully though, many pro players do remember where they came from, understanding and appreciating the value of a dollar.

Unfortunately, it only takes a few athletes who, through their undisciplined lifestyles off the field, give professional sports a black eye. Violence, drug abuse, criminal records, loose living, and lips that lash out in the media are all public relations nightmares for those teams wishing to project an endearing image to the community. Indeed, fortune and fame can be heady wine, intoxicating and addictive. These twin narcotics can exact a costly toll from a person, dulling the senses and eventually distorting reality altogether. But that is precisely what made Colts owner Jim Irsay and Head Coach Jim Mora so enthusiastic about having landed a catch like Brandon Burlsworth. What was apparent from their scouting report became evident at mini-camp — Burlsworth was the complete package, on and off the field. He was not only a total player but also a terrific person. Through their draft pick, they felt confident that with Brandon, there were no moral or public relation concerns anywhere in the immediate or distant future. No drunken brawls. No DWI's. No arrests. No broken curfews. No clandestine payoffs. No pregnant girlfriends. No scandals. Just those gaudy glasses … and an all-American guy.

With Burlsworth, the Colts organization was getting a throwback player of sorts, a one-of-a kind guy reminiscent of a time when photographs were in black and white and character was lived out in color. Apart from his glasses, Brandon would have looked just as natural 40 years earlier in a leather helmet. With Brandon, the Colts didn't get a guy who had a propensity for trouble. They got a guy who had a burning passion for football, a passion still smoldering from Saturday afternoon sandlot games. They just signed a man who possessed a simplicity of character we long for in our role models.

Fortunately, he was a part of a football club whose leadership was committed both to the play on the field and to the people who played there. It was apparent that owner Jim Irsay desired more than just numbers in the win column for his team. He was striving to help create a family atmosphere as well among the players. In many ways it was a young organization, with Irsay being the second-youngest owner in the league. In only his third year of ownership, he had spearheaded a rebuilt Colts football team. From their sudden move to Indianapolis from Baltimore in 1984, the Irsay family had sought to bring back the Colts' confidence that characterized past years of the team's history. Expanding the team's headquarters and building a multi-million training complex and state-of-the-art facilities, the Colts positioned themselves to once again become respected NFL contenders. After a dismal 3-13 finish in the 1998 season, the team reversed direction and went 13-3 the following year. This ten-game turnaround was the best by any team in the NFL's 80 seasons.

Clearly, with the previous year's addition of superstar Peyton Manning and a roster which included some of the leagues' premier players, the future of the Indianapolis Colts could not have looked any brighter. And for one young man from a small town in Northwest Arkansas, that bright future became his focal point. As far as it concerned him, he was set on making Colts history rather than just remembering it.

Colts' president Bill Polian had his eye on Brandon beginning the summer before his senior year. Again, the same things that were catching others' attention were causing Polian to raise an interested eyebrow in Brandon's direction. As a result, he put Burlsworth in his "guys to watch" file. As Brandon gained more notoriety as the Hogs' season went on, there was no question in Polian's mind as to whether to take him in the draft. In a retrospective glance, it would appear as though there was simply a cause-effect relationship between having taken running back Edgerrin James in the first round and Brandon later. It makes good sense that if you're going to spend your only first round pick on a running back that you would follow it up by drafting someone to block for him, protecting your investment. But for Polian and the Colts, there was much more to their thinking than that. In the words of the Colts' president, Brandon was "our kind of player, with his work ethic, character, professionality, and accent on preparation." It was Bill Polian who had the duty and delight to be the first to call Brandon the previous Saturday, congratulating him on his new status as an Indianapolis Colt. Mini-camp would begin four days later on the following Thursday.

Head Coach Jim Mora was also impressed with Brandon months before he put on a Colts helmet. Along with his position coaches and scouts, Mora had watched a lot of game film regarding Brandon. They immediately saw he was the real deal. For offensive line coach Howard Mudd, Brandon was the first guy he looked at selecting in the draft. In fact, so impressed was he with Burls' scouting report that he compared every other potential draftee to him. After the draft on Saturday, Mudd would meet his new player soon, as Brandon was to report to Indianapolis the following Thursday, April 21st for the Colts' mini-camp. Mini-camp, which includes both rookies and returning players, serves several purposes. For the rookies, it's their orientation to the team, giving them an initial taste of the NFL. It's the first time to practice as a team, as well as a chance for players to learn the system and add new plays. It also allows coaches to evaluate individual players and the team as a whole.

One of the first things the rookie Colts did at mini-camp was to report to head trainer Hunter Smith and answer questions on a comprehensive medical history form. Smith is the chief coordinator for the entire health care system for the team. His job includes preventing, treating, and rehabilitating players' injuries, taking care of illnesses, broken bones, sprained ankles, diseases, etc. Brandon compliantly responded to every question with a "yes sir" or "no sir."

Smith was a close friend with Dean Weber, who serves as head trainer at Arkansas. Because of this friendship, he already had plenty of background information on Brandon. And Smith explicitly trusted Weber's judgment. He was aware of his walk-on status, his work ethic, and "do whatever it takes" attitude. But in spite of his all-out commitment to prepare, practice, and play hard, Brandon had managed to avoid any serious or potential career-threatening injuries. Smith also knew from Weber that Brandon lived a "squeaky clean" lifestyle, taking care of his body outside of football. That meant no drugs, alcohol, or illegal training supplements. The only thing physically defective about Burlsworth was his eyesight, being both near-sighted and far-sighted at the same time. That afternoon, following the physical exam, Smith approached Brandon concerning his glasses.

"Brandon, I would prefer that you wear contacts if at all possible. On the offensive line, your glasses are likely to get smudged, dirty, have a finger poked through them, or even broken."

Smith was doing his best to persuade Brandon to shelve his old spectacles and convince him of the advantages of wearing contacts. But though the head trainer had learned much about the former Razorback, he was yet to be educated in the elementary ways of "Burls 101." Lesson number one: Once Brandon finds a successful and comfortable routine, you had better just go ahead and give up rather than try and change his established pattern. School was in session as Burls responded with a kind confidence. "Well, sir, I appreciate you offering that. But I can just wipe the sweat off my glasses if I need to. And if they break, I can use a spare pair."

"Well, okay," Smith consented. "But my job is to offer you the best things possible to help you play well. If you want to wear the glasses, that's fine, but let's just make sure they're Plexiglas." Hunter then thought to himself, *Well, Eric Dickerson played with Plexiglas goggles and they didn't prevent him from becoming an all-pro, Hall of Fame running back.*

This orientation process was followed the next morning by a complete physical exam by the Colts' team doctors. Lasting some four hours, this exam was thorough, time consuming, and tiring. Once again, Brandon was poked, prodded, and physically scrutinized in an effort on the Colts' part to accurately evaluate their new draft pick. This was a laborious process, especially considering the athletes had come to the complex at 6:30 a.m. to have their official Colts "mug shot."

When Brandon arrived that morning, he put on his new team jersey and his trademark glasses. Then he was led to have his photograph taken in a room not much larger than Brandon himself. As he sat down, it became apparent there was some problem with the glare of the lights reflecting off Brandon's glasses. While the team photographer attempted to reposition his camera angle and readjust the lighting, Brandon simply took his glasses off, popped the lenses out of the thick, black frames and replaced the glasses on his face, smiling for the camera. No reflection problem now, and after a few flashes he popped the lenses back in and proceeded to his next assignment.

Since players wear no pads while at mini-camp, they are partially graded on their overall athletic ability. Though he couldn't actually hit anyone without pads, Coach Mudd could see Brandon was put together well and he made a strong first impression with his eager and enthusiastic approach. Mudd noticed how Burlsworth distinguished himself from the other linemen with his style of play, always looking for something else to do rather than waiting for Mudd to tell him the next thing.

Free agent and returning offensive guard Waverly Jackson played beside Brandon at the mini-camp and was struck by Burlsworth's lack of cockiness, a trait sometimes exhibited by high-round draft picks. Coach Mudd never had to repeat himself to Brandon as he worked hard on each assigned task. There was a sense of brotherhood which had been developed among the Colts offensive lineman and Jackson looked forward to having Brandon as one of those brothers.

Offensive tackle Adam Meadows knew there were a few missing pieces in the Colts offensive line and after only a few days felt like Brandon would more than fill in those gaps. One of the things that impressed Meadows about Brandon was that, untypical of young rookies going up against veteran linemen, he didn't hold anything back. Burls wasn't intimidated or even really concerned about who was lining up against him. There was a leadership quality Adam saw in Brandon. Of course, in Brandon's mind he was doing what he had always done, leading by example. He was speaking with his life, while others only do so with their lips. Meadows recognized this maturity as a sign of needed stability in a league where many fail to handle the tensions and perks of being a professional athlete. With all the people who suddenly want to know you, it is easy to forget who you really are. Fortunately for Burls, he had never been one to think more highly of himself than he ought. His identity was grounded in God and in what He could do through him. Having such a solid life foundation was something with which Meadows could identify. Being a Christian in the NFL is not the easiest thing in the world, considering the lure and lusts that accompany a six- or seven-figure income. Nevertheless, professional football has an ample share of men who hold their faith in Christ above their career in football. Meadows was excited because there was a growing spiritual presence among the Colts players. They had been experiencing a strong move of God on the team, with players' lives being reborn and transformed, including Meadows himself. From what he knew of Burlsworth's character, it encouraged him to think that this move of God would continue to grow with Brandon now on board.

In addition to his faith, there was something else that impressed Meadows about the Colts' new rookie. Adam made a mental note that though Burls was reserved, he exuded an unusual confidence. He observed that his humble spirit harmonized well with his fierce work ethic. "You could tell there was something different about him," Meadows said. The 6'5", 295-pound lineman developed an immediate respect for Burlsworth before even knowing him very well.

Respect is a quality players need for one another, especially offensive linemen. In many ways, these guys are different from the other members of the team. It is perhaps the most unselfish position to play. In order to function well they have to function together as one unit. Selflessness is a requirement in this "team within a team." No lineman can work independently of the others or as an island unto himself. They have to blend in, forming one cohesive unit. Another difference is that, unlike their other offensive teammates, they don't get to play with the football. After the snap, they never see the ball or even look at it, except in the event of a fumble recovery, though they must have a perception and understanding of where the ball is at all times. Only perhaps a handful of the 70,000-plus paying customers are watching them during the game. Their eyes are following the ball. The vast majority of fans usually cannot even name an offensive lineman. The only time an offensive lineman is noticed is when he makes a mistake, such as an off-sides penalty. Then everyone notices, and many boo in response. It only takes one holding penalty or quarterback sack to erase 40 previous perfect blocks in the minds of fans and armchair quarterbacks.

These guys are the original blue-collar boys of the NFL. The incredible hulks of football. Administering bone-crushing blocks, play after play, they exert upwards of 1,000 pounds of pressure on their tree-trunk legs. The line of scrimmage is an intersection witnessing hundreds of head-on collisions over the course of a season. And in the pile-up, it becomes a literal survival of the fittest. Grabbing and gouging. Pushing and pounding. Blocking and bloodletting. It's gladiatorial gridlock on every play. With every snap of the football, somebody is gonna feel the hurt. To survive in the position and make a career out of it, a man has to have a certain instinct and inner drive. The will to win must be strong, and Coach Mudd immediately noticed in mini-camp that Burls had all of the above qualities. During that mini-camp, Mudd had special meetings with his linemen and at times tested them by giving them a large amount of information. His purpose was to reveal their true interest and retention level. As a coach, his job, as he saw it, was to take complex things and make them simple. If a player responded properly to Mudd, he would then be able to internalize the teaching, making it second nature, and thus "slow the game down for them."

Burls was soaking all this information in like a sponge, taking copious notes. Another aspect of Brandon's eagerness showed up as he approached Mudd before leaving camp, requesting the team's playbook. As one might imagine, there are many plays to learn as part of an NFL offense, with lots of added techniques to learn at the offensive line position. Asking for the playbook was not an unusual request, as players often obtained it to impress a coach. But Brandon wanted it so he could be prepared when he returned for training camp in the summer.

But mini-camp is not all work and no eat, which was good news to Brandon. The Colts have their own cafeteria facilities equipped with cooks and a full-time, professional dietician. This ensures that while at mini-camp, players eat the proper foods. So when lunchtime came, Brandon went through the chow line and grabbed a food-filled tray. Heading to a room, he found an open table and sat there by himself. Walking by that room at about the same time was Craig Kelley, who is head of the Colts' public relations department. Kelley normally ate his lunch in his office, but on his way that day he happened to glance through the window on the door and spotted Burls sitting alone. Hesitating, Kelley decided to change his lunchtime routine and go sit with the rookie from Arkansas. Looking up from eating his first meal as a Colt, Brandon noticed Craig, who introduced himself. Burls' eyes widened upon learning Kelley had gone to LSU, another SEC school. They made light conversation about their respective schools and home states. It wasn't a long dialogue, just long enough to last through a lunch. But Kelley could tell the time spent together really meant something to the former Razorback. Being so far away from family and familiarity, Craig Kelley represented to Brandon a faint link to his life back home. He was one of the first acquaintances he had made in the city that would become his new residence. Though only a brief encounter, that random meeting helped to begin building a bridge from Harrison to Indianapolis. Both Burlsworth and Kelley felt it was the start of a future friendship.

Especially taken by Brandon was Coach Howard Mudd. The offensive line instructor was drawn to the shy, but intense, Burlsworth and discerned that though he wasn't originally blessed with an abundance of raw talent, he got a lot out of himself. He played to his potential and beyond. "He's the kind of person that would play better than you coach him, and those are the kind of players you are looking for," Mudd later reflected. Dropping back to defend the quarterback, Brandon played with his "head on a swivel," constant looking from side to side, daring another man to get into the backfield. He possessed a heightened sense of alertness to play. "Brandon had the instincts and the drive necessary to get the job done. A dream to coach," said Mudd. And that's precisely why Mudd and the Colts' scouts had him ranked way up at the top of all the offensive linemen in the draft.

Of course, the media was present at mini-camp, interviewing both new and returning players. When it came time to interview Brandon, they all specially requested that he wear his glasses. Though he normally just wore them to play, Burls smiled and agreed. Many of the early rounds of questions were about the glasses. This provided them with a needed angle and story. Apart from his outstanding play, the glasses were what distinguished him from other players, giving him "character." Some professional athletes wear special shoes, colored headbands, bandanas, or hairstyles. Brandon didn't really have that much hair, having buzzed it down — another sign of his dedication to simplicity. And though he wore the big glasses for the practical purpose they served, brother Marty had recently told him, "Bran, don't let it bother you when people kid you. Next year fans all over the NFL are going to be wearing those glasses." So it didn't upset him when sports reporters asked him about his solid black specs. He was good-natured about it and laughed with the reporters in the locker room. He told them what he had told all the others. "The defensive linemen may make comments in the first quarter. But after that they pretty much shut up when I knock 'em down a few times."

Soon, however, the questions turned to his new role with the Colts. Brandon's eagerness showed through loud and clear in his response. "I'm very glad to be with this team. I know [the Colts] are an up-and-coming team, a young team with a lot of young players. And I think they are a team that will be successful in the future," he said, adding, "I'm just looking forward to going downfield and putting Edgerrin James in the end zone."

As the newest member of the Colts' offensive line, Brandon rightly recognized that it was his job to protect Peyton Manning and Edgerrin James. His was not a glory position. The glory would come when one of their teammates got in the end zone. Then he could run down the field, high-five the others, and celebrate. Until that time, however, there was business to take care of on every play, a job to do. And it was a job Brandon relished.

Even at mini-camp it was evident through his initiative that Brandon was ready to play. At the end of the three days, Coach Howard Mudd took Brandon aside and dropped a huge piece of good news. "Brandon," Mudd said.

"Yes sir."

"Brandon, you should begin preparing yourself between now and the time you come back for training camp for the eventuality that you will be running through the goalposts the first game of the season. That's a big thing, to start as a rookie, but don't be afraid of that."

"Yes sir." It was indeed a big thing. Based on his college play and mini-camp alone, the Colts were telling Brandon he was destined to be an immediate starter in his rookie year.

"Brandon. There's just one more thing," added Mudd.

"Yes sir."

"We're all adults here in this world of pro football. And my dad named me what he named me for a reason. I prefer my players to call me by my first name, Howard. You don't have to call me 'sir' anymore. Okay?"

"Yes sir."

Mudd would join Hunter Smith as a fellow freshman in learning Burls' way of doing things. In the "world according to Burlsworth," you were supposed to address men in authority as "sir." It was just as important to him as where he parked his car each day or how he arranged his room. These were life patterns to Burlsworth, habits that are hard to break. It was just part of his personality and his character to show respect in this way. Though his name may have been Mudd to others, to Brandon he would be "sir" for a long, long time.

Mini-camp was now officially over, and Brandon was heading back to Arkansas for a while before reporting back to training camp in July. At the conclusion of the final practice, players gathered around in a large group huddle for a final few words before hitting the showers. At that moment, a photographer snapped a frame of the team all together. From the angle of the shot, the picture shows the backs of nearly every player … every player but one. There, in the center spot of the photo is #66. Wearing an intensely focused and attentive expression, Brandon's is virtually the only visible face in the entire crowd of Colts.

Already, he was beginning to stand out.

Already a natural leader, Brandon (in his trademark glasses) facing his new teammates at the Colts' mini camp, April 1999.

SIXTEEN

QUALITY TIME

Returning back home to familiar territory in Arkansas, Brandon was not particularly fond of the attention he was drawing all across his home state. His growing status as a sports celebrity dictated headlines and lead articles in newspapers. Particularly around draft day there were numerous stories and pictures reporting the celebration of his new job as a professional football player. In addition, Burls graciously granted television and radio interviews, becoming a common face to Arkansas sports anchors. *Hawg's Illustrated*, a well-known Razorback sports magazine, had earlier run a picture of a little boy who had dressed up like Burlsworth on Halloween. Wearing a replica Razorback uniform and helmet, the boy even had his own version of the thick, black glasses. After the picture was published, the boy's family sent Brandon a copy of the article, which he autographed with a smile and sent back, along with a personal note and two signed football cards. Of course, with this kind of notoriety, it came as no surprise that Brandon's friends began ribbing him about how he was now about to make a lot of money playing in the National Football League.

Former teammate Russell Brown called just after Burls had returned from the Colts' mini-camp. Brandon joked with Russell, telling him how "ignorant" he was for not going out for the NFL and trying to play. Even though he had enjoyed an exceptional career at Arkansas, Brown was considered by many scouts to be too short at six feet to play as an NFL lineman. "You could have made it," Brandon chastised his buddy. "If I did, you could, too." But Brown had already begun settling into another career, entering the world of financial planning. Because he had always felt most comfortable in a small circle of friends, Brandon saw no reason not to throw some business Brown's way. He decided pretty quickly he wanted his friend to assist him when it came to managing his upcoming wealth. "I wanna do all my business with you," he told him. Brandon had trusted Russell with so much else the past several years. There was an interdependence between them on the football field, working together to become one of the most outstanding front lines the SEC had seen in many years. Brandon knew Russell. He was a friend.

Former teammate Grant Garrett also called Brandon to congratulate him following his being drafted by the Colts. For some years, Garrett had been one of the ringleaders in the practical joke department, with Brandon more than once finding himself the target. When he wasn't doing that, Grant was riding Brandon on account of his many quirks and idiosyncrasies. It was all done in good fun to rib Burls for his eccentric behavior, as the two had developed a close bond. Theirs was a back-and-forth bantering which often Brandon himself instigated, grinding his thick knuckles deep and hard into Garrett's hip, making the former Hog lineman grimace in pain and cry out for mercy. But all kidding was laid aside this time as Garrett told Brandon what he really thought, telling him, "Burls, nobody has worked harder or deserved it more than you." It was a moment of transparency for Grant, a time to let down his guard and let his friend know how much he appreciated him.

The two had begun their college football careers together under Danny Ford, the man Garrett gratefully credits with giving him the opportunity to be a Razorback. They had grunted through countless hours in the weight room together, suffered through two-a-days, enduring Coach Knight's "vision-provoking" mile runs. Together with the rest of the Arkansas offense, they had made the adjustment to a new coaching regime and blocking strategy. They had weathered back-to-back losing seasons, then re=bounded to help give the Hogs their best start in ten years. They had fought each other for leg room on the team bus and in Garrett's truck, with Grant always getting the short end of the stick. It was more than just a coincidence that their lockers in the Razorback athletic complex were close together. Symbolically, so were their lives. Though it wasn't their style to get emotional about their friendship, the emotion was nonetheless there. For Garrett, it went way beyond that. It wasn't just #77's nearly flawless performance on the football field that he respected. He admired Brandon Burlsworth the man. And now that the rest of the professional sports community was about to realize it, too, Garrett wanted Brandon to know just what a great guy he really was.

Burls felt the same way about his teammates and friends. A few months earlier, on January 1, following the Hog's tough loss to Michigan in the Citrus Bowl, Brandon was (as usual) the last one to leave the locker room. As he was making his exit, he was talking to Ron Higgins of the *Memphis Commercial Appeal*. "I wish I had another year to play for Arkansas," said Burls, picking up his duffle bag for the last time. "All I ever wanted to do was play for the Razorbacks. I love the coaching staff here." Then he added, "I love the players." Though he was clearly excited about playing in the NFL, there was almost an anticlimactic tone to the transition between college ball and the pros. It wasn't due to there being less of a challenge. In fact, it would be just the opposite, as the level and caliber of professional play would call upon Brandon to prepare himself for head-on collisions with some of the meanest, strongest, and most experienced athletic defensive players on the planet. The NFL would have him calling on all his talent and skills to compete. These were not 19-year-old college students, but rather seasoned professionals who routinely ate rookie linemen for afternoon snacks. That wasn't the anticlimactic part for Brandon. What caused him to be so reflective in that empty locker room on New Year's Day was that, perhaps more than any other time, he realized how much he had loved being an Arkansas Razorback.

The wonder of it all sank in as he contemplated his playing days at Fayetteville. He had developed great respect for his coaches for reasons other than their ability to produce winners on the field. He had followed them with unspoken allegiance, accepting their every word as law, embracing their approval as his motivation. In the solitude of that moment, Brandon grasped the enormity of the honor which had been his to wear a Razorback jersey, to have represented the university, his family, and his faith before hundreds of thousands of people each week during football season. It occurred to Brandon that that day had been the last time he would ever shout, "How bad do you want it?" to a huddle full of Hogs. No doubt about it. Brandon knew what Grant Garrett was trying to say with his congratulatory remarks. He loved and admired his Razorback teammates just as much as they did him.

Over in Harrison, no one could have been more proud of Burlsworth than was Grant Williams, his former high school business teacher. More than a friend, Williams was also a huge fan. And so was his son, Austin, with whom Brandon used to play chase around the desks in Williams' classroom after school. Now it was Austin who was chasing Brandon ...in newspapers, magazines, and television. At his teacher's urging, Brandon had joined FBLA (Future Business Leaders of America) his senior year in high school. As Williams was the adviser of the local chapter of the organization, he had previously asked the future NFL star to consider making an appearance and short speech to an audience of FBLA delegates at the State Leadership Conference held in Little Rock that April.

Brandon had agreed to wear the "motivational guest speaker hat," though he was bashful about speaking to a large audience. Williams told him not to worry, that he would help him prepare his speech. "Just talk about what you do, how you had your goals and worked hard to accomplish them. Tell them that dreams can come true." Unfortunately, the dates of the conference fell at a time between the combine and the draft, and Brandon was unable to make it, though he gave Grant his word he would do it for him in the future. Williams had no doubt Brandon would make good on that promise. He had always tried to motivate his students to think beyond the present and plan for the future, encouraging them to set goals, understand the meaning of opportunity, have determination, and believe in themselves and their faith. "It's okay to be different than the rest," he told his students. "You can overcome all the odds through being a Christian. By never giving up, living a simple life, learning the importance of habits, being humble, showing respect for your parents, showing respect for God, and never being afraid of trying the unthinkable, there is almost nothing you can't do." Though a high school teacher's words can often fall on deaf ears, with more students yawning and staring at the clock than listening, apparently somebody had listened. And sometimes it only takes one, letting you know you've made an actual difference in a life.

Brandon was looking forward to making a difference in others' lives as well. Part of the benefit package which comes with being a professional athlete is a platform of influence from which to speak. It's like having automatic accessibility into tens of thousands of people's lives by mere virtue of the fact that you get paid to play sports for a living. However, the type of influence an athlete makes is his own decision. Agents, publicists, front offices, and even friends may have an opinion in the matter, but when it boils down to the bottom line, it is a personal decision. He can use his professional podium to teach many different values, some by design and some by accident, depending on the athlete and the circumstances.

But another difference a pro athlete can make is through the new influx of cash coming his way. Knowing that Uncle Sam expects a generous cut of the profits, many pro players make large tax-deductible contributions to charitable organizations or even set up their own foundations. This not only keeps the government's hands off the money, but also enables the player to use his money to aid good causes. Brandon was aware of the fact that within a matter of weeks he would be getting a hefty signing bonus from the Colts. Almost certainly ranging somewhere between a half to three-quarters of a million dollars, this would be a lot of money for a guy who used to squirrel away $18 per-diem checks in the glove compartment of his car. Because the amount of his contract was as of yet undetermined, Brandon and Marty spoke with a number of sports agents in an attempt to find the one they felt would best represent his interests. After interviewing several, both brothers concluded none of them really offered the level of attention and care to Brandon's future they desired. In the end it was decided that Marty would represent Brandon at the contract negotiating table. That was just fine with Brandon, who had always allowed his big brother to take care of things "off the field" anyway. He had stayed busy during his post-draft days serving as Brandon's unofficial "official" spokesman and public relations director, sending faxes and website addresses containing information about Brandon to brother Grady in West Virginia. Signing an NFL contract was something Brandon began working on with Marty, but it wasn't an urgent matter since he had already been drafted. It's not as if he was a free agent and still promoting his talents with a team. He was "in." Besides, the more the Colts saw of him and his excellent play, the more they would be highly motivated to offer top dollar to the All-American standout.

Of course, there was no avoiding the subject with Burls' close friends. Only they had the freedom to kid him about what a rich man he was about to be. Mike Bender, Brandon's former line coach with the Hogs, jokingly told him, "Brandon, now that you're a pro, I expect you to take *me* out to Ryan's Steak House." For Burlsworth, he wasn't enamored with all the hoopla of hundreds of thousands of dollars. He planned on living fairly frugally anyway, probably buying a house for himself and his mom in Harrison and renting a big enough apartment in Indianapolis where the family could stay when they came up for games. For certain, he planned to purchase a new truck, and at last would have a vehicle he could fit into instead of shoehorning himself into his '93 white Subaru. When asked about his excitement regarding making big money in the NFL, Burls told a friend, "I'm just really ready to go play."

In reality, others were far more concerned about the NFL and making money than he was. Given his personality and past track record, Burlsworth was not likely to blow his money on material possessions. For him, the draft was never about the money, but about being the best at your position. That was just one more thing about Burls which made him appear "too good to be true" to some folks.

Though he was now a member of a professional football team, Brandon refused to sit back and soak in the satisfaction. There were now new goals to set. "I wanna make the all-Rookie team, and maybe even be the Rookie of the Year," he told brother Marty. Knowing they didn't merely draw names out of a hat or hand out the honors to the first in line, Brandon began preparing himself even harder for life and competition in the NFL. He knew all too well that weights don't lift themselves and muscles don't automatically get stronger unless there is someone there to make it happen. Consequently, that meant he would have to work for it. And work hard.

Because of his familiarity with the Razorback weight room, Brandon decided to split his time between Harrison and Fayetteville, spending a few days each week working out. Since college rookies were not allowed to return to their respective

NFL teams until the spring semester was officially over, Burls figured this would be a perfect time to concentrate on maintaining his weight room regimen. While in Fayetteville, he again stayed at Jeremiah Washburn and Joe Dean Davenport's apartment, sleeping on a foldout couch. Though both men knew better than to touch Brandon's stuff, they, of course, did it anyway. Being very particular about neatness, Brandon did not take kindly to people messing with his things.

During his final season with the Hogs, in the locker room after a game, Brandon was packing up his things in a travel bag. Because he was the last to leave the locker room and board the bus, a new team assistant grabbed up the rest of Burls' pads that night, hurriedly stuffing them into the bag. Brandon sat, staring at him in disbelief as if to say "I cannot believe what you just did." Burls promptly turned the bag upside down, dumping its entire contents out onto the locker room floor. Then systematically repacking the entire bag, he meticulously folded each article of clothing, taking his sweet time as a subtle way of communicating his displeasure.

Having lived with him before, Washburn and Davenport were all-too-familiar with Brandon's predisposition to compulsiveness. With that knowledge as his weapon, combined with a history of hoaxes and pranks in his repertoire, Joe Dean took Burls' prized 1995 NFL calendar, turning it backwards. Brandon came home and threw a fit at Davenport, who naturally proceeded to blame the whole incident on Washburn.

In spite of annoying moments such as this, in between workouts Brandon loved nothing more than to hang out with his former football buddies, some of whom were entertaining their own NFL offers. The guys spent part of their free time going out to eat, usually somewhere with a buffet of course, like CiCi's Pizza, where Burls consumed his standard three-plate minimum. Or it was Ryan's Steak House where Brandon sprinkled bacon bits on his food, which prompted an immediate ribbing from Jeremiah and the rest of the crew.

When they weren't eating, they simply hung out at different guys' apartments watching television. The channel of choice was typically ESPN. However, during baseball season Brandon always watched the Cardinals, knowing virtually everything about them. A month earlier they had all been glued to the NCAA basketball tournament, with the guys excitedly filling in their own brackets ahead of time in an effort to predict the 1999 National Champions. That first-round betting pool lasted only as long as the first few games. But the Connecticut Huskies lasted all the way through the tournament, dethroning the defending champions from Duke University. For a while Burls and his buddies grew fond of watching "professional" wrestling, with each man pulling for his favorite WWF warrior.

For Brandon, it wasn't so much what the guys did together that was important. The main thing to him was that they were just hanging out together. He loved spending what he referred to as "quality time" with his best friends, often telling them, "Hey, we need some 'QT.' "

Because Joe Dean's family owned a farm in nearby Tontitown, just north of Fayetteville, he spent much of his time taking care of the family's livestock investment. It's not hard to imagine the 6'7", 270-pound Davenport tossing around bales of hay on a farm. An all-around athlete, Joe Dean had also seen playing time on the Razorback basketball team. His size and agility made him an asset to Coach Nolan Richardson. But off the court and back on the field, Joe Dean had caught 18 passes for Houston Nutt's team that year. Because of the tight end's enormous frame, the football resembled a miniature toy as he cradled it in his huge hands. Jeremiah Washburn however, had other things on his mind, and they had nothing to do with farms or football. His energy instead was focused on his fiancée, Susan, whom he was to marry in June. With the wedding just two months away, "Wash" was enjoying his final weeks of bachelorhood. As a freshman, Jeremiah had mistaken

Brandon's quiet, reserved nature as being "stuck up." But the more he got to know the big boy from Harrison, he learned just the opposite was true. Though Brandon had many faults, being proud and stuck up were nowhere on the list.

In their apartment, the guys had mounted a dry erase board on the refrigerator, which they used to take down phone messages for each other or to post reminder notes. It was a good thing there was something on the outside of the fridge because, like typical college guys, there was rarely anything on the inside. That refrigerator message board became a playing field of its own as the three launched verbal barbs back and forth at each other. Due to Burls' propensity to retaliate for all the kidding he endured at their hands, he sometimes chose more passive methods to exact revenge against Joe Dean and Jeremiah.

One particular rainy evening Davenport returned home around 10:00 p.m., wet and worn out from a long day working at the farm. Heading straight to the fridge, he discovered a message left for him on the dry erase board. It was a crude, primitive drawing depicting a little tractor driving across a field in the dark and in the rain. The caption above the artwork read, "Joe Dean Davenport, the only farmer that cuts hay in the rain at night." Burls' editorial cartoon was meant to suggest Joe Dean was in reality out doing something else on that rainy night. After several minutes, Davenport gave up trying to explain himself to Brandon, who blamed the cartoon on Washburn. Davenport's defense fell on deaf ears to Brandon, who kept saying, "Uh huh. Yeah, right. You were cutting hay in the dark. Sure you were."

Their tongue-in-cheek joking was just another thread which helped weave the strong chord of friendship between them. No one ever doubted for a minute that beneath the laughing there lay a bond greater than the one that brought them together as teammates. Theirs was a common ground, more stable and sure-footed than the stadium turf on which they had played together. Deeper than any of them realized at the time, their common love for God had grown their young lives closer together like interwoven root systems, strengthening and supporting one another. Whether shy or gregarious, tall or short, obsessive or obnoxious, walk-on or scholarship, it really didn't matter with these guys. They were more than fellow players on the football field. They had become teammates in life. They were brothers.

After his return from mini-camp, Brandon was walking across the parking lot of the Broyles complex when freshman Josh Melton spotted him. Driving up to Burlsworth, Melton rolled down his car window.

"Burls, guess what? Guess what? I've got your old locker! Number 247." Josh had been in awe of Burlsworth since first stepping on campus, the senior lineman's work ethic having already achieved legendary status. From that time on, he had tried to pattern his life after the All-American football player in his conditioning and Christian character.

Though Brandon appreciated the compliment that Melton was honored to now occupy his old locker, he diverted the attention off himself, saying, "Nah. It's *your* locker now. It belongs to you," adding a postscript word of counsel to the young player, "Just take care of it."

It had been Brandon's custom to go home every weekend since he had left for college. Each time he came home he would stay just as long as he could on Sunday, sometimes getting up at 5:00 a.m. to drive back to campus for his Monday classes.

Like any college boy will do, Brandon brought his laundry home for his mom to wash. That bag contained the only kind of dirty laundry ever associated with Brandon, as he never had anything to hide about his personal life. "You can dig all you want," Tommy Tice is fond of saying, "but you'll never dig up any dirt on Burls." Because of his regular trips home each weekend, his Fayetteville friends rarely ever saw him after classes dismissed on Friday. Except during football season, he would be back in Harrison, hanging out at home. Eating his mom's cooking and sister-in-law Vickie's desserts. Talking to Marty about the future. Playing with his three nephews. Just spending his own style of "quality time" with his family. He missed out on a lot that goes on at college on the weekends — parties, outings, fraternities, etc. But in Brandon's mind, he didn't miss a thing. He was unable to comprehend why a student within driving distance of home would want to stay cramped in a tiny dorm room when he could be at home in his own bed, eating his mom's food, and seeing his family.

The whole concept of "home" to Burls wasn't something he believed a person eventually grew out of, but rather grew closer to as time went on. While some young adults mark off the days, like inmates, until they are released out from under the roof of their parents, Brandon was quite the opposite. If there were any days to count, they were the ones which led up to the time he would make that drive down rural Highway 412 every Friday. Some may have thought him a "home boy," and to some degree they were right. But no matter. After all, "It doesn't matter what others think. It only matters what I think." Had he only listened to what others thought of him, he would never have walked on at Arkansas and become one of America's outstanding college football players.

But his weekend trips home to Harrison were not the only time Burls saw his mom. He also met his mother every Tuesday night in a tiny roadside town called Marble. There's not much there in Marble, but there is a little country store and they chose it as their meeting place. There Brandon would receive his duffle bag full of cleaned and folded laundry and linens from his mom. Barbara usually got there first, as the tiny crossroads community was a little closer to Harrison than it was to Fayetteville. This Tuesday night custom began when Brandon started calling his mom after the weekend at home, saying "Uh, Mom. I left something at home, would you bring it to me?" They agreed the most equitable thing was to pick a halfway point between them, and thus Marble was the chosen location for the ritual rendezvous.

At that country store, Brandon bought a Diet Coke and a Three Musketeers bar each and every time. Then the two sat outside on a wooden bench, even in cold weather, and spent a few minutes just talking. "Mom, do you think I'm fat?" he would ask.

"No, honey, you're just fine," was Barbara's standard reply.

Sometimes they sat in silence except for the sound of crickets chirping or the occasional Doppler effect of a car passing by. Because of the depth of love between them, not a whole lot needed to be said for the mother and son to communicate. Barbara knew exactly what her big boy was thinking because she was having the same thought. For them, it was a few moments of rare satisfaction in life when it sinks in that "all is well"... just sitting on a bench with your mom, who also happens to be your friend, and eating your favorite candy bar. What could be better? Beside you is the woman who raised you, put you up, and put up with you. She's the same person who tied your shoes when you couldn't lace them yourself and took you to football practice in junior high when you couldn't drive. She's the one who threw a 16th birthday party for you at Pizza Hut, inviting only your immediate family and your best friend Ed, 'cause that's what you really wanted. She was the person you cited as being the best influence on your life because, you said, "She is always willing to help." The same woman who had once changed your diapers still cared enough to drive down a country road to bring you your clean laundry. And though he had severely tested her nerves in the early years, looking at her son on a Tuesday night that spring, Barbara knew she wouldn't change a single thing about her boy. Adding to her contentment was the knowledge that her 22-year-old genuinely appreciated her, and demonstrated it by the way he honored her. For Barbara and Brandon, it was their own personal "quality time."

No mom could ever want more.

Brandon shared more than just his mother's initials and last name. The two shared a common spirit, combining character and compassion. Brandon loved his mom, and he was not afraid for his macho teammates to know it either. And they all did know it. They loved hanging out with the Burlsworth family while in those road game hotels. He was not embarrassed to have his mom do his laundry, either, or to drive 35 miles to pick it up on Tuesday nights. And he was not ashamed to sit with her on a wooden bench at a country store in Marble, Arkansas. Theirs was a love as solid as the namesake of the community where they sat.

Finishing his Coke and candy bar, Brandon picked up his duffle bag and threw it into his car, giving his mom a hug and telling her he loved her. Then they got into their cars and began the drive back in opposite directions. But their final Tuesday night ritual occurred just before they vanished out of sight in their respective rearview mirrors. Glancing up at the mirror they would each tap on their brakes as a means of saying goodbye, a last way for them to simply say,

"Love you, Bran"….

"Love you, Mom."

Talking to the press after a win over Kentucky,
October 3, 1998.

SEVENTEEN

"It's Over"

On Wednesday, April 28, Coach Houston Nutt saw Brandon at the athletic facility and invited him to join the rest of the team that afternoon, as they were to receive their SEC Western Division Championship rings. Burls was on his way to meet Brent Bender, his former line coach's son, for lunch. "Coach, I really appreciate that," he said. "But I have a previous commitment to go to church tonight with my mom. You let the other guys enjoy that."

It was the only time Nutt ever saw Brandon not be totally dedicated to the team, but Burls had a commitment more important than football, and that was something Nutt completely understood. Meeting Bender for lunch was a treat for Brandon, as the two had become friends through his relationship with the coach. In fact, Brandon was close to the entire Bender family, having shared a number of meals at their house. Brent and Brandon also shared a similar penchant for retaining trivia. Both young men were described by their families as "walking dictionaries." But this lunch wasn't a time to exchange insignificant information about sports or history. Brent knew this was his last chance to hang out with Brandon for a while and wanted to treat him to lunch. The two talked about making plans for Bender to come to Indianapolis to see Burlsworth play. With overtones of gratitude to God, Brandon told Bender, "I can't believe how fortunate I am that things have worked out for me like they have."

After their meal, Bender dropped Brandon off at the apartment. As he was getting out of the car Brent remarked, "Brandon, you're about to be a very rich man. Famous."

Pausing, Burls turned and responded, shaking his head, "No, Brent. I'm just Brandon Burlsworth from Cherry Street in Harrison, Arkansas. I just wanna go back there one day and live on Cherry Street."

Arriving back inside the apartment to pack up his things before returning home, Brandon sat and spent a few final moments of "QT" with Chris Chalmers and Jeremiah. They talked to him about the Colts, the NFL, and mini-camp, but Burls really didn't want to talk about it that much. He just wanted to talk normal stuff, just like they always did. They watched some TV together with the guys all the while kidding Burls about being rich. About 3:30, Brandon decided it was time to go and he finished packing his bag. Chris walked him out to the car to say goodbye. Chalmers had looked up to Brandon in more ways than one. Being only 5'10" and weighing just around 180 pounds, the defensive back looked undersized compared to the 6'3" plus, 308-pound Brandon. For Chris, it was an ordinary afternoon, with nothing special about it except that his good friend was about to begin what was expected to be a long career in the National Football League. Shaking his hand, Chalmers quipped, "Well Burls, I guess the next time I see you, it'll be on TV."

He had no idea how right he was.

Even though he had completed his career as a Razorback, Brandon still made the trip from Harrison to Fayetteville about every other day to work up a sweat in the Hog's weight room. Crashing on Jeremiah's couch, he would get up the next morning and head back home. This particular Wednesday in April 1999 saw the Fayetteville campus sweating over final exams while the country was still reeling from an altogether different kind of testing. It had been just nine days earlier that two angry teenagers blazed into Columbine High School at lunchtime with semi-automatic weapons, sawed-off shotguns, and home-made pipe bombs, submerging their campus in carnage and chaos. Upon exhausting their fury, the two assassins executed the same sentence on themselves that they had pronounced on their innocent victims. Covered by every television network, the unforgettable images and soundbites flooded the airwaves, overflowing into America's homes and hearts. Stored for all time in our nation's vault of grief are the horrors of that senseless bloodbath. As that Wednesday came, we had only begun to grieve that tragic loss of life.

The Burlsworths had experienced some grief of their own the past 18 months as Leo Burlsworth had died in 1997. Not long after, Brandon had attended two more funerals. Vickie Burlsworth's mother passed away, and then shortly afterwards, Brandon's grandmother went home to be with the Lord.

At his grandmother's funeral, Marty turned to Brandon and said, "That's it. No more dying."

Brandon replied, "You're right. I'm tired of going to funerals."

But on that Wednesday there was no thought of grief as Brandon was traveling along Highway 412, going home for dinner and then to church with his mom. Meanwhile, over at the athletic complex, Razorback football players were celebrating as they received their rings for being 1998 SEC Western Division Champions.

Arriving home late because of the traffic jam on Highway 412, Tommy Tice had hardly come through the door when the phone rang. It was the principal of Harrison High calling. "Tommy, is it true about Burlsworth being killed in a wreck?"

Shocked and a little offended, Tice shot back. "No! Absolutely not. That's somebody's idea of a cruel joke." Hanging up the phone, the coach's thoughts immediately turned to Barbara Burlsworth. If this were a rumor, then she needed to be reassured. If it were somehow true, she would need a lot more than that. Ringing the Burlsworth home, Tice's worst fears were confirmed firsthand.

Vickie Burlsworth was working late in her husband's photography studio when the phone rang. Marty had already left for the day and gone to pick up their three boys to bring them home. Normally, she didn't answer the phone after business hours, and it was now ten minutes to six, but for some reason she was drawn to respond to the incoming call. The caller on the other end of the line identified herself as a state policewoman. "Are you Vickie Burlsworth?" the officer asked.

At first, Vickie suspected it was a prank call or a gag made by a friend, but the tone in the woman's voice was anything but amusing. "Yes, I'm Vickie Burlsworth," she said, somewhat confused.

The policewoman continued. "I need you to come to Barbara Burlsworth's house right away."

"Okay. Why?" Vickie wondered.

"I can't tell you why, ma'am," was the response.

It was then Vickie heard loud wailing in the background which told her the officer was calling from the Burlsworth home. At first, she thought the background voice might be Joe Don, her 12-year-old. Rapidly trying to make sense of the call and put two and two together, she speculated he had been hurt or had done something bad enough to involve the police. Racing in her car the short distance to the house, a thousand thoughts were flashing through Vickie's mind all at once. "Lord, what's happened? … What could be wrong? … Where's Marty?" Pulling up at the house, Vickie sprinted across the yard and through the front door. Once inside, she saw a scene she would never forget. There in the living room was Barbara Burlsworth, crying out, "He's dead. He's dead. My baby's dead."

With her body in shock and her mind in confusion, Vickie froze, struggling as she spoke. "Who, Barbara Ann? Who is it?" She was unsure who "he" was, thinking maybe it was one of her boys.

Barbara responded through the tears and pain as if the words themselves ripped out her soul. "It's Brannie. Brannie's dead."

One might expect there to have been a brief instant of relief upon learning her own sons were safe and sound, but the impact to Vickie was just as devastating. The tragic news blindsided the two women, weakening them both emotionally and physically. Barbara's words knocked the breath out of Vickie, causing her to fall to the floor, where she embraced her mother-in-law. In that moment of initial grief, composure fell victim to emotion, and understandably so. It's the kind of news every mother dreads. Initially it seemed too bizarre that something like this would happen to a guy who was almost too good to be true.

Amid the pain and panic in Vickie's mind she knew she had to get in touch with Marty as soon as possible before someone else called him or he heard it on the radio. After several failed attempts, she finally reached her husband on his cell phone. "Marty, something has happened. I'm at your mom's. Please come now."

Marty had earlier driven by his mom's street and glanced down toward the house as he passed by, glimpsing a brief sight of a white car parked out front. Since the family was expecting Brandon home at any time, he assumed the car was his brother's. Folding up his cell phone, Marty began rewinding his thoughts back to that white car. Since he had already picked up his boys and spoken to Vickie on the phone, he knew the only family member out of his grasp at that time was Bran. Marty remembered thinking Brandon was already later than expected in returning from Fayetteville. Pulling up in front of his mother's house he saw the white car again, this time concluding it must be an unmarked police car. When he walked in, Vickie met her husband with a somber countenance. "It's Bran, Marty."

For the eldest Burlsworth brother, news of global destruction could not have been any more devastating than those words. He flashed back, remembering his last conversation with his kid brother only hours earlier. He had spoken to him at lunchtime when Brandon called to ask if Marty would help him find a hubcap for one of his wheels. It was simply unbelievable that this could be happening. For a fleeting moment, denial set in, disallowing Marty from admitting any of this could be true. "Not Bran. Not now." Perhaps it was a mistake. Maybe he was hurt and in the hospital. Maybe there's still hope. But denial and doubt wouldn't linger long. As soon as they had come, they vanished as the dark and painful truth began to set in.

It's a terrible black night of the soul, losing a family member. The passing of someone we love affects us all in different ways, with every individual's response being as different as the people themselves. Though overwhelmed with sorrow, Marty realized that he would have to act as the family spokesman, as the task of contacting relatives and family friends would fall to him. Regaining his composure momentarily, he took a deep breath and picked up the telephone to break the news to brother Grady.

At his home in West Virginia that Wednesday evening, Grady Burlsworth was downstairs working in his office when the phone rang. Jeannie was upstairs and heard the ring, but Grady made it to the phone first. Being brothers and having grown up together, the Burlsworth boys knew each other well enough to know when something was wrong. Grady could always tell things weren't right with Marty because his elder brother would talk in short, succinct sentences. Pressing the receiver to his ear, Grady heard his brother's voice on the other end of the line.

"Hey," Marty began.

"What's going on?" Grady asked.

"Well, it's not very good," Marty continued. "Bran's been in an accident."

"Don't kid with me about that," Grady said, mildly reprimanding his older brother.

"I'm not kidding," Marty said matter-of-factly.

Grady could now tell that Marty was very serious. Grady's castigating tone quickly changed to grave concern. "How bad is he hurt?" asked Grady, probing for more information.

He was unprepared to receive what his brother said next. Two words that would change the rest of his life. Bluntly, Marty simply replied, "It's over."

Within a fraction of a second, in between the time it took for his brain to transmit the message to his heart, a tidal wave of feelings immediately began swelling up within Grady's body. Knowing he was about to surrender control of his emotions to an oncoming wave of grief, Grady managed to utter only a brief sentence. "Marty, let me call you back." And with that he hung up the receiver, disconnecting the phone call.

Feeling like he had been hit by an oncoming locomotive, Grady could feel his knees weakening beneath him. Unable to support his own weight any longer, he collapsed to the floor and the floodgates of tears opened wide. Crawling to the stairs and crying uncontrollably, he began climbing one step at a time, calling out to his wife, Jeannie. Hearing his gut-wrenching guttural cries, she ran out of the bedroom to discover her husband on the stairs, sobbing and wailing. "Brandon's dead," was all he could say. Immediately Jeannie embraced her husband, joining him on the floor. Crushed under the weight of grief, they did the only thing they could do at a time like that. They just cried.

Soon church members began showing up at the house, consoling Grady and Jeannie. Initially wanting to jump in the car and drive straight through the night to Harrison, Grady was persuaded otherwise by discerning friends. "Bad idea," they counseled. And they were right. He was in no state of mind to safely make the all-night drive. But because Jeannie's sister worked for an airline, the two of them could obtain tickets and fly out first thing in the morning, which is what they decided to do.

Back in Harrison, word had leaked out about the accident and had been reported on local radio. In a small community like Harrison, news spreads quickly whether it be good or bad. And this was bad. Really bad. Both Barbara and Marty's church families interrupted their services that Wednesday evening to pray for the Burlsworths. They then dismissed their congregations so that friends could go and lend support to the family. For the Burlsworths, there was an outpouring of comfort from those in their churches and community that clearly let them know their burden would not be carried alone. People began coming by Barbara's home, giving her hugs and offering her help. Some would sit and say nothing more than what their hand on her shoulder communicated. "We love you and we're here for you." There is really not much to say at a time like this. For that matter, not much actually needs to be said. Words are hollow at such times and cannot begin to fill the massive void the empty heart feels. Try as some might, the best comfort comes through the loving presence of a friend who cares. No words. Just being there mainly, that's all. Some who came by that night simply sat and held Barbara's hand. Some evoked memories of happier times with Brandon. All of them cried.

Coach Tice had arrived at the Burlsworth home, eyes flooded with tears. "I was there, Marty," he said, referring to the accident. "I was there and didn't even know it."

Family friends Jamie Holt and Bennett Horne began handling the increasing contacts from the media as radio and newspaper stations began inundating the family with calls. They spoke for the family at a time when they were unable to speak for themselves. They were with the Burlsworths every step of the way as the night wore on. The hour grew late and after everyone had given their last hug and said their final goodnight, there were just the three of them left — Barbara, Marty, and Vickie. It seemed like it had been a month since hearing the news earlier in the evening, so great was their sadness. Time seemed suspended in a cloud of sorrow. It was dark both outside as well as inside the Burlsworth home in Harrison that night. Though they were together as a family, someone was missing. None of us realizes how big of a space a loved one takes up until they are gone. They had always included Brandon, whether it was a trip to Branson or an evening at the movies. The past four years he had been the focal point of the family, receiving perhaps a lifetime's worth of attention during that time. Brandon became somewhat of a "glue," binding them all together. He rounded out their family, made them feel complete. But it wasn't football that made Brandon so special to his family. They knew him long before he set foot on the field or picked up a weight.

In many ways, the Burlsworths couldn't understand all the media interest and celebrity-like status everyone else seemed to attach to the young man who avoided the limelight. To them he was just their "Bran." His days as a Razorback, his All-American honor, his NFL draft and status as an Indianapolis Colt — none of it mattered in the least at the moment. They would have traded it all without a second thought just to have him back. But he wasn't coming back. This awful nightmare was a reality for the Burlsworths.

For Barbara, she had to begin the coping process of losing her baby boy. She would have to work through the inconsistency and seeming cruelty of life. Parents weren't supposed to outlive their children. It just wasn't right. Nothing was right about that night. It was a confusing blur seen through a haze of tears. For Marty, he was dealing with his own brand of grief. Bran was more than just a brother to him. He was his best friend. Watching his mom effectively raise Brandon without a father, Marty stepped in and filled the gap as much as he could. He looked out for him, forecasting his future, oftentimes pushing him in an effort to ensure he had one. Marty wore the patriarchal hat when it came to Brandon. But he was also his coach, personal trainer, agent … and biggest fan. There was a connection Marty had with his little brother, a kind of relationship that teeters precariously on the edge of extinction in today's families. Here were two brothers who loved each other, trusted each other, and cared for each other. They could read each other's thoughts. Marty and Vickie both were confidants to Brandon. But more than that, he looked up to them as role models. And role models they were for him, as adults, Christians, and parents. But all that changed in an instant as they went from being mentors to mourners.

It was close to midnight when everyone left Barbara's house. The three remaining family members were exhausted and drained from the energy expended in receiving those who had come by that evening. They were tired. Spent. Mentally, emotionally, and physically depleted. They would have to sleep just to recharge so they could survive what would prove to be very difficult days ahead. Recognizing their condition and the low state at which they found themselves, Marty knew there was only one direction to turn in a circumstance like this. Looking to Barbara and Vickie, Marty said, "We need to pray." Falling to their knees, they gathered in a tight circle, holding hands. There, in the darkened loneliness that seemed to fill the living room, Marty led them in prayer. The three of them poured out their hearts to God, confessing their utter desperation and need for Him in this critical hour.

Early the next morning, Grady and Jeannie left their home in West Virginia, flying first to St. Louis and then on to Springfield, Missouri. Once they arrived there, someone would pick them up and drive them on to Harrison. On the initial leg of that journey, Grady wore a zombie-like stare, still reeling from the shock of the tragic passing of his kid brother. Death and loss brought to him what it does to others who face similar circumstances. Feeling somewhat disoriented and disconnected, he sat on the plane to St. Louis, thinking to himself, *I don't know if I can take this*. Having been in ministry, he had counseled and comforted others, but "when it happens to you, it's a different story." He pondered the popular saying "It's better to have loved and lost than never have loved at all." *I'm not so sure that's true*, he said to himself. Losing Brandon was a heavy hit to the heart. His spirit acquiesced, resigning himself to the fact that he was totally helpless to do anything about all this.

Changing planes in St. Louis, Jeannie and Grady had time to grab a bite to eat in an airport restaurant. Sitting down, Grady took one bite, then began to weep.

"Hold on, sweetheart," Jeannie gently comforted her husband as she steadied his hand with hers. "We're gonna get through this."

Because of their status as standby passengers, the Burlsworths were forced to take their chances on obtaining seats, as all the flights out of St. Louis were booked solid. The first flight to Springfield left. No seats. Then the next one, and still there was no room. By this time Grady was growing anxious, desperately trying to keep his composure and manage the storm of emotions that swirled inside him. Finally, he could take no more and approached a lady, with tear-filled eyes all but begging her to give up her tickets so he could get to his grieving family. But it was to no avail. Overhearing his pleas in the gate area was an elderly couple who had somehow heard about the accident through the media. Without so much as a second thought, the aged couple gladly and graciously gave up their seats to Grady and Jeannie, enabling them to board the flight to Springfield.

The Burlsworths never knew who that couple was or why they made the sacrifice they did. Perhaps they had lost a son themselves years ago. Or maybe they were just kind people who reached out like Good Samaritans. To Grady and Jeannie however, they were guardian angels watching over them in the hour of their greatest need.

Brandon's boyhood best friend, Ed Robinson, picked the couple up at the airport and drove them home to Harrison. Grady thought to himself as they drove, *As bad as I feel, I know Mom has to feel ten times worse.* It had been just two months earlier that Barbara had lost her mother. Now, in just a matter of weeks, she had lost her youngest son. Arriving at the house, the emotions resurged again as Grady was reunited with his mom and brother. Seeing one another caused them to relive all over again an encore of tears and sorrow they had experienced the previous night.

Grady looked across the room and saw Marty sitting almost motionless in a chair. Unshaven and obviously suffering from lack of sleep, Grady could see the effects of losing Brandon deeply etched in his brother's face. "Marty, a lot of people are coming over soon. Go home and take a shower and then come back," Grady encouraged his brother.

By this time, word about the accident was rapidly spreading as the major network affiliates began airing reports of the tragedy. Arkansans woke up on April 29 to read the story in their newspapers. In a matter of hours since the accident, concentric circles of grief began emanating from the tiny town in the Ozarks, sending shockwaves of sorrow across an entire state. Brandon's time here had ended in a matter of seconds, and as Marty had accurately declared, it was indeed "over."

But getting over Brandon Burlsworth was entirely another matter altogether.

The trophy clock given to Brandon by his family at Christmas 1998: Brandon Burlsworth, 1997-98 All-SEC; 1998 All-American

EIGHTEEN

A State Of Shock

Danny Ford was enjoying a restful retirement in upstate South Carolina. Living on his farm in the foothills of the Smoky Mountains, Ford had fallen in love with the area while coaching at Clemson University years earlier. It had been some time since he had heard from Tommy Tice, so when the Harrison High football coach rang him up late that Wednesday evening, the first words out of Ford's mouth were, "Who died?" Upon learning of Burls' passing, Ford immediately began making arrangements to fly out to Arkansas.

Houston Nutt was at home when he got the phone call that devastated him. Nutt knew Burls and had greatly admired him for his work ethic, attitude, and heart, but mostly because of his Christian character. From the first day he met him, the coach noted that Burls was courteous and quiet, and that he was a leader by example rather than exhortation. Nutt appreciated Brandon's role as the backbone of the Hog's offensive line, the way he dominated on the field, his attention to detail, and the way he never had a false step when they were in the red zone. He even admired him for the way his locker was arranged down to the last detail. In Nutt's words, "Everybody on the team had an awesome respect for Brandon Burlsworth." Recalling his last conversation with Brandon that day, it occurred to him that the accident took place, almost to the minute, when the other Razorback players were getting their division championship rings. He thought how Brandon would rather give up glory in order to return home and go to church. "He was everything you wanted in a friend, a son, and a football player. He was the total package."

Inwardly, the coach made a vow to himself right then, silently declaring, "He will never, ever be forgotten." The following day the Arkansas coach called a special team meeting in the same room where just 24 hours earlier they had celebrated their championship season. Only now the mood in that room was markedly different. High fives were now hugs as the college athletes did their best to console one another. Nutt led the somber meeting, attempting to make some sense of the unexpected tragedy. Mainly though, he just allowed everyone to grieve and love one another, spending their time remembering their fallen teammate. Many of them referred to Brandon as "one of God's warriors." Most just called him "Burls." It was hard for the young men to associate such a bad thing happening to such a great guy. Suddenly, many of the highly conditioned, thoroughbred young athletes realized they weren't invincible. As Nutt noted, "None of us is promised tomorrow."

As the team meeting ended, Josh Melton walked over to the Razorback's equipment manager, Tim Cheney, and said straightforwardly, "Let's go get my stuff out of Burls' locker." Later Melton confessed "I knew I didn't have any place there. It was Burls' locker."

Back in Harrison, the Burlsworth family was wrestling with the unwanted task of making the arrangements for a service on Saturday. Football was past tense for the Burlsworths. Now they would have to talk about a funeral. Instead of negotiating an NFL contract, Marty was making funeral arrangements. Rather than helping Brandon choose an apartment in Indianapolis, they were picking out a burial plot for him. Planning the service, choosing a location, deciding who would speak, etc.

— it was not the way they had intended to spend the upcoming weekend, but they were being made acutely aware of the fact that death is no respecter of persons and that life was anything but "fair." Their minds were filled with unanswered questions about what had happened, and it wasn't until later that they were able to get all the details concerning the accident.

The Arkansas State Police post in Springdale received a report of the accident at 4:17 p.m. that Wednesday afternoon. Brandon was traveling eastbound on Highway 412, a two-lane highway he had driven hundreds of times. It was on a flat stretch of road near a curve that, for reasons unknown, Brandon's 1993 Subaru apparently veered left of the center line and clipped the left front fender of a semi-truck towing a flatbed trailer. The state police reported that first contact involved only four inches of Brandon's front left bumper. That initial impact sent the car back into his own lane only briefly, then the car crossed the center line again and hit a second 18-wheeler that was trailing behind the first one. The head-on collision immediately reversed the direction of the Subaru, sending it over 160 feet backwards in the opposite direction. The Carroll County coroner on the scene commented that the evidence indicated Brandon was killed instantly, noting that he was wearing a seat belt.

In a matter of only a few seconds, everything changed. All the things his future might have potentially held vanished. The NFL. Indianapolis. Fame. Money. Marriage. A family. Four inches made the difference between life and death. A cruel epitaph to a life lived in an almost obsessive pursuit of perfection. He was just a half hour from Harrison. Thirty minutes away from home, church, and family.

At first, some outsiders initially wondered if alcohol had played a part in the accident. But they apparently had not done their homework on Brandon. The absurd suggestion was immediately dismissed. However, those who did know him well were also forced to begin dealing with their loss. This process included their own brand of speculation as to what might have happened. It was incongruous for them to think that a young man so dedicated to detail would have made such a fatal mistake. Burls was not one to have any loose ends lying around. There was nothing messy about him, his room, or his car. Everything was in its place at all times, his life displaying a meticulous order. It just didn't add up that Brandon would have made such an error on a road he knew so well. But after the official investigation and with all the evidence recorded by the Arkansas State Police, it was concluded that, for reasons unknown, Brandon's car crossed over into the opposite lane and into the oncoming truck. Did he drop a cassette tape and momentarily reach down to pick it up? Had he taken his eyes off the road for a second, swerving ever so slightly to the left? Did his familiarity with the route he had driven so many times over the years lull him into a brief complacency? Did the effects of rising early in the morning and working out tire him to the point that he slowly drifted off to sleep, causing him to veer over the line?

Unfortunately, we will never know what actually happened that Wednesday afternoon. The Burlsworth family began resigning themselves to the fact that there were only two who knew the truth — Brandon and God. But for those left behind, it remains a mystery just as frustrating as why he was taken at all. With questions still lingering about the recent past, Marty and Barbara were forced to deal with the immediate future and funeral. It was decided that since there would likely be a huge turnout for the funeral service of someone as well-known as Brandon, they would hold the service on Saturday, May 1, in the high school gymnasium.

Meanwhile, up in Indianapolis, the Colts were dealing with the loss as well. Head Trainer Hunter Smith had gotten a call that Wednesday night from friend and Arkansas' head trainer Dean Weber. "Hunter, I've got some bad news. Brandon has been in an accident." It then became Smith's job to make phone calls to Colts' President Bill Polian and Head

Coach Jim Mora. Coach Mora informed the team the next day. Polian contacted Colts' owner Jim Irsay who told him in no uncertain terms, "Brandon is a Colt, and I want him treated as a Colt. I want you to do whatever we need to do." Based on his boss's instructions, Polian assembled a contingency from Indianapolis to fly down to Arkansas for the funeral, which included himself, Howard Mudd, Hunter Smith, and center Jay Leeuwenburg.

Coach Mora was home when Hunter Smith called informing him of the tragedy. Mora remembers having a horrible feeling wash over him. Though the football club had high hopes for Burls as a player, and though they had only 11 days with him on the team, the personal loss was much greater than the professional one.

For Colts' offensive line coach Howard Mudd, Brandon was exactly what he thought he would be as the former Razorback reported to mini-camp just days before. "The reason you scout," Mudd reflected, "is to get a guy just like this. You maybe come across someone like Brandon every four or five years. We knew we were getting the kind of player and person we wanted on this football team. We felt he was perfect."

Just that Wednesday, Mudd had been raving to his wife about Brandon, telling her how impressed he was with him. That night the "Drew Carey Show" came on television, a show Mudd had never watched, but he had heard about the comparisons between Brandon and the sitcom's star. Calling for wife Shirley to come, Howard pointed to Drew Carey. "That's what the guy looks like. Get used to that look because you're going to see it a lot around here." It was only a little while later that evening that Mudd received the call regarding the accident. Later, the coach reflected on Burlsworth, "The whole purpose of sports is to give those who aren't gifted with natural talent to earn, through hard work, a chance to get there. If you're going to be a great football team, you really need people like Brandon. They are the bedrock of this game."

For some who have been in a management role in the NFL for years, it's easy to grow cold and calloused as one is immersed in the business end of the league. Bill Polian reflected, "You read that there are no heroes anymore, but guys like Brandon renew our faith in the belief that the heroes are still out there. The human element is the real thing in this business, the real reason we do what we do." Ironically, at the same time they were driving from the Springfield airport down to Harrison for the visitation and funeral, the Colts' representatives were forced to talk via their cell phone to agents regarding player holdouts, contract negotiations, and the corporate end of pro football. Arriving in Harrison, the crew from Indianapolis understood for the first time what Brandon meant to the small community and state. They were amazed by the outpouring of people at the visitation.

The image which stood out in Polian's mind is of that visitation, seeing some of America's hard-working middle class standing in long lines outside the high school gymnasium. There, with their ball caps in their hands in reverence, having just come from work in area fields and factories, they came to pay their last respects. Jay Leeuwenburg came to the funeral representing Colts' players. He had only known Brandon four days, but later explained, "It was clear he was the kind of guy we all wanted to get to know. It was my loss that I could not become friends with him." At the Colts' club facilities in Indianapolis, flags flew at half-mast. Club owner Jim Irsay sent a letter expressing his condolences. He also pledged to honor Brandon's memory in an appropriate fashion. That was a promise the Colts would keep.

Not content to merely make a consoling phone call to Barbara Burlsworth or just send flowers, Danny Ford instead sent himself. Purchasing a plane ticket, he flew to Fayetteville, got in a car, and drove to Harrison so he could be at the funeral. To Ford, Brandon had been one of those players that represented the tough-minded work ethic drilled into his mind by legendary Alabama football coach Paul "Bear" Bryant. Burls, thought Ford, was the kind of player the "Bear" would have loved to coach. Fundamental. Teachable. Committed. Competitive. Joining Ford there in the gymnasium were hundreds of local residents, all hoping for a chance to squeeze into the building. That Saturday service was attended in full force by the entire Razorback football team. The university chartered two buses which carried the team and their coaches to the small Northwest Arkansas town. Normally when the team enters an arena, it's amid the deafening cheers of over 50,000 football fans. But this was another occasion. Game day was replaced by one dominated with grief. Instead of suiting up in their uniforms, they wore suits and ties. Rather than charging onto the field, they marched silently into the gym. No one present that day will forget the moving image of seeing the Razorback football team file into that room and take their seats. Members of the Harrison High football team came as well, wearing their blue and gold team jerseys, a tribute to the former Goblin lineman. All told, more than 2,000 mourners packed themselves into Harrison High School's gymnasium that Saturday.

Just prior to the funeral Marty and Grady had discussed whether or not to view the body. Marty had personally not wanted to see Brandon's body and did not want a public viewing. "Bran never did like all the attention of people looking at him, and he sure wouldn't want us to do that to him now." Grady agreed with his brother concerning the public viewing but deeply felt, for his own sake, he personally needed to see his baby brother one last time. Having lived away from Arkansas for several years, Grady didn't have the opportunity to spend time with Brandon like Marty and the rest of the family did. For him, viewing the body brought a sense of closure for him and his wife, Jeannie. It would be his own way of saying goodbye. Because he believed what the Bible says about death and beyond, Grady was confident he was merely viewing the body in which Brandon had lived while here, not Brandon himself. Burls was now in the presence of the One who loved him, had died and rose for him, and who had saved him. Grady noticed there was hardly a blemish on the body. It was nearly perfect. Just like Brandon.

With that final visit, Grady bid a tear-filled farewell to the chubby little kid he remembers growing up with in Harrison. Though it was a painful experience, for Grady it was the right thing to do, his greatest comfort being the confidence of a reunion one day in heaven.

Several people spoke at the funeral that day, including Reverend Arlis Thrasher of the Faith Assembly of God Church in Harrison. As Barbara and Brandon's pastor, Thrasher had come to know the Burlsworths fairly well. The pastor chuckles when he recalls some of their services where some would raise their hands and become vocal as they worshiped the Lord. But in stark contrast to the liveliness of the congregation was Brandon Burlsworth. Standing in the back of the crowd, with arms folded and wearing a face of simple contentment, he just soaked it all in.

The pastor's job that day was to declare the mind of God regarding death, to comfort those who grieved, and to give them hope of a future resurrection. And that's exactly what he did. Hearing his words that day were those who had no hope for a life after this one. They learned that what was most special about Brandon Burlsworth was not his accolades, academics, or achievements. What ultimately made Brandon unique was that God made him that way. Without God in his life, Burls would have simply been another tragic end to a promising life. But though he left us, Pastor Thrasher wanted the over-2,000 in attendance that day to know that Brandon's life did not really end on April 28, 1999. Brandon was still living, only in another place, a place Jesus had been preparing for him for 2,000 years.

Tommy Tice, Houston Nutt, and Bill Polian also gave eulogies. Nutt observed that Brandon was a man prepared for everything. Prepared for practice. Prepared for games. Prepared for the NFL. And though he was taken unexpectedly, Nutt wisely pointed out, "He was even prepared for this."

Polian remembers, "Here we come, in our rental cars and suits, big time guys, and I thought to myself, if only '60 Minutes' could see this. This is real America." Polian realized that what was happening there in a hillside gym in Harrison was more than just something for the ten o'clock news. To him, it seemed it was a place from which greatness springs. It is the America that America longs to be. Having grown up in a close-knit community himself, Polian was reminded of the values imparted when townsfolk genuinely care for one another and their families. After going down to the funeral, members of the Colts' organization came away with a renewed belief in what got them in the business in the first place. "It made us proud to say we were associated with people like him." The Colts' president called Burls a "shining example." "Brandon represented everything we want in a Colts uniform. He was a Colt. Others will play for us," he said, "but we won't replace a Brandon Burlsworth." Polian missed the confirmation of a co-worker's daughter because of the funeral. Arriving back in Indianapolis just after the confirmation service, he reflected on the irony of his weekend experiences. One was just beginning her life and introduction into the faith while the other had died, his faith turning into sight.

Longtime Arkansas Athletic Director Frank Broyles commented, "I wouldn't have missed it for anything. It was such a special time. I wish everyone in Arkansas could have been here." On the stage was Brandon's #66 Colts jersey, along with a framed picture of him sporting his now-famous trademark black glasses. There also on the table was an Indianapolis Colts helmet, a silent reminder of a hope and a dream that would never be. The day before, the University of Arkansas Athletic Department announced they would officially retire Burlsworth's #77. Coach Nutt had approached Broyles the day after the accident, making the unusual and rare request. And although the university had only retired one other jersey in the over-100 years the sports program had existed, Broyles immediately agreed to Nutt's request. The athletic director believed it was both a great idea and a fitting tribute to the person and player Brandon was. As one might expect, plans were already being made to retire his high school jersey as well.

At the funeral service, a grief-stricken crowd was shown a highlight tape of Brandon delivering bone-crunching blocks to defensive linemen, opening holes for running backs, and providing much needed protection for quarterback Clint Stoerner. A letter was sent from Arkansas Governor Mike Huckabee honoring Brandon's play on the field as well as Barbara's efforts in raising him. At one point during the service, Jeremiah Washburn noticed teammate Chad Abernathy crying. It was startling to see the normally even-keeled Abernathy publicly display that kind of emotion, and the sight hit Washburn hard, producing a swell of tears in his own eyes. Indeed, all across the players' section, giant physical specimens were wiping away the tears. *Arkansas Democrat-Gazette* writer Bob Holt later wrote, "For one more Saturday, Brandon Burlsworth was with his Arkansas football teammates and coaches, surrounded by family and friends. Except this time, there were tears instead of cheers."

Meeting that day for the first time on the floor of the Harrison High gymnasium, Grant Williams introduced himself to Mike Bender, Brandon's initial offensive line coach at Arkansas. Williams had been out on his cattle farm that Wednesday afternoon when his wife came running across the field, delivering the news that crushed his heart. Speaking to Bender, Grant told him what Brandon had said about him, how he had admired him and considered Bender a great influence in his life. They stood there, shaking their heads, bewildered concerning how or why something like this could have happened to Brandon. Bender had thought about what some were saying caused the accident, agreeing with Williams that Brandon would have never tried to pass with double yellow lines. Coach Bender said when he first heard news reports he knew this could not be right, because if the road signs said "do not pass," then Brandon Burlsworth would not try to pass and break the law. He would never do anything he was not supposed to do! It wasn't characteristic of Burls to do that.

Coach Bender, trying to make some sense of the whole scenario, guessed the only justification for Brandon's leaving was that "God must have needed somebody special for a big job, somebody that He could really depend on. So he came and got Brandon." Here were two of Brandon's mentors, men whom he revered and loved, men who had helped instill within him a craving to succeed and the character needed to do it.

They all came there that day to say goodbye to #77.

Ten of Brandon's former teammates served as pallbearers. This included Chad Abernathy, Russell Brown, Chris Chalmers, Grant Garrett, Nathan Norman, Ed Robinson, Clint Stoerner, Jeremiah Washburn, Bobby Williams, and Ryan Hale. Hale had asked for and obtained special permission to leave the New York Giants mini-camp so he could be present at the funeral. None of these young men had ever imagined they would one day be a pallbearer for a fellow player. It was a dreaded and sobering duty, but one they all willingly embraced. These were the men who had sweated buckets of perspiration beside Brandon. They had fought with him. Run with him. Bled with him. They had won and lost with him. Brandon had helped carry Stoerner and those men to victory in so many games. Now it was they who would carry him. Try and imagine what it's like to bear the casket of one of your best friends.

One of the pallbearers was childhood friend and mentor Ed Robinson. Ed had a long history with Brandon, beginning in elementary school as the two had shared both work and play, laughter and sorrow… and a lot of pizza. Ed Robinson's emotions ran deep that Saturday. A big boy himself, more than once he lost the fight to hold back the tears which kept rising to the surface. How can one not weep when saying goodbye to a guy who was like a brother for most of your life?

Filing past a table near the casket that displayed photos and memorabilia from Brandon's football career, Grant Garrett noticed a picture taken featuring Brandon at the Arkansas High School All-Star Game. Examining the photograph more closely, Garrett noticed himself standing in the background. He thought nothing more about it until several weeks later when he called the Arkansas athletic department asking for some old game photos. One of those pictures arriving in the mail prominently featured Garrett in the foreground. Again, upon a closer look, he this time spotted Brandon in the background, slightly out of focus. Burls had indeed somewhat faded into the background with his death, and maybe now it was Garrett's turn to shine in his own way.

The line of cars leading to Gass Cemetery outside of Harrison filled the rural road for miles, calling to mind a scene out of *Field of Dreams*. It would be the second time in a week Brandon had caused a traffic jam. It was a near-perfect day, weather-wise, as the mourners crowded into the small area near the gravesite. The family had put a great deal of thought about what Brandon's headstone would look like. When the final decision was made, it read:

Brandon Vaughn Burlsworth
Sept 20, 1976
April 28, 1999
Harrison Goblins #54
Arkansas Razorbacks #77
Indianapolis Colts #66
1998 All-American
1997–98 All-Southeastern Conference
SEC Academic Honor Role 1995–98
Our loss is great, but God is greater

Shortly after the accident, cartoonist Vic Harville of the *Arkansas Democrat Gazette* illustrated a deeply moving sketch in which he depicted a Razorback with head bowed standing before a framed #77 Burlsworth jersey. In truth, all across the state, heads were bowed. In Scripture, seven is considered the number of perfection. Who better to wear double sevens than Burlsworth?

Tommy Tice knew he had to be strong during the funeral as he would be drawn into many conversations with friends and media concerning his favorite former player. But though he had to be strong, he didn't want to be. Following the funeral on Saturday, Tice went home for his own private mourning. So heavy was his heart that he went to sleep on Saturday night, not getting out of bed until Monday morning. It was a tremendous blow to the man who had watched Brandon grow from being a skinny-legged uncoordinated member of the Goblins practice squad to the All-American, future NFL star he would have surely become. His thoughts were filled with the familiar sight of seeing Burls sitting outside the weight room in the early morning darkness, waiting for the coach to arrive and unlock the door. Tice had been close to him in life, and unbeknownst to him that Wednesday afternoon on Highway 412, he was close to him in death as well.

After the graveside, everyone returned to their homes and the Razorbacks headed back to Fayetteville, with their buses passing the very spot of the accident. That evening, several players went out to eat at Ryan's Steak House as a tribute to Brandon. To them, the term "Hog heaven" began taking on a whole new meaning. Though the funeral was now history, the process of grieving and remembering had, in reality, only just begun. Weeks and months would pass before his family, friends, and fans could get beyond what had happened. Life does go on, and as coach Tice said, though they would eventually get over his death, they would never get over his life.

They loved you, Brandon. You'll never know just how much.

Following the accident, Harrison business owners paid tribute to their fallen hero by displaying his jersey numbers.

NINETEEN

Where Are the Heroes?

May 10 was designated "Brandon Burlsworth Day" in Harrison by the town's Chamber of Commerce and Razorback Club. A memorial service was held at Pioneer Pavilion in the north Arkansas College gymnasium in Harrison. Harrison High School Athletic Director and Head Football Coach Tommy Tice spoke, as did Coach Nutt and Harrison Mayor Bob Reynolds, announcing that the local youth center in Harrison would be renamed in Brandon's honor. Coach Nutt presented Barbara Burlsworth with a large framed picture of her son in action on the football field against LSU.

A host of personalities were on hand, including Colts' Vice President of Public Relations Craig Kelley, who presented Colts jerseys and footballs to be included in a display case located in the foyer of the center. "Nobody would have worn the blue and white [of the Colts] better than Brandon Burlsworth," Kelley said. Houston Nutt added, "He left something behind that nobody will ever forget." What he left behind was a huge hole — a 308-pound hole. Stores and schools all over the area displayed the numbers 54, 77, and 66 on their business signs, expressing in their own way how much Burls had meant to the area. At a local auto shop the marquee read, "Harrison will always remember 54, 77, 66." At the sign outside Harrison Junior High, the words were: "Inspiring Example for Our Youth. In Loving Memory of Brandon Burlsworth." One sign perhaps spoke for a whole community, simply stating, "Lord, Help Us Understand." For weeks, you couldn't eat a hamburger or get your oil changed without remembering Brandon Burlsworth.

Marty Burlsworth in turn donated a pair of Brandon's glasses to the university to be placed inside his locker at the Broyles Complex. Shortly thereafter they would permanently enclose the locker in glass. In that locker is Brandon's Razorback uniform, jersey, helmet, and pads, his playing shoes, a large photo composite of him in action, and a pair of his black glasses. Also included are his practice shoes, the same ones he wore for five straight years! Burls' earlier words to Josh Melton concerning his old locker proved unknowingly prophetic as he had encouraged the young player to "just take care of it." And that's exactly what they did. While Burls wouldn't particularly like the almost museum-like attention drawn to his old locker, he would appreciate the fact that it was perpetually kept the same, and in perfect order — a perfect tribute to him.

As the grieving continued, local residents tried to make sense of Brandon's passing. The entire community had come together, helping in any way they could. For a while, it seemed the waters in Crooked Creek stood still.

Cards, letters, and flowers flooded the family mailbox. E-mails were sent from as far away as Japan and Germany. Former Razorback football players, students, children, and adults from all walks of life sent their condolences, pledging their prayers for the family. One former player, now a coach, wrote promising to instill Brandon's work ethic into his players. Over 700 responded to the online condolence site set up by a caring Colts fan.

Well-known sports writer Rick Gosslin wrote an article in the *Dallas Morning News* on May 9, referring to Brandon as a "footnote in NFL history." And technically, he was right. Brandon never took a snap, played a down, or suited up for the Colts. He never got to play professional football in the NFL. He never saw his dream fulfilled of blocking linemen for Peyton Manning or Edgerrin James. He never raised his hands high in the air following a triumphant touchdown. He never walked down the tunnel of the RCA Dome in Indianapolis on game day or heard his name announced over the PA system as a part of the starting lineup. THAT would have made him happy.

He wasn't about to be blinded by the lights and attention of the NFL. Instead, he would have been an added glow to the lights at the Colts' home stadium. Joining him in shining that light would be other Christians of like character on the team.

Because Brandon had earlier stated he wanted to use a portion of his NFL salary to help children, the family set up a foundation to help do just that. The foundation was designed to help achieve the realization of Brandon's dream and is based on the belief that every child is a gift. The Christian organization's mission is to support the physical and spiritual needs of children, in particular those children that have limited opportunities. It encourages developing positive values, strong faith lives, and a life pattern that would exemplify "doing it the Burls way." Brandon felt very fortunate to have the many opportunities he was afforded. When asked about his success, he would simply say, "I've been blessed." Marty, determined to do his part in keeping Brandon's dream alive, took on the role of executive director of the foundation.

Brandon believed very strongly in setting the right example for our youth. He also felt that he had been extremely blessed and wanted to give back. The foundation takes 25 underprivileged children from various communities across Arkansas and Indiana to Razorback and Colts home football games.

Another part of the foundation's goal is a chance to provide a fun way to spread Burls' message. "Most of these kids have had very limited opportunities in a lot of ways," Marty says. "Giving them a chance to be on TV or meet football players or go to games is certainly an exciting thing for them. But they also get a chance to hear about Brandon and the things that he stood for, like education, perseverance, a strong work ethic, and staying positive." Sometimes Marty delivers those messages personally. When he is unable to attend games, someone else familiar with Brandon conducts the session with those known as "Burls' Kids," who each wear a pair of trademark black horn-rimmed glasses just like Brandon wore. Some players might have considered those glasses a joke. But on Burls, they became a cult fashion statement. Still another desire of the foundation is to show kids a role model in Brandon, someone they can remember and emulate. To let them know there are still some heroes left in the world today.

At halftime of the opening game of the Colts 1999 season, club owner Jim Irsay held a small ceremony at midfield in the RCA Dome where he, on behalf of himself, Bill Polian, and the Colts organization, presented Marty and his mom with checks for scholarship funds in Brandon's name.

The team wore the initials "B.B." surrounded by a miniature Colts horseshoe on their helmets that season, and also declared that no one would wear #66 for the entire 1999 season. Because they considered Brandon an Indianapolis Colt, and out of their desire to honor him, the football club has partnered with the Burlsworth Foundation, participating each year in its mission.

Brandon's friends were also dealing with the loss. Chris Chalmers thought back to his final goodbye to Burls, speaking what would be the last words Brandon would ever hear. "I guess the next time I see you, it'll be on TV," he said. In a macabre sort of irony, Chalmers words came true as he watched reports of the accident on television.

Brandon was to be in Jeremiah Washburn's wedding that June, and at the ceremony he was cognizant of his former roommate's absence. After returning from the honeymoon, Jeremiah was walking into the athletic complex one morning when he turned and spotted a white Subaru almost identical to the one Brandon drove. Oddly, it was parked in nearly the exact same spot Burls had used for five years. Up until that point, Washburn had managed to remain fairly composed when his thoughts turned to Brandon. But on that summer morning, the grief that had been chasing him for months finally caught up to him. With his emotions coming to a head, Washburn broke down and wept for the first time since the accident.

Not long afterwards, Jeremiah and his dad, then a coach with the Tennessee Titans, got together to look at tapes of Burlsworth's Senior Bowl practice drills. In those drills he was pitted against a defensive lineman to see who would gain the upper hand. After getting beat the first couple of times, Brandon came back strong and began dominating his opponent, even driving him to the ground. Watching that tape brought back a whole library of memories for both father and son, prompting the elder Washburn to comment, "Boy, that little kid from Harrison sure grew up, didn't he?"

The two sat in silence for a while without a word, huge tears welling up in the eyes of both men.

Jeremiah couldn't forget the way Brandon's death had affected his dad on the night they had first heard about the accident. "It was the worst night of my life," Jeremiah remembers. "I saw my dad cry." Upon further reflection, Jeremiah and his father concluded that the brief Senior Bowl film was an accurate microcosm of Brandon's whole life — short, but long enough to overcome the odds and become what nobody thought he would be. Later in the year, while in Buffalo where he was working on an internship with the Bills, Jeremiah received a card from the Burlsworth family. Upon hearing the name, some of the Bills' players asked, "Is that THE Burlsworth?" Though he never set foot on the field at the pro level, many of the Bills players said they were really looking forward to competing against Burls and how they had thought he was a remarkable player.

Occasionally, Jeremiah and his bride still go to Ryan's Steak House for dinner. And when they do, he makes sure he sprinkles a few bacon bits on his food, just to remember Burls.

"He hated two-a-days," Washburn remembers, "but he did them anyway. He hated the work as much as the rest of us. But for him, nothing was going to stop him from his goal. He was a man's man, and though he drove us crazy with his idiosyncrasies, we loved him. All the press he received never went to his head. Brandon was just a normal guy in many ways, but Christ shined through all his imperfections. He was a great Christian who knew the Scripture. In fact, he was a much better Christian than he was a football player. To be honest, I don't miss Burls the football player or Burls the all-American. I just miss my friend."

Brandon was indeed a "man's man," a huge physical specimen. No one had a problem picturing him side by side other linemen in the NFL. He was a bulldozer for running backs. He was a grizzly bear, a Kodiak with character. A joy to watch play. Failure wasn't an option to him. He didn't have a "stop" button. The word "mediocrity" wasn't even in his dictionary. When asked by the media, he described himself as a "basic person," adding, "People say I'm sophisticated, but I don't know about that. I'm not flashy. I pretty much keep to myself." And he was no dumb jock, either. His small-town-boy accent and sometimes stammering speech betrayed a deep intellect. He was a fact machine. His feet were firmly planted on the field and in life. He exuded a humble confidence and was the near-perfect balance of an athlete, student, and person.

He was a small town kid with a big time heart, a heart "big enough to fill three Razorback stadiums," protégé Josh Melton noted. Even before the accident, Josh had patterned himself after Brandon, imitating him in the weight room, on the field, and in his academics, as well as spiritually. "How many people," Melton added, "make that kind of impact in all those areas?"

Coach Don Decker summarized, "Brandon was honorable in all he did. In fact, he was more honorable than the rest, and not just because of his death. He was honorable in his lifestyle."

Brandon was a coach's dream, doing exactly what he was told to do, and then some. He became an all-American football player, not because it was handed to him, but because he simply wanted it bad enough. His stubborn, bulldog approach to routine molded him into one of the toughest competitors in college football. For Burls, it was all about desire and passion. He didn't like attention drawn to himself, though ironically that is exactly what happened when he began wearing the glasses. "I just wanted a basic pair of glasses," he once told a reporter. "I guess the rest is history." It is now, Brandon.

In his position on the team, Burlsworth blocked for others in a role of relative obscurity. Helping others succeed on the team is what he did through his life and example. Clint Stoerner commented, "Everybody wanted to be like him. He was as close to being the perfect Christian, student, and football player as anyone I know." Football was the third most important thing in Brandon's life behind his faith and family, and look what he accomplished. What does that tell us about the kind of Christian, son, and brother he was? Reflecting on that '98 season, Houston Nutt recalls, "We had team. We had unity. We had Brandon Burlsworth!" No wonder the coach exhorted the whole Razorback squad to "just be like Brandon," originating the memorable catchphrase, "Do it the Burls way."

He practiced line drills when nobody was looking. But even this practice of privately working on the fundamentals didn't begin with football. As a young teenager, Brandon often sat in his room at youth camp, reading his Bible ... again, when nobody was looking. It wasn't about glory for Burls, at least not about his own glory. He wasn't the first to get in the limelight, but he was the first to give back to the community whenever he could. It's what separated him from all the rest. You can throw all the awards and Razorback stuff away because they don't hold a candle to who he was as a person. To Brandon, the small things mattered and according to those who knew him best, "There wasn't a weak part of his game."

Burls had only 11 days with the Indianapolis Colts, so little time for them to evaluate and work him into the Colts game plan. But apparently it was long enough for them to forecast him as a rookie starter. Craig Kelley, Vice President of Public Relations for the Colts, said, "We have a file on every player. Brandon's file is thicker than players who have been here with us for five years." The Colts also devoted a page to Brandon in their *1999 Media Guide*. Pictured in his official Colts "mug shot," Brandon is smiling while wearing the infamous glasses. Though unintentional, Brandon's memorial in the Colts' book falls on page 77, his old Razorback number. That 1999 season, Kelley, who had become the Colts' key liaison to the Burlsworth family, called Marty before the first Colts game, just to talk. Soon the pre-game calls became a routine, almost a ritual. Brandon would have been proud of them.

In a league where some guys get second and third chances for questionable conduct, Brandon never even got one. Across the NFL, players and coaches alike shook their heads in disappointment. Oakland Offensive Line Coach Jim Erkenback said, "The NFL is the loser here. It's guys like Brandon Burlsworth we need in this league." Burls had the work ethic, the academic profile, the "intangibles" which pro coaches look for in order to make that level. Being a professional athlete was never about big bucks for Burls, as teammate Anthony Lucas confirmed a few days after the funeral. "I saw Brandon last week and said, 'Are you ready to go make that big money?' He said, 'No, I'm just really ready to go play.' " He was sometimes hard to believe in his "backward" approach to things.

But that which made him unique also made him even harder to forget. His biggest impact wasn't when driving defenders back onto turf on the football field, but it was through the legacy he left behind after his death. It was a legacy of faith and a fierce will to be the best.

Fantasy creator Walt Disney once said, "We can achieve our dreams if we have the courage to pursue them."

Courage was something Burls had reserve tanks full of. No fantasy here. He made his dream a reality. From childhood friends to former teammates to professional coaches, there is hardly a person who can talk about this extraordinary individual without exerting a laugh or shedding a tear. To be sure, there are others who share some similar qualities with Brandon in college and pro football. Men with the same focus. Same fierceness. Same faith. Those are the guys who deserve an extra ovation. And so does their God.

Greatness is something bestowed on those who are the first, the best, or who last the longest. Heroes are born, not out of mere accomplishments, but out of a life lived. How tragic these days when our images of heroes are stained and shattered by headlines of drug abuse, arrests, and criminal charges. Where are the young men and women who are worthy role models for our kids? Where are those who make footsteps in which America's youth can follow? When will we realize that heroes aren't made in the signing of a multi-million dollar contract, or the piling up of sports records? We have lowered the standards for our heroes. It used to be that only a professional player could wear the official team uniform. Now anyone with $75 can own an authentic game jersey. Somehow that cheapens the honor and privilege that go with that jersey. In reality, only the players themselves have earned the right to wear it. But we have done the same thing with our heroes. We throw the term around and slap it on just about anyone who has attained even a modicum of celebrity status, whether it is in the world of sports, music, or entertainment. But greatness is not merely for those fortunate enough to gain public notoriety. It is not for those who seek grandeur or personal glory. Rather it should be for those who, through quiet strength, demonstrate character on and off the field or the stage.

A person's name is more than just how we identify them on a class roll, mailbox, or credit card. A name becomes synonymous with who a person is — his or her character. Some names come with preset images and perceptions — names like Rockefeller, Walton, and Gates. These are names calling to mind wealth and economic empires. Other names are more common, but by virtue of the ones bearing them are forever associated with greatness — names like DiMaggio, Montana, and Jordan. Brandon Burlsworth never played a single down in the NFL, but his life and legacy were already defined well before he suited up before millions on television.

Through his example on the field, in the dorm, at home, on Saturday night, and Sunday morning, Brandon left behind a name that will be associated with integrity, perseverance, faithfulness, gentleness, humility, goodness, kindness, and excellence.

And that is part of a real hero's test. He must pass through the fiery trial of a life lived. Not a perfect life, but a life worthy of imitation. That being the case, let it be said that by all accounts, Brandon Burlsworth qualified. That almost storybook quality he possessed is what motivated a secretary in the Colts' organization to drive to Harrison, Arkansas, while on vacation in Missouri, just to visit the grave of the young man about whom she had heard so much. It's the example that inspired a young boy to permanently display a Sports Illustrated article about the former Razorback on his bedroom dresser. Opened to the page featuring Burls' picture, the article stands as a silent sentry, encouraging him to always "do it the Burls way."

In addition to retiring his number and enclosing his locker, the University of Arkansas also commissioned a painting to be done, a large mural located in the Broyles Center meeting room. This is the same room where the Razorbacks have their team meetings. Painted by Fayetteville artist Nancy Couch, the mural took 268 hours to complete. Depicted is an actual charging band of wild razorback hogs. Galloping in the same scene is running back Madre Hill, with Brandon out in front of him, leading the charge. Every freshman football player who sees that mural hears Coach Nutt say, "Son, look at that back wall. Understand that as a part of this team, you're representing a very special guy. Never forget that."

Up in Harrison, you can still see evidence of Brandon's ongoing influence. The kids in town play basketball and do some of their growing up at the renamed Brandon Burlsworth Youth Center. The outdoor mural at Goblin stadium reminds players and fans alike to "do it the Burls way."

The legacy also lives on through the Brandon Burlsworth Foundation, which helps hundreds of kids each year in various ways, including raising money for academic scholarships to the university. To help the foundation, two Little Rock businessmen produced replicas of Burls' glasses as a fundraising vehicle for the foundation. The glasses are inscribed with #77 on one earpiece and "Do It The Burls Way" on the other. Football camps taught by former Razorback players volunteering their time and fundraising golf tournaments help keep the dream alive as well. His presence is still felt in that weight room at Harrison High and over in Fayetteville as well. If a player considers cutting a corner or stops short of achieving his potential, he is reminded of the example of one who never quit until he did his best and beyond.

But there is no tangible way to measure the personal impact Brandon's life left in his hometown. Though he had coached him for years and helped to mold him into the future star he would become, Coach Tice is quick to say, "Tommy Tice could have never done for Brandon Burlsworth what Brandon Burlsworth did for Tommy Tice." To many, Burls personified everything that is good about high school and college athletics. In a world clamoring for heroes, Burlsworth was more than just a breath of fresh air.

He was a whole new way to breathe.

For the family, the grieving lingers on, sometimes more difficult to bear than others. There are photographs they still can't look at, videotapes they have yet to watch. At the time of the accident, Marty stated, "We can't make sense of this. Who could? An untimely death defies reason, especially when it happens to someone so young, so promising, so talented, and hopeful. It seemed that everything was lining up perfectly for Brandon. His future could not have been any brighter."

Brandon was just reaching his stride when his life was tragically cut short. This made it particularly hard for Marty to let go of Brandon. For a solid year, he visited the grave daily where his baby brother was laid to rest. Sometimes he would visit more than once a day. He still goes to the site periodically, cleaning up around the headstone, keeping it neat and tidy. He knows Brandon would like that. On occasion Marty drives out at night, shining his headlights on the stone. He prays while there … and remembers. Sometimes he talks to his brother as if he had never left. It's a kind of therapy for Marty. He has decided he will never allow the memory of his little brother to fade. He will never fully let him go. How could he?

Just when Brandon was becoming a man, Grady was looking forward to finally spending more time together. *The best times for us were still to come*, he remembers thinking. At the second fundraising golf tournament held by the foundation, Marty and Grady paused and looked at each other, realizing somebody big was missing from the picture. Brandon would be a missing piece of their lives that only God himself would be able to fill in time.

Even now, it's hard for Barbara, and she still gets emotional when the Colts' starting offense is introduced at games. She longs to see her big #66 rumble from the tunnel and onto the field he never saw. She, too, visits the grave where her son was laid to rest, buried next to his father. Separated much of their lives, in death and in heaven they are finally together. The anniversary of Brandon's passing brings a renewed sadness and grief to Barbara's heart, but it's not a grief without hope. She knows she will see him again. In just a matter of years, just a tick of eternity's clock, Barbara will reunite with her boy. Still, every Mother's Day reminds her of the fact that one son won't be there.

When Brandon was elementary school age, he played imaginary football games out in the front yard of his house. His sole teammate was his pet dog, a dachshund named Cricket. As the day wore on and it began to get dark, Barbara, who had been watching him from the kitchen window, walked to the front door, calling him to come inside for the night. Of course, a little boy playing rarely understands the "night rule" of front yard football. To a child, it's a seemingly arbitrary time for a parent to call a halt to play. An irrational interruption. And why should he comprehend it when, in the theater of his mind, he is about to score the winning touchdown in the Super Bowl? It just didn't make sense. "Not now, Mom." There is more game to be played. To a kid like Brandon, playing football in the front yard, it was ending all too soon.

On April 28, 1999, Brandon's Heavenly Father, who had lovingly watched him for 22 years, walked to heaven's threshold and called Brandon's name. It wasn't the end of the game in Brandon's mind or in ours. There were still plays to be called, touchdowns yet to be scored. A career to have. A wife to love. A family to enjoy. A lifetime to live.

But nonetheless, God's call came. And for Brandon, it was simply time to come home.

A gray day in Starkville, against the Mississippi State Bulldogs — November 21, 1998.

TWENTY

"How Bad Do You Want It?"

Writer Henry David Thoreau hit the proverbial nail on the head when he wrote, "The mass of men lead lives of quiet desperation." What he failed to mention was that some also live their desperation out loud, as men and women, boys and girls frantically search for a lifeboat of hope on a sinking planet. Some people are born, live their lives, and pass on without anyone hardly noticing. Without knowing their purpose for being here, these lost souls spend the better part of their lives either in a desperate search for meaning or struggling just to survive day by day. But every so often an individual comes along who goes against the grain of mediocrity. Someone who defies the ordinary. Brandon Burlsworth was such a young man.

But in spite of this comfort, the nagging question remains. Hovering over us like a threatening rain cloud on game day, we would be less than honest if we didn't ask "Why?" Why did this happen? Why Brandon? Why at such an early age? Why at such a promising time in his life? More pointedly, why, since God is supposed to be in control of all things, did He allow this tragedy to happen? Couldn't He have prevented it? Is He not powerful enough? How could a loving God let something like this happen? Definitive answers at a time like this are scarce and, at best, speculative. In our human frailty we desperately grasp for some semblance of rationale amid the confusion. There are those who search for a satisfactory explanation and, upon finding none, grow bitter towards heaven. It's natural in the grief process to question. Like the undeserved suffering of the biblical character Job, unexpected death is a loss that defies all powers of human wisdom.

Put simply, it is beyond us, and that which we cannot understand we typically reject. It's no different with the untimely death of such a promising young man as Brandon. Regardless, the truth remains. Death is an awful reality, and an inescapable part of life. As Paul Azinger so accurately put it when eulogizing friend and fellow golfing great Payne Stewart, "We live in the land of the dying, but we are going to the land of the living."

Brandon Burlsworth's departure remains a perplexing puzzle for us to piece together, especially considering that some of the key pieces are still missing. From all outward indications and human reasoning, his season ended way too soon, pre-empted by divine allowance. The timing seemed to fly in the face of sound judgment. It just didn't make sense.

But unknown to us mortals is a wisdom greater than all human knowledge combined — past, present, and future. Admittedly, God's ways intersect in a plane far above our tiny, miniscule intellects. And unfortunately for us, He is not in the habit of consulting flesh and blood in His decisions. Incidentally, that's why He's God and we're not. If we understood all His ways, we would be His equal and thus wouldn't need Him. After all, a man's got to know his limitations, and part of sound judgment in life is recognizing those human frailties. God isn't obligated to share with us the reasons behind His unsearchable ways. This side of heaven, there is no question-and-answer session where all of life's irreconcilable issues are settled. Some things will always remain in the category of the unknown … at least for a while. Until that time, when all the whys are swallowed up by understanding, there is something we can do. We can trust in God by faith even when we are unable to figure out His plan. Even in the midst of life's unexpected trials, we can gain from Him the strength to carry on in spite of the pain and confusion. Then, through a retrospective lens we can see through the fog, drawing conclusions and realizing a death such as this was not the result of a random tragedy.

Even in his short 22 years, Brandon's life had a genuine sense of purpose. There was a reason he was here with us. If his life teaches us anything, it's that a person's legacy is not measured in length of days or in wealth accumulated, but rather in the quality of days lived.

Brandon found his purpose in life as he realized a personal God created him. That same God had patiently endured for centuries the self-centered pursuits of a human race bent on self-destruction, spiritual anarchy, and rebellion. Brandon understood the biblical concept of sin, and that he himself was a sinner. He knew the penalty for this sinful self-life is an eternity of separation from God. But in spite of this eternal consequence for man's rebellion, God amazingly still loves us. This is not some sort of sentimental, emotional love that exists in word only. On the contrary, it's the kind of unconditional love rarely seen in our world today. It's a love that does more than just feel something for someone. It is compelled to do something. It's a love that demonstrates itself to mankind in the clearest way. In fact, God's love for us is so great that He chose to send His Son Jesus to die on a cross, receiving in himself the awful penalty for our sin … in our place. He suffered the eternal death sentence that was meant for us. Through His payment of our sin debt, He satisfied the righteous demands of God the Father. The debt is now paid, and nothing is left for us to do but receive the free gift of forgiveness, an abundant life here on earth, and eternal life in heaven.

The Bible states that as we confess our true identity as sinners and embrace the person of Christ as our new life leader, God reconciles us to himself and we become His friends. But more than just friends, we are adopted into His royal family and begin the relationship for which we were created. We become new creations. A new life begins. The slate is wiped clean. Our past is forgotten. Our present is secure and our future is full of hope. There is real meaning now. Direction. Purpose. Fullness. No more searching. No more uncertainty. No more "quiet desperation" of which Thoreau wrote.

Hopefully, this book has brought many things to you. Perhaps it has made you a more avid Razorback fan. In that case, great! Go Hogs! Or maybe it has caused you to appreciate your family members in a new way, to more deeply love your parents, children, brothers, and sisters. Or it could be that it has inspired you to incorporate some of the lessons learned from the life of this extraordinary young man — to persevere against adversity, to be an overcomer, to never give up, or to treat others as you want to be treated. Any of these results would equal the price of the book. But may I challenge you to think about this: If one day someone happens to read your life story, what would they walk away with? What would you want them to take with them after having been led on a tour through the "archives" of your life? Through watching your personal "game film," would the audience clearly see your purpose for having been on the "team"? For Brandon, beyond all the good of the things you have read about him, he would want you to know the same God he knew. Brandon is now spending eternity with the One who loved him, died for him, saved him, and gave him 22 years to accomplish his purpose in this world.

Mission accomplished, Brandon.

Now and forever, Burls is enjoying the presence of the One who was willing to pay the ultimate price to give him a relationship with God. In heaven, Brandon has no doubts, no fears, no what-ifs, no regrets. He fully understands why he was here for just 22 years. He now knows why he was born in America, raised in Harrison, and created to play football. He now knows exactly why he was taken, though we may remain behind with our questions. Through his life and the legacy he left us, he now influences thousands of adults and young people alike to "do it the Burls way." That is an impact that cannot be measured in book sales. Changed lives were Brandon's objective. And you know by now that he would settle for no less.

Brandon did not have the privilege of experiencing what all of us dream of — a long life, a family, of growing old with someone you love. It wasn't length of days or an NFL all-pro selection, or a successful pro career that he accomplished. But his death and untimely passing unexpectedly force us to examine something deep within ourselves. Whether athlete, parent, child, brother, or sister, we all have a race to run in life, and none of us knows how long our individual race will be. Together with the rest of humanity, we all race toward invisible and unforeseeable personal finish lines. Not one of us is promised a tomorrow. Brandon began his race in life well, not anticipating it would be a short one. Nevertheless, he ran it with the only pace he knew — full speed. When he stepped onto the football field, all the pistons were firing. He gave 100 percent on every play, something no teammate, coach, or opposing defensive lineman would ever debate. But housed inside his 6'3", 308-pound, muscle-bound frame was a quiet spirit, a humble heart, and a devout soul. It's true that still waters run deep, and Brandon's waters proved to be a river of life.

Football was a major passion for Brandon. He enjoyed it and excelled at it. He pursued it with all his might because that's what he was made for. "I feed off other people's success," he once said just before the NFL draft. "I want to go to a football team that wants to win and help that team win. I have a burning desire to succeed and I want the team that I play for to have that kind of desire, too. I know I can help a team like that." But he wouldn't have worn his blue and white

Colts jersey as an opportunity for self-attention or adulation. He knew that any success or celebrity he received was a gift of God. That's why, in his own focused manner, he lived each moment to the fullest. Brandon hardly passed up an opportunity to demonstrate his love and appreciation for his mom. That was just Burls' way. Like him, all any of us has is the reality of today and the memories of yesterday. Whatever we aspire to do, we should do it now. Burls' life ought to motivate us to love and appreciate our family and friends, especially while we still have them.

His is a story containing almost fairy tale overtones, nearly unbelievable, virtually too good to be true … but thank God, it was true. It's the kind of story that keeps you believing in high school and college athletics. Burlsworth gave new definition to the term "All-American." He modeled the character we as parents wish for our kids and the passion and champion spirit we as kids long to embrace. It may be argued that it's a bit premature to speak of Brandon using words like "legacy" and "legend." After all, how do we apply these words to a young man who only lived 22 years? The answer is found by asking the citizens of Harrison, Arkansas, and a few hundred thousand Razorback fans. Ask those from all over the country who, through letters and e-mails, sent their tributes to the Burlsworth family. Ask the university's athletic department and coaching staff. Ask the men who played with him and lived with him. Ask his buddies. Ask the adolescent athletes who today are sweating it out in the Harrison High weight room. Ask their football opponents who continue being "baptized" in nearby Crooked Creek on Friday nights. Ask the thousands of underprivileged kids who benefit from the foundation which bears his name. You can merely live a life or you can leave a legacy. It's a choice each of us faces on a daily basis.

In death, Brandon was buried in a simple, obscure cemetery, one you would never really notice; that's just the way he was and the way he would want it. Though somewhat of a loner in real life, he never played alone on the field. There was always a silent "partner" present, giving Brandon the strength to "do all things." "How bad do you want it?" was more than just a motivational metaphor for Brandon. It was a way of life. Everything he accomplished in college was because he wanted it badly enough. Brandon said, "When you're on the line [of scrimmage], not much is said. It's all in the eyes. They see the determined look in my eyes, and that tells the whole story. I know then they can't stop us." Brandon had the eyes. They were the eyes of a champion.

His senior year at Harrison High he announced, "I'm going to try and walk on at Fayetteville. I want to be a Razorback." He became much, much more than that. He wanted a chance to play professional football. He wanted heaven and a relationship with God more than anything. And he got it. "No question where he went the second he died," teammate Nathan Cole said.

This book's purpose is not to glorify Brandon Burlsworth. He would never have wanted that. This book is a tale of hope, a story about what it means to dream and to see your dreams realized. By no means does it purpose to unduly exalt Brandon. But on the other hand, it is entirely appropriate to honor the man and the life he lived. As Americans we spend much of our energy glorifying musicians, actors, and athletes while ignoring or neglecting those who excel in true leadership and character. This story is intended to encourage others through the example of a life worth imitating. Some people cast long shadows. I guess that's because they stand so tall. Looking back, it's easy to see, there really was a reason for his season.

The fall following Brandon's death, in 1999, the Arkansas football team once again faced their new rival, the Tennessee Volunteers. Only this time it was at Razorback Stadium in Fayetteville instead of Knoxville. In the minds of Hog players and fans, it was payback time. Throughout that season, Brandon's former teammates had talked about him in the huddle during key games and drives, especially mentioning him that day against the defending national champions. With just over three minutes remaining, the Razorbacks sealed their victory, avenging their loss from a year earlier. In an ironic twist, the final score was 28-24, the exact numbers of the previous year's game. Only this time they were reversed in Arkansas' favor. The Hogs had executed revenge and the Razorback fans exacted redemption, storming the field and tearing down the goalposts. "We felt like Burls was with us in that final drive," said Kenny Sandlin, playing in Burls' right guard position. From Indianapolis, Craig Kelley called Marty to share in the victory, knowing that win brought the eldest Burlsworth a special joy.

Later that fall, in the same War Memorial Stadium where Brandon had sat with his mom, prophesying himself to be a future Razorback, Marty watched with satisfaction as the Harrison High Goblins won the state championship. Following the game, Marty dialed Kelley's number on his cell phone, calling him from down on the field in the midst of the celebration.

Immediately afterward, in the Goblin's locker room, amid the high-fives and cheers of sweaty teenage boys overflowing with victory and adrenaline, Coach Tommy Tice was asked if he believed Burlsworth was watching the game from heaven that day. "No," Tice said matter-of-factly, "He was here, riding on every one of our shoulders."

As you read these words, Brandon Burlsworth is completely content, enjoying the presence of God and the company of all those who have gone before him. He has been inducted into the highest hall of fame there is. He's finally perfect. "Hog Heaven" takes on a whole new meaning now.

Every football season, some 70,000 Razorback faithful gather inside Reynolds Razorback Stadium in Fayetteville, Arkansas, to celebrate an annual ritual. Just prior to kickoff, red-clad radicals will perform a time-honored tradition as they "call the Hogs." But it's more than just a liturgical repeating of the words "Woo! Pig! Sooie!" You can be sure they'll draw deep breaths, filling their lungs with the autumn mountain air, letting out a war cry whose echo will reverberate all across the Ozarks.

And someone will be listening.

AFTERWORD

BY MARTY BURLSWORTH

We truly believe "that God causes all things to work for good" (Rom. 8:28), but "the accident," as it is called, totally devastated our family. The prayers from around the country were all that helped us make it through this tragic time.

The Burlsworths are a tight-knit family with Brandon being the very center of our lives for the last five years of his career. We were all so happy to be along for the ride with him. As most football families know, priorities and schedules are adjusted for the football season; it was a wonderful time.

Our family was overwhelmed by the attention and the many stories of people whom Brandon had inspired, and how his example had changed their lives. After the initial shock of Brandon's accident slowly wore off we knew that his story needed to be told. His example could inspire so many, young and old alike. He had already inspired so many during his short time on this earth. To us he wasn't superhuman, he was just Brandon, living his life the way he always had.

Our family wanted Brandon's story told. We wanted people to know the person who worked so hard and had such great faith to get where he was. Many times I've witnessed him studying at the dining room table at one or two in the morning. Getting by was just not in his vocabulary, whether that be on the football field, in the weight room, in the classroom, or most impressively, in his devotion to God.

When I first met with Jeff Kinley concerning the prospect of doing this book, I had the immediate impression that he was the right person for the job. We had prayed for someone with conviction and a Christ-like attitude to tell Brandon's story. Jeff wanted to tell Brandon's football story but he was also very interested in his priorities of faith, family, and football.

Jeff, along with New Leaf Press President Tim Dudley, continually kept our family updated on the progress of the book and allowed us to proof the manuscript as the book progressed. Every effort has been made to insure that the pages of this book contain factual accounts of the events in Brandon's life.

I want to thank all parties who made this book possible: Brandon's friends and teammates who knew him so well and shared stories of their time with "Burls" — the Arkansas Razorback athletic department, the Indianapolis Colts football club, and the people of Harrison and the state of Arkansas who loved him as we did. And Colts' fans in Indiana who also continue to rally behind his example today.

Coach Houston Nutt and Frank Broyles have been extremely helpful in making this book a reality. Jim Irsay, Bill Polian, and Jim Mora of the Indianapolis Colts also made huge contributions to the content of this book. Colts' public relations director and my good friend Craig Kelley had a big hand in arranging interviews and also sharing his own personal stories of his time with Brandon. It would be impossible to recognize everyone individually who contributed to this book in this small section. Suffice it to say that many miles were traveled and countless interviews conducted with so many friends, relatives, coaches, and teammates. We appreciate you all.

Shortly after Brandon's accident we came across an outline for a Bible lesson he prepared for church just days before. It just seemed to fit the situation in which we all found ourselves with this great loss. I thought it fitting to include it here.

The Lord Has a Plan

New Living Translation
James 1:2–4

Dear brothers and sisters, whenever trouble comes your way let it be an opportunity for joy. For when your faith is tested, your endurance has a chance to grow. So let it grow for when your endurance is fully developed you will be strong in character and ready for anything.

- We all go through trials at some point.
- Being a Christian is by no means easy.

James 1:12

God blesses the people who patiently endure testing. Afterward they will receive the crown of life that God has promised to those who love him.

- The Lord will bring those through trials who persevere and believe in Him.
- Trial of being away from home.
- You don't have to enjoy the trial but realize that something good will result from it.
- The Lord has a plan for our lives.

Zechariah 13:9

I will bring that group through the fire and make them pure, just as gold and silver are refined and purified by fire, they will call on my name and I will answer them. I will say these are my people and they will say the Lord is our God.

Brandon Vaughn Burlsworth
September 20, 1976
April 28, 1999

THE BRANDON BURLSWORTH FOUNDATION
brandonburlsworth.org
Our Christian organization's mission is to support the physical and spiritual needs of children, in particular those who have limited opportunities. The foundation encourages a strong faith, character and sportsmanship, developing positive values, and a life pattern that would exemplify "Doing It The Burls Way".
You Tube
119 W. Central Avenue • Harrison, Arkansas 72601

Jeff Kinley is a graduate of Dallas Theological Seminary and has spent over three decades empowering people with God's vintage truth. He is the author of 26 books, and speaks all over the country. See jeffkinley.com for more information about his ministry.